METHODS OF TEACHING COMPUTER SCIENCE

METHODS OF TEACHING COMPUTER SCIENCE

By

Moturi Ravi Kumar

M.Sc., M.Ed., M.C.A.

Lecturer in Mathematics & Computer Science

R.V.R. College of Education

Guntur–522 006

General Editor

Dr. Digumarti Bhaskara Rao

M.Sc., M.A., M.A., M.Ed., Ph.D.

Reader

R.V.R. College of Education

Srinivasa Nagar Colony

Guntur–522 006

Andhra Pradesh

India

DISCOVERY PUBLISHING HOUSE

NEW DELHI-110002

Published by:
Namit Wasan

DISCOVERY PUBLISHING HOUSE PVT. LTD.
4383/4B, Ansari Road, Darya Ganj
New Delhi-110 002 (India)
Phone : +91-11-23279245; 23253475; 43596065
E-mail : discoverybooksindia@gmail.com
discoverypublishinghouse@gmail.com
namitwasan9@gmail.com
web : www.discoverypublishinggroup.com

Edition: 2020

ISBN: 978-81-7141-823-7

Methods of Teaching Computer Science

Printed at:
Infinity Imaging Systems
Delhi

Foreword

Teacher education is quantitatively marching ahead towards quality education. The central and state governments through the NCTE and the Directorates of School/Higher Education are rendering their legitimate service in improving the quality of teacher education by formulating and implementing various academic policies and educational programmes. Along with these policies and programmes, the teacher educators and the prospective teachers teaching and studying in teacher education institutions need good curriculum and quality books.

The methods of teaching each subject play a pivotal role in enhancing the efficiency of their practitioners. Identifying the very importance of the methods of teaching and the quality of books, a series of books on the methods of teaching different subjects have been developed by experienced teacher educators for the benefit of teachers in making in teacher education institutions. Thanks to the authors.

Valuable suggestions for the improvement of these books are welcome from fellow teacher educators, prospective teachers and other academicians involved in the arena of teacher education.

The authors and the editor dedicate this series of books on the methodology of teaching to Mr. Tilak Raj Wasan, Proprietor, Discovery Publishing House, New Delhi, for taking up this commendable task of publication to meet the felt needs of teacher education faculty and clientele.

Dr. Digumarti Bhaskara Rao
Research Director in Education
Nagarjuna University
br_digumarti@rediffmail.com

Contents

1

Introduction

The computer should be used as a learning tool within the student's college classes. Students need to experience how one learn via computer. At WOSC we are in our third year of a National Science Foundation Comprehensive Assistance to Undergraduate Science Education grant titled, "Infusion of Computer Science into Liberal Arts, and teacher faculty member per year concerning the potential of the computer as an educational tool. This is accomplished through a two week summer workshop during which time the faculty member defines a project to be implemented doing the course of the following year with grant support. Through these activities we have begun to incorporate the computer as a teaching tool in several courses in various departments on campus. The most successful applications to-date have been in the Music, Dance, English Composition, Biology, Mathematics, Education, and Psychology areas.

Special Education/Psychology-computer-aided testing, software programmes for lab experiences, and student scoring of their own personality inventories.

Music – Pitch and interval ear raining and multi-voice score training.

Physics – Wave motion demonstration programme.

Mathematics – Intermediate Algebra competencies and data research on testing.

Chemistry – Organic compounds nomenclature practice.

English – Composition editing using word, processing.

Education – Application of on-line computer-administered testing.

Psychology /Special Education – Statistical teaching packaged.

Economics /Business – Record keeping system, simulations of running a profitable business, and fiscal management.

Biology – Use of pre-packaged programmes in General Biology and demonstration of various programmes to elementary teachers.

Mathematics – Graphing programmes for trigonometry and vocabulary.

Education – Collection and analysis of student data and transfer of that data to a statistical package.

For the education majors, additional training is required to lay the foundation for using computers as an instructional tool. Very few instructors write primary textbook materials, yet almost all instructors create supplementary materials.

The typical classroom instructor will not be writing computer programmes, but will be creating or managing supplementary materials. The focus is on helping the instructors learn to choose and use good application software in their classroom and to use the computer as a management tool. The following topics are covered in the foundation block for elementary and secondary educational:

1. Computer managed records–
   (a) Grade book;
   (b) Test banks of questions;
   (c) Achievement records.
2. Drill and practice material–
3. Tutorials.
4. Entire curriculum packages.
5. Video/computer interface.
6. The computer as an exploratory tool.
7. Software evaluation and selection.

For students who wish to develop a computer science emphasis the following courses are available at WOSC.

First year

CS 101 Computers and Society 4 credits.

CS 133 Computer Coding - BASIC 4 credits.

Second year

Cs 211 Introduction to Computer Science 4 credits

CS 212 Techniques of Programming- PASCAL 4 credits

CS 215 Computer Organization 4 credits

CS 213 Symbolic Language- FORTRAN 4 credits

CS 217 Into to Data Processing -COBOL 4 credits

Third year

CS 311 Symbolic Language Programming 3 credits

CS 371 Applications Programming I 3 credits

CS 372 Application Programming II 3 credits

Fourth year

CS 430 Data Structures and Management 3 credits

CS 406g Special Topics 3 to 4 credits

MTH 406g Extended BASIC 4 credits

Students who wish to become the managers and area specialists on computers within speed need to have much of the same basic training as any other computer science person on the lower division level. Their upper division work should be directed toward the area of teaching about computers or the development of instructional material. To provide for this need WOSC offers the following courses—

ED 451g Microcomputer Systems 3 credits

– The building of a working vocabulary dealing with microcomputers. Essential hardware and software components and their functions are studied. Applications of microcomputer systems within the classroom are investigated.

ED 452g computer Based Education 3 credits

– Characteristics of computer-based education illustrating the advantages to be derived from using computer-managed and computer-assisted interactive systems. Most of the work in the class will be focused on the microcomputer. Prior classwork in ED 4518 and/or CS 133 is required.

ED 461g Computer -Assisted Instruction 3 credits

– The design of computer-assisted instruction lessons and interactive systems will be studied. Students will be asked to design a set of computer-assisted lessons for classroom use.

ED 466g Computer-Managed Instruction 3 credits

– This course is designed to introduce students to a computerized method of testing, record keeping, and decision making that will assist administrative, classroom, and individual learner management. The student examines how computer-managed instruction can solve the management problems of individualized instruction.

A revised education technology masters degree programming incorporating up to 18 credit hours in computer application courses has received committee approval and is in the process of being implemented. Supporting our underlying philosophy that the computer is an instructional medium available to all students, WOSC has one central facility consisting of 13 APPLE II microcomputers, 10 of which are connected to two CORVUS hard disk drives.

Two of the systems have printers attached to them. In addition there are three free standing units, one of which has a video interface. This facility is located in the college library providing, access to all. There are also six microcomputers located around campus for faculty development of programmes and classroom demonstration. During the course of the school year over 50 per cent of the college population interacts with these computers.

The CAUSE Grant has allowed us, as Western Oregon State College, to begin acquainting faculty and administrators with microcomputers. The faculty has begun to examine the curriculum to see how to make use of computers as a teaching tool and to determine the degree of exposure a beginning teacher needs to be prepared for tomorrow's classroom.

Public education is in a period of dramatic change; we believe that all aspects of teacher-education must be examined to insure that we can help future teachers not only gain skills in working with people but also gain the skills needed to use the developing educational technology. Curriculum must be continually examined and adjusted or teacher education risks being out of phase with both students and society itself.

Before listing some of the things being done for teachers using the resources of the School of Education at the University of Michigan, we should describe the basis for our interest in and approach to serving education through computers. In general, we strive for balance among teaching, research and service' we hope to develop, apply and share knowledge about the use of computers at all levels of education, elementary school through college. We choose to give special attention to school and community resources, and then make the most of the special resources of the University of Michigan and the School of Education.

Focus on School and Community Resources: The things most important to effective learning with computers are happening today in schools and homes, not in universities and the colleges. What we do for teachers using the resources of the School of Education must serve them well in their own schools and communities. Therefore the pre-service training, as well as in-service programmes and consolation, is carried out with an eye for the facilities and situations which will be found in the local schools.

Computers, Education and Teachers: Inexpensive computing facilities that are easy to use will be one of the more important things to happen to education in this century. We believe that she experience of teachers and the availability of technical support will be the most important factor in determining how well computers are used in schools. The need is now, and growing more rapidly than institutions are professional organizations can respond.

A Role for School of Education: Colleges and universities can translate interest in computers and education into actions to meet the needs of students, teachers and administrators by going out into the schools and communities to assist with operational programmes, by maintaining high standards for professional development and practice, and by nurturing appropriate interest in research, e.g., to increase knowledge about teaching and learning processes. More specifically, we recommend that schools of education provide practitioners with skills in teaching and administration of computer-related curriculum as well as information about computers, and arrange for continuing support of on-going programmes as well as one-shot training to get them started. Action-oriented research is appropriately included in all training and support activities, that is, professionals should get involved in planning for, collecting and interpreting data to aid in decisions in their schools.

Resource of the Colleges and Universities: Training and support offered to teachers through colleges and universities should take advantage of the special resources available there. Microcomputers are used throughout the University in many different ways—information systems, process control, laboratory equipment, specialized graphics, etc.

Students have a unique opportunity to learn about current and future uses of microcomputers, and as teachers they need to know about computing in their areas, in jobs, and in society, not just in the classroom. Exploration of microcomputer applications opens doorways onto the entire world of computing. The university of Michigan has been a leader in computers and education since a Food Foundation grant in 1956 for curriculum development in engineering education. Nearly all parts of the University have been involved, humanities and the arts as well as sciences and professions.

Various units provide courses as well as software and applications, Research and development throughout the University contributes to the quality of the programme in the School of Education, and education faculty help other units using computers in teaching give appropriate attention to matters of leaning and teaching. We believe the most effective uses of computers in education today, are well based in the subjects taught and in supporting disciplines, so we do not treat "Computers in education" as a separate discipline.

Overview of this Report: The first section describes the academic programmes in the School of Education—degree programmes, courses, independent work, and cooperation with other teaching units. The second and third sections summarize service and research activities. The facilities for educational computing are describeb briefly in the last section, and we close with a brief statement about future directions.

The University of Michigan School of Education is organized in five large units: administration and policy planning; development, learning and teaching; higher science. Computers are used in all the programmes, but they get particular attention in "development, learning and teaching" as part of literacy. Special topic such as problem solving, learning strategies and social relations are considered in all four areas of literacy. Computing in education is not treated as a separate degree programme because the University gives only one masters degree or doctorate in education, and more importantly, because computing in education is considered in context rather than as a separate subject.

Microcomputers and Education provides an overview of computers in education with special attention to instructional design, testing and evaluation. Microcomputer Programming for Educators serves as an introduction as well but leads to specific skills is one or more languages and the development of specific programmes for use in ones teaching. These two courses are offered every term and enroll about 30 students each time. Microcomputers in the classroom integrates programming, instructional design and classroom management. Seminar in the Use of Microcomputers in Education provides for advance project work. These two courses are scheduled once each year and are restricted to graduate students; typical enrollment is 20.

Because the field is growing and changing more rapidly that a school of education can respond with new courses, and because the student learning about computers in education come from varying backgrounds and situations, the College offers many opportunities for study of special topics by individuals and small groups in addition to regular courses. Typically students will define topics for independent reading or research, often derived from questions raided during one of the regular courses, and sometimes based on experiences in their own teaching, research of administration.

One or more faculty members will assist in redefining the topic and identifying resources for independent work. The results often are reported through informal seminars as well as in publishable reports. About ten students use this option each year. These opportunities for independent work provide some of the flexibility needed in a new area of study, and help determine what topics later students should study as a more formal programming is developed. That is, some of the following topics may become regular courses:

- Computer use in science, match, social studies, etc.
- Planning and administration of computer labs and programmes.
- Curriculum science and education.
- Information sciences and education.
- Social amplifications of technology.
- State and regional programmes for computers in education.
- Learning theories and technology.
- Research and evaluation.

The need for practitioners helping with computer applications and studies in schools is considerable and immediate. The linkage between research and practice is of immediate benefit to operational programmes as well as long-term research. Therefore, practical experience is very appropriate in a graduate study of computers in education. We encourage practicums and project experience, either in association with on-going projects in the School of Education or elsewhere in the University, or in the schools in which the candidates presently work. We know no better "examination" than that provided by experience in the field—managing a microcomputer lab, developing instructional applications in one's discipline, or helping teachers to use computers more effectively in their classrooms. We expect about ten students a year to enroll for credit in a practicum; presently the only students in this category are working on doctoral dissertations.

Undergraduates in our teacher preparation programme have ample opportunity to use computers in their regular classes or independent work. In addition to trying computer applications in the relevant discipline, students are likely to be signed other interesting activities, such as using a microcomputer to carry out a readability analysis of text materials and designing a computer-based learning activity. A microcomputer resource center provides machines, software, publications, and other materials for individual work, as well an opportunity to observe learners from pre-school to adult working with computers individually or in classes

Diffusion of computing through methods classes began with a grant from the "faculty development fund" at the Center for Research on Learning and Teaching. We went to the instructors with suggestions for computer use in the various disciplines, demonstrated the applications, and offered to assist. Virtually all methods courses now include computing activity directed by the individual instructors, with technical assistance form the staff of the resources center. Students can go on to teach themselves more about computers; some enroll in the undergraduate classes.

The School of Education draws on the resources of other units that work with computers and information systems, and also coordinates its efforts with others interested in computers in schools. The School of Library Science shares resources for demonstration and research; working together, education and library science prepare students for serving a support function in the schools. The College of Engineering has set up microcomputer classrooms for undergraduate courses in programming and applications. At scheduled times these classrooms are available for demonstrations, workshops and special classes.

The PET shop is available for other uses, especially for summer institutes since only a few chemistry lab sections are scheduled in the summer. The Department of Computer and Communications Sciences helps staff several courses off campus for teachers needing a sound basis in computer science. The Department of Psychology has several laboratories working on learning and instruction using computers, providing graduate students in education access to a wider variety of research opportunities. The Center for Research on Learning and Teaching helps provide the resources for demonstration and research, and in return, the School of Education helps faculty elsewhere in the University explore computer applications in their own teaching and scholarly work, a task beyond the resources of the Center. The communication among faculty using computers began with a series of workshops and "faculty seminars" organized by the Center for Research on Learning and Teaching. Later the same series was offered on the site of the resource center in the School of Education, establishing it as the new site of information and advice. The Apple users group meets regularly at the School of Education, further identifying the resource center as a focal point for communication.

The School of Education offers many lectures, demonstrations and consultation on the use of microcomputers for schools. These include;

- faculty orientation sessions;
- intermediate district or country school board sessions; and community meetings.
- At times faculty members help the staff in the planning of computer systems and curriculum to be used throughout a school or district. We are always conscious of helping share experience among organizations and agencies. For example, we helped establish a state task force on computers in schools, we work with regional

resource centers in the public schools systems throughout the state, and, of course, we share software through professional associations and user groups.

The University also offers specific in-service programmes for schools system.

Researchers at the University are active in a variety of studies and plan a comprehensive research programme on the use of computers in education. A microcomputer research collaborative established in the summer of 1979 has encouraged and participated in research on attitudes and values; learning with computer assistance; social structures; and futures. CAI, per se is not given much attention, but the researchers focus instead on aspects of learning, procedures for curriculum design, social context for learning, or other disciplines which contribute to effective use of computers in education.

The realities of computer-use in schools for the next few years dominate research planning. For example, attention is being given to conceptualizing how a single microcomputer is best used with a group of students where the institution cannot afford enough machines for everyone individually or in pairs. The programme of research assumes more computers will be purchased for homes that for schools and so explores ways to exploit home computing for education. Research is encouraged in many innovative uses of computers in education. Such uses include but are not limited to attitudes that those using computers in education have towards:

- learning;
- careers;
- educational institutions;
- technology in education;
- lifelong learning;
- creative activities supported by technology;
- family activities.

Learning with computer assistance, including aspects of:

- efficiency;
- effectiveness;

- long-term effects;
- thinking and problem solving;
- learning skills;
- skills for handling information.

Social structure, involving:

- classroom structure and activities;
- friendships;
- interpersonal relations;
- teacher-student relationships;
- teacher role;
- parent role;
- implications for family.

Futures, research, including:

- anticipating new technology and its impacts;
- assessing social implications;
- shaping alternative futures.

The computer education resource center is housed in the Instructional Strategy Services unit of the School of Education, providing an appropriate context, technical support, and ready access for students, faculty and the teaching support, and ready access for students, faculty and the teaching community to explore a new technology in education. Other programmes of the Service unit provide links with graphics, video, curriculum review, information services, and the like. Of course, other units in the schools of Education also use microcomputers in their work; students use machines in the Statistical Laboratory, the Center for Evaluation Research Training, and a special programme in education and psychology. Both the manager and assistant manager of the resource center know the computer field well, along with their own specialities in library science. Workshops, demonstrations, and open access fit well within its domain, and the unit provides the larger context of teaching and learning.

The lab includes at least one of each common microcomputer along with documentation and a library of applications. About seven Pets, ten Apples, and a dozen Atari's can be assembled so that workshops and classes have one computer station for each of two terminals on time sharing systems, and one additional terminal is dedicated to special uses in graphics. Typically half of the machines are out in faculty offices or field research. The equipment kept in the resource center is arranged about the periphery of the space for individual work but it can easily be shifted for group use of classroom demonstration.

A second classroom is used when we call in extra machines. Group viewing is accommodated through use of large monitors: black and while monitors for applications which are primarily text, and colour where that is helpful to the demonstration. The same monitors are used for viewing material from videotape for more convenient use in group demonstrations as well as easy access by individuals. The resource center also has two vediodisc players, one consumer model and one industrial for experiments with computer-controlled videodisc.

The staff person who handles other equipment for the Resource Centre also takes care of computer connectors, cables, and the like. Some time is required for the cleaning and repair of disk and cassette media, the diagnosis of equipment problems, and minor repairs. This person also makes arrangements for outside repair as needed.

The computer lab maintains a large set of materials in cooperation with the Center for Research on Learning and Teaching. The center manages to maintain:

- a comprehensive programme library;
- a substantial reference library;
- most of the relevant periodicals;
- manuals for each of the machines;
- most of the recent textbooks;
- media materials:
  1. video tape
  2. tape-slide
  3. computer programmes;
- annotations on programmes and applications;
- self-help posters.

The resources center is supervised by experienced library and media staff. The manager, assistant manager and laboratory aides together provide service to both faculty and students, comparison of equipment options, such identification and review of software, advice on development of applications - - and assistance with preparation of graphics for use in papers and other presentations. That is, the resource center provides computer resources for any scholarly work by students, as well as a site for study of computers in education. In addition to the regular staff and faculty, undergraduates are hired as aides and programmers to extend the support staff to serve more people at modest cost.

The students use their work as a learning experience. About twenty undergraduate student benefit from this opportunity each term. Graduate students help with review application programmes and publications. Workshops, short courses and programme review are carried on by faculty members on a regular basis.

Service to other units, organizations and informal groups have proved mutually beneficial. For example, the University of Michigan Apple users group meets regularly, and typically some education students who happened by, get "hooked" and leave with some new ideas of software for innovation or use.

Graduate students have gained excellent experience staffing special courses for the University Children Center, and education classes have observed young children exploring computers. The resource center is a resource for local teachers, providing the full tango of information and examples maintained for University students and faculty, and offering demonstrations in an "open house" format and instruction through institutes and workshops In addition, and academic programme for talented students offered by the Gifted Students Institute each summer since 1978 provides one example of the "computer camp" idea that has becomes so popular recently. "Properly designed, can allow students to formulate hypotheses, test them, analyze results, and refine their conceptions. Moreover, they can provide the student with a record of the course of his or her investigations, permitting greater self-awareness of thinking and, learning." There are, however, many barriers to realizing this potential, among them a lack of consensus on the definition of higher-order thinking and an incomplete understanding about the use of technology to promote it. We explore both issues in this chapter.

There are diverse views about the components of higher-order thinking and no adequate and agreed upon theory from which to derive a definition that would elicit consensus. Although a number of researchers have developed theories, definitions, and criteria for higher order thinking, a consensus remains elusive. For instance, Feurstein emphasizes "autonomous learning" and the importance of logical reasoning, recognizing relationships, classifying and comparing concepts.

Foshay stresses the importance of learning to learn, which he labels the "pursuit of meaning," and includes such components as learning facts and findings, learning techniques, learning sources and processes interpreting information. Zacharias is more practical, emphasizing heuristics such as determining whether a problem can be solved, pushing possibilities to the limit, even to absurdity, asking for help, changing scale to achieve a different perspective, and bringing in outside information. Each perspective is valid, but they do not combine to provide a consensus.

For the purpose ot this chapter, we suggest that higher order thinking occurs when a person is engaged in active and sustained cognitive effort directed of solving a complex problem and when the person makes effective use of prior knowledge and experience in addressing the problem. The problem must be complex for the person; many problems will meet this criterion for some people but not for others. Problems may be well-structured with clear definition, rules, and goals or ill-structured with unclear definition, ambiguous rules, and subjective goals. By sustained effort we mean engagements requiring anywhere from ten minutes to many hours or longer.

Cognitive effort includes activities generally identified in the literature on problem solving, such as integrating and synthesizing different bodies of information, making critical judgments, and developing and testing hypotheses. We include the concept of effectiveness in our definition because an important overall pedagogical goal is to improve the student's capacity to succeed in solving increasingly complex problems. We believe that a novice problem solver, although engaged in active and sustained cognitive effort, may not use strategies of the same efficiency as those used by an expert.

On the other hand, an expert who very quickly reaches the correct solution to a problem that to other might be complex would not be engaged in higher-order thinking. We believe that effectiveness in higher-order thinking necessarily involves making appropriate use of prior knowledge and experience relating to the problem. This conception of higher-order thinking enables us to think about ways of realistically challenging students of different ages and with different levels of knowledge as they deal with problems they perceive to be intellectually complex.

Although we can not precisely specify the components of higher-order thinking, we have a good idea of what such thinking is not. While higher-order thinking may be involved, it usually is not evident when the central activities of students are (a) memorizing, (b) learning isolated facts and findings (c) using algorithms rigidly or automatically, or (d) answering problems with solutions already known to them. Such activities do not involve higher-order thinking because they do not represent "complex" problems nor do they require sustained cognitive effort for most students.

Our definition of higher-order thinking suggests that much of what goes on in schools bears only an indirect relationship to higher-order thinking. Evidence of lack of instruction in higher-order skills comes from a variety of places. Studies of reading instruction find that 90 percent of instruction is directed at the learning of isolated words and only 5 percent is focused on understanding text. Surveys of textbooks indicate the tremendous emphasis on vocabulary learning and the superficial and fragmented nature of the material. Studies of mathematics instruction report that early instruction in arithmetic may even drive our some of the effective problem-solving strategies that students bring to school.

The nature of standardized achievement tests discourages teachers from focusing on higher-order skills. Items on such tests typically require responding with discrete bits of information in a multiple-choice format. Domains for these tests are often rigidly defined and rarely require students to synthesize information across defined domains. Recent work by a small group of educators and cognitive psychologists has resulted in school-based curricula designed to improve thinking skills. Like others, Sternberg has argued for the necessity for training students to think: Each program should provide explicit training both in the mental processes used in task performance and in self-management strategies.

Techniques for teaching these skills cover a wide range of options and philosophies. Glaser and Sternberg have described and analyzed several of the more touted instructional programs and their reported successes. These programs range from teaching ways to structure problems and generalizable heuristics in a nearly content-free environment to training strategies within a specific content domain.

Generally, computer software for the schools is similar to other instructional material in its focus on imparting factual information and on low-level algorithmic skills. There is evidence that students can learn factual information effectively by using computers in academic subject areas. For instance, the effectiveness of computer-aided instruction has been consistently demonstrated in foreign language and in science.

Across subject areas, computerized instruction is associated with greater or equal gains in learning when compared with traditional instruction. Furthermore, this achievement is obtained in equal or less time than is needed for regular classroom learning. An experiment carried out in the Los Angeles Unified School District shows some of the potential for computer-assisted instruction.

In conjunction with the Educational Testing Service, the district conducted a five-years longitudinal experiment using the Computer curriculum Corporation's drill and practice software that was originally developed by Patrick Suppes. The purpose was to determine whether these computer programs could improve performance of students in compensatory education programs in mathematics, reading and language arts. Compared to a control group, students using the CAI materials showed large and significant gains.

The use of CAI curricula helped students to improve standardized test scores significantly. Nearly all the research on effects of computer-assisted instruction in schools focuses on knowledge development programs similar to the programs in the Los Angeles schools. Such programs account for the greatest use of computers in elementary schools. There is little evidence however that computer software stimulates higher-level thinking. This lack of evidence is one of the reasons that software to promote higher-order thinking is used in schools only to a very limited degree. Another reason is that few programs are available, even though the quality of such programs is beginning to improve.

2

Learning Computer

Assuming that the societal changes wrought, by microelectronic technologies would have greater implications for changes in educational programs than would the instructional potential of these technologies. Second, since future scenarios about life in the developing computer culture will, in the final analysis, be written by individuals, the capacities of schools to enhance self-realization will become increasingly significant. Third, all of the important issues related to uses of microcomputers ultimately reside beyond technology in human and social domains. Finally, the objectives of computer literacy programs cannot be permanently fixed; they change as societal values and technology change.

Various Concepts

At a general level, differences in the conceptual and practical meanings of computer literacy exist within and across nations, at a specific level, they are found in the multiple programs offered in given school. Diversity expresses itself through the scope and depth of computer literacy programs, the objectives they seek, the outcomes they produce, and the places they occupy in curricula. Computer literacy programs now found in schools are not easy to classify, in part because they are usually defined in general terms. In addition, those describing programs often fail to distinguish clearly between concepts and their uses, and the resulting obscurities make classification difficult. Nevertheless, the categories of literacy elaborated below do help document and clarify the diverse expressions of current programs.

Those who have acquired "operational" literacy can define the basic components of hardware and software and can demonstrate the machine-related skills needed to make computers work. Designed to introduce students to the computer, this approach is often implemented through daily exercises during a period of several weeks. When the exercises are effective, students understand such concepts as "monitor", "keyboard," and "central processing unit" and how the components labeled by such concepts work together with other parts to make computers function.

Students are also able to turn a computer on and off, load software, show proficiency at the keyboard, demonstrate the use of storage devices, and acquire "minimal" troubleshooting techniques. Operational literacy, then, emphasizes "hands-on" experiences and simple concepts. Directed at elementary understandings and skills, the approach demands neither extensive teacher training nor substantial amounts of instructional time. Nor does it require much change in existing curricula or major investments beyond those made in hardware and software.

The minimal demands of the approach may account for the fact that many school districts have opted for it in their initial literacy efforts. The approach, while limited, provides an entry into the world of the computer and a potential bridge to more significant learning experiences; more easily than other literacy alternatives; operational literacy can be made available equitably to all students. Learning produced through operational literacy, critics argue, are both trivial and subject to quick obsolescence. They might contend, for example, that teaching students how to turn computers on and off is just as trivial as teaching them how to turn television sets on and off. Both activities squander valuable time. Critics also argue that operational literacy outcomes are immediately out of date, hardware and software are changing so fast, they say, that today's operations are obsolescent tomorrow.

In addition, future computers, with their enhanced "friendliness," intelligence, and simplicity, will require only the most elementary skills. Why waste students' and teachers' time, critics ask, by providing trivial and obsclescent learnings? Is the assumption about obsolescence as sound one? Since students of technology typically underestimate, often substantially, the time required to realize new developments, a note of skepticism is in order. Put differently, projections made about impending achievements in intelligent and friendly computers by critics of operational literacy, especially the highly optimistic ones, are likely to be in error. If the new technologies have potential for enhancing learning, then a pertinent question arises—why wait years for more powerful computers while immediately closing the door on opportunities for all students to acquire potentially useful entry skills and concepts?

Is the "triviality" argument sound? If the learnings acquired through operational literacy offer no foundation for new learnings, they can be classed as trivial. However, if the elementary and first-stage learnings facilitate the attainment of more advanced ones, they are not necessarily trivial. To be sure, research is needed to determine if the "operational" learnings acquired in fact enable students to realize more sophisticated learnings. Further, do students from diverse backgrounds actually use the initial learnings to acquire more advanced ones?

Instrumental literacy approach to literacy computers are used as instruments for acquiring stipulated learnings or bodies of subject-matter. In Sweden, for example, leaders have used computers in high schools to teach mathematics and civics. They chose these subjects in parts because they "are taken by all compulsory school pupils, and they are included in most lines of upper secondary school". The approach enables all enrolled students to learn to use computers as they acquire content or skills; in addition, the computer can be used as an instrument for "modernizing" subject-matter teaching.

In the Swedish plan, for example, computer-supported projects produced, according to one observer, a variety of subject-related outcomes among which were new insights by students into mathematical relationships, into "connections" among subject matters, and into the analytical aspects of mathematics. In addition, teachers coordinated instruction in physics and mathematics more effectively. The Swedish approach reflects the instrumental use of computers in selected subjects. Some high school leaders have aspired to use computers in all subjects taught. Those taking clerical courses, for example, might acquire word processing skills;

skillful programmers, they move the posits, beyond passive contexts to richer and more self-actualizing ones. Some advocates of programming cast a critical eye on instrumental literacy because it places students in a passive role. As programmers, students can use computers in the active pursuit of their own learning objectives. If their responses are limited to those in programs developed by others, their imagination and learning are sharply constrained.

Papert and Kemeny, as advocates of programming, speak and write as trained mathematicians. Algorithmic reasoning, an offspring of mathematics, can resolve precisely defined problems. It has repeatedly demonstrated its capacities to resolve technical problems associated with the development and use of microelectronic technologies. In fact, the expansive array of digital artifacts that lies at the heart of the computer culture is in one sense the product of algorithmic thinking. However, the task teaching students computer programming differs markedly from that of teaching them to address effectively the human, social, occupational, and civic problems created by microelectronic technologies. These latter problems lie outside the rational world of computer programming and in the emotion-laden contexts of political organizations, work settings, family milieus, and other locales.

Surrounded by conflicts, these formidably complex problems cannot be fully resolved through algorithmic reasoning. The contentions that all students should acquire computer programming skills, then, should be viewed critically. To make computer programming a literacy standard for all students reflects a questionable strategy. Even if the standard is one which can feasibly be met by all students-a proposition that is far from self-evident-major investments in time and resources would be required to produce a narrowly based set of skills.

Significant Ideas

Noble has identified "consumer literacy" "worker literacy," and "citizen literacy" as the major role-related concepts. Although writers do not always define these terms in the same way, the concepts do accurately reflect prevailing views about which roles are being altered by computers and which ones can serve as foci for developing computer literacy. Consumer literacy carries two meanings, one linked more to hardware and the other more to software. The first stresses that individuals should be effective acquirers and users of computers and associated hardware.

Since almost all families will eventually spend large sums of money on home computers and peripheral equipment, advocates of consumer literacy reason that schools should teach all individuals how to handle such expenditure wisely. The second meaning of consumer literacy centres upon the "applications" individuals will be making "as part of their strategies for information retrieval, communication and problem solving". Advocates of this view optimistically project rapidly increasing flows of information out of, into, and through home computers. Individuals using the expanding sources of information will need requisite knowledge and skills. They will need to learn, for example, how to enhance their education through electronic media, exchange ideas through computer networks, and use shared databases to solve individual and community problems. Schools, then, should provide students with the literacy skills required to function in tomorrow's microelectronic environments.

Worker literacy is defined, on the one hand, as the skills needed to perform specific jobs and, on the other, as generic cognitive and information skills. The first definition presumes that the trend away from industrial jobs and toward information jobs will continue and, further, that career and vocational programs should teach individuals to perform such specific information jobs as computer repairing, systems design, and data processing.

The second definition of literacy presumes that future job requirements will always be changing and that schools, more than ever before, should provide students basic skills which they can apply as their jobs undergo change or as they move into new ones. Workers in information-related jobs, in other words, need higher-level mental skills than industrial workers traditionally have had. During the last decade, the impact of computer technologies on political environments is so far-reaching, some argue, that new approaches to citizen literacy are sorely needed. Today space and time no longer constitute barriers to national and international communication.

However, television and satellites are increasingly communicating political events through images, leaving it to citizens to search for the deeper political meanings behind appearances. Further, as the new technologies take over an ever-expanding number of government and business functions, they are posing far-reaching questions related to the privacy of individuals, equity of citizen access to the new media, and the role of computers in politics. All of these conditions, proponents of computer literacy argue, highlight the need for citizen literacy. Actual descriptions of well-developed programs directed at consumer, worker, or citizen literacy are not as prevalent as are descriptions of other types of computer literacy programs.

For one thing, they are more difficult to design and implement than are operational, instrumental, or algorithmic reasoning programs. Since the definitions of role-related needs are still ambiguous, organized content to support instruction is not yet widely or conveniently available. Finally, support for the idea that schools should provide students generic or higher-order learnings for use in consumer, worker, citizen, and other roles is growing. Role-related literacy has not escaped criticism.

Modern Technologies

Computer enthusiasts, some contend, have exaggerated the impact of the new technologies on job requirements, consumer demands, and citizen responsibilities. Levin and Rumberger, for example, suggest that the number of "information" workers required will be relatively small as compared to the number of janitors, cashiers, secretaries, and other service, workers needed. Others contend that school and community leaders have launched literacy programs without adequate reflection. Some have blamed an "uncritical press" not only for exaggerating the need for literacy programs but also for providing "free advertising in the guise of objective reporting".

Many educators have tended to accept the claims of computer enthusiasts uncritically. Thus, criticism is needed to develop more realistic views about the educational significance of the new technologies. However, the claims of the critics can be accepted as uncritically as those of enthusiasts. Stated another way, criticisms that lack logical or evidential support need to be viewed skeptically.

Critics of role-related literacy may be correct within an immediate time frame and incorrect within a longer-range time frame. Expanding computerization is changing consumer, worker, and citizen functions, even if slowly. Thus, today's critical messages about role related literacy not only may prove to be errant; even worse, they may reinforce outmoded patterns and stifle the creation of needed new ones.

Advocates of computer literacy, then, have stimulated considerable thought about the concept during the last decade. Witness, for example, the analyses that increasingly dot the educational literature. By aggressively defining and diffusing multiple definitions of literacy and by skillfully linking them to diverse learning objectives, they have contributed significantly to the development and diffusion of literacy programs. However, the mixed messages elicited by computers have slowed the diffusion of the concepts.

Some, seeing nothing new in computer technologies, indifferently dismiss them; in so doing, they rule out the "Whither" question. Others, sensing a computer-created "revolution," urgently call for major adaptations in school programs and a thorough answer to the "whither" question. Given such disparate views; the first question facing those studying computer literacy is whether or not computer uses in schools indeed reflect another passing fad.

The indifferent, who "have seen it all before," believe firmly that the microcomputer is just another in a series of technologies without impact. They point to the high but disappointed hopes past educational leaders have had for programmed texts, televisions, and related innovations. They conclude that after a period of uncritical use the microcomputer will have an uninfluential ending as have past instructional technologies. Since it is only one more in a long series, they ask why one should assume that it has more than passing significance. The "passing fad" argument is erroneous because it is based upon a false assumption, namely, that the capacities and effects of microcomputers are similar to those of previous technologies.

Microcomputers in fact differ substantially from past technologies. Because of their greater versatility and flexibility, they can be put to many more instructional uses. In additions, they can help manage instructional processes; versatility access subject-matter from libraries, information utilities, and other electronic sources; and facilitate the development of programs by students to meet their own objectives-feats that past technologies could not perform.

Computers differ from past technologies in a more fundamental way, namely, in their far-reaching effects on society. The impacts of programmed texts, for example, were confined to educational contexts. Even television, with its widespread influence, has not moved as deeply into society's institutions as has the computer. Microcomputers populate homes. work places, business enterprises, government agencies, social agencies, and other non-school organizations. Having spawned a powerful array of novel industries, computers are now stimulating new dreams and aspirations, redefining human machine relationships, shaping cognitive psychology, and altering modes of thinking.

As computers change society, they create new educational needs, as already noted. Microelectronic technologies, then, represent much more than new educational means, they are surfacing profound questions about the ends of education. Therefore, they cannot be blithely dismissed. The conclusion that the computer is not another passing fad does not imply that school purposes and programs will change rapidly. Powerful barriers constrain technological change. The new technologies do demand much more learning and change on the part of school personnel than have past technologies.

The high costs of implementing literacy programs will slow diffusions processes. The clashing tides of positive and negative opinion, which surround decisions about computer uses, will complicate adoption decisions. Finally, it is significant that much larger private-sector investments are currently being directed at 'offices of the future' than at 'schools of the future', and 'at functions performed in business, military, telecommunication and government agencies in contrast to educational ones."

The new technologies have evoked both dark and bright scenarios. Optimists, emphasizing effective uses, see computers producing beneficial outcomes; pessimists, emphasizing misuses, see destructive and even dire consequences. While enthusiasts make expansive claims, skeptics decry these claims and cast them aside. Hope, optimism, and enthusiasm clash with fear, pessimism, and skepticism. The result is bifurcated views. That these views impinge directly upon the 'whither' question can be shown with some specific examples. The first set of examples is linked to current computer uses; the second, to presumed future impacts of computers.

Sherry Turkle has referred to the "Computer as Rorschach." The phrase is an apt one; computers do tap deep human emotions and elicit contrasting perceptions about their meaning and significance. Applications of computers in the political arena, for example, bring dissonant views. Some examples relevant to citizen literacy can help clarify the point. Some have probed the impacts of the new technologies on individual liberty and privacy and have discovered an "electronic nightmare." Others, after studying national experiments in "teledemocracy," have concluded that the new technologies can help citizens influence public policy decisions.

In a similar view, some have observed that the power of "technological elites" constitutes a threat to democratic decision making; others see in the diffusion and use of microcomputers a new means for advancing decentralized communication and democratic action. Or while some argue that linear thinking can be effectively applied to political problems, others contend that intuitive thinking will be required to solve these problems. Some believe that expanding international databases will enable leaders to address worldwide political problems more effectively; others contend that leaders from developing nations will suffer even greater inequalities in political opportunities because they will be unable to access the data.

While the less sanguine stress that large technological systems, with "lives" of their own, cannot be controlled through political processes, the more cheerful contend that humans, as creators and users of these systems, can control their effects. Contrasting positive and negative views, such as those just noted, have implications for research. Inquiry is needed to shed light on actual in contrast to presumed outcomes of computer uses.

Some of the differences in view can be explained by the fact that scholars, in drawing their conclusions, use data about different but related phenomena as, for example, the computer's impact on a process (learning) in contrast to its impact on a value (privacy). However, a more fundamental problem is that the factual premises to support generalizations tend to be weak; effective research could uncover unreliable findings and false conclusions.

Perceptions about future consequences differ just as much as do those about immediate results. Thinkers often hold antithetical views, for example, about the long-range impacts of computers on the economic sector views which have implications for "worker literacy" programs. Some, looking at the steady infiltration of robots into industrial settings, conclude that the result will be a permanently unemployed "underclass"; others, examining the impacts of past technologies on unemployment, assert that the new technologies will create at least as many jobs as they eliminate.

Some contend that the new machines will inevitably dehumanize work; others argue that computers, by taking over the routine, will bring shorter work weeks and that this, in turn, will lead to more educational, social and other humanistic activities. While the optimists believe that ongoing research will make it possible for robots to perform increasingly "intelligent" functions, the least hopeful maintain that research break-throughs in artificial intelligence will be extremely limited. The act that leaders and scholars hold such sharply divided views about the immediate and long-range significance of new technologies signals in still another way the powerful forces unleashed by computers. By surfacing conflictive and vital issues, the forces are stimulating and encouraging proactive throughout.

The precious discussion has stressed that computer literacy is a young concept, that educational leaders have defined and implemented it in diverse ways, and that sharply clashing views surround its uses. At this point an important issue arises, namely, what framework can be used to analyze the newborn, diversely, interpreted, sharply contested and complicated concept of computer literacy? Since the history of the concept is short and relevant research is scarce, analogies offer one framework. Thus, acquiring computer literacy can be compared with the learning of a foreign language or the attainment of "book" literacy. Book literacy offers one fruitful analogy for probing the "whither" question.

Notably, book literacy and computer literacy are both similar and interdependent. The various symbols on the keyboard used to write this chapter are immediate indicators of the reciprocal relationships between written literacy and computer literacy. Other symbols, which appear from time to time on the screen are additional reminders of the interdependencies between books and computers. These linkages underline a significant fact, namely, that individuals cannot acquire computer literacy without literacy in written language. Since one-fifth of the population of the United States is illiterate in written language, when more demanding measures are used, millions are locked out of computer literacy.

Printed and Electronic Words

The linkages between computers and books, then, suggest an important policy generalization, namely, that when school leaders make commitments to computer literacy they should not do so at the expense of traditional literacy programs. Those comprising today's large illiterate population tend to be members of disadvantaged social, economic, racial and other groups. Since as a rule they have had limited access to written materials in their homes, they have long experienced unequal learning opportunities. Such inequalities, which still persist 500 years after the invention of the printing press, offer another lesson to those concerned with policy related to computer literacy.

The opportunities available to students pursuing computer literacy will undoubtedly be more inequitable, at least for the foreseeable future, than will those available to students pursuing book literacy. Since computers and associated peripherals are much more expensive than books, educational agencies and parents will find it more difficult to provide children and youth the equipment needed to ensure equal opportunities. In addition, there are already public institutions that can diminish inequities in reading opportunities; however, public institutions to nurture computer literacy are not yet widespread.

If support for the concept of computer literacy continues, equity issues will increasingly find their way onto the agenda of school boards. Some educational leaders are already addressing the issues. Affirmative programs directed at computer literacy during the summer, after-school scheduling to expand computer learning opportunities, and the use of such concepts as "student-access ratios" all reflect responses more random than widespread and more inchoate than well developed. The concept of "public information utilities" highlights the access question in the larger context of society. According enable all interested individuals to use large electronic databases to pursue educational, citizenship, and related purposes.

The implementation of this idea is at best a long-range possibility It could not be realized until more advanced technologies are achieved, new information norms and habits are developed, and the transmission of computer-based information becomes much less expensive, nevertheless, the adjective "public" that stands before "information utilities" denotes an already emergent sensitivity is society to the equity issue. Given the very slow diffusion of reading skills during the last 500 years, public funds to support electronic information exchange will likely come slowly, if at all.

The first to achieve new skills are usually not eager to transfer them to others. Thus, when individuals, centuries ago, acquired written language skills, they became members of an elite group; as elites, they opposed the broad sharing of literacy skills. For example, the reading elite in England in the nineteenth century "viciously criticized" the idea of free libraries for the common people. Arguing that such libraries would cater to the "popular passion for light reading, above all for light fiction," the elite contended that the mass reading of such books would deter human progress, the common people would simply read the wrong things. It is possible that even today those who have acquired highly sophisticated computer skills tend to look down upon the use of games and drill and practice routines in schools..

Those opposing and those supporting the mass diffusion of literacy skills have confronted one another for centuries. Leaders on the side of the people, including the most disadvantaged, have prevailed, even though their struggle is not yet ended. Aided by powerful institutions, especially governmental agencies, they have repeated and acted upon a simple message, namely, that if individuals are to be enlightened and effective, they must be literate. If computers fulfil their educational promises, the struggle to eradicate inequitable learning opportunities will continue. As computer-utilities, and international promises, the struggle to eradicate inequitable learning opportunities will continue.

As computer-driven interactive cable, electronic universities, information utilities, and international networks are increasingly used, equity issues will become more salient. Since microelectronic technologies are more complex, expensive, and mutable than books, the equity issues they raise will likely be even more difficult to resolve than those associated with written language.

The five-century story about book literacy is broader than that of ever-expanding learning opportunities; it also encompasses a long struggle to define and redefine the goals of literacy in ways that reflect changing societal values. Thus, Patricia Graham, writing about literacy skills in the early 1980s, observed: "literacy... is what everyone needs in late twentieth-century America, both for their own good and for society's good." However, Horrace Mann argued, from a nineteenth-century perspective, that if students acquired literacy, vice would be reduced and morality would be improved a view that in today's climate would strike many citizens as incredible. In Mann's time, however, morality was such a salient value that school leaders could not easily ignore it. Given the secularized public schools of today, Mann's definition of literacy is no longer highly relevant. Definitions of computer literacy will probably follow in the footsteps of traditional literacy; they will, in other words, be temporary and impermanent.

Rather than, policy makers will need to seek definitions and objectives that mesh with the needs, of their time. Since the information society is much more mutable than previous societies, computer literacy objective will likely undergo more frequent changes. Given the many fearful messages about robots and related machines and their deep cultural roots, computer literacy decisions will also likely be more controversial. Witness, for example, the currency of the dark omens expressed a century and a half ago in Shelley's Frankenstein.

Given the long evolution of book literacy, what features best describe its patterns of growth? For one thing, literacy definitions over time have become more complex—a pattern already reflected in computer literacy. For example, the simpler concepts of operational and instrumental literacy are associated more with the 1970s while the more complex concepts of computer programming and role-related literacy are linked more to the 1980s while the more complex concepts of computer programming and role-related literacy are linked more to the 1980s.

The move from the uncomplicated to the more complex can be seen as follows: operational literacy requires minimal machine skills; instrumental literacy requires minimal machine skills; instrumental literacy, the skills to learn from programs developed by others; algorithmic reasoning, the skills to create one's own programs; and role-related literacy, the skills to perform as competent consumers, workers, and citizens in the developing information society. Given the pattern just noted, another question arises: What features best denote literacy's developing complexities? For one thing, more varieties of radiant skill are now assembled under the literacy tent; for another, the functions served by literacy have multiplied.

Why are the meanings of literacy more encompassing today than they were earlier? Today's meanings stem from a multicentury trend toward an ever more varied content disseminated in a widening array of books, monographs, newspapers, magazines, and journals. When Martin Luther translated the Bible into the German language in the sixteenth century, he provided a powerful new stimulus and a popular means for the citizens of his nation to acquire literacy. At that time, however, literacy was by necessity defined largely in relation to one book.

With the spread of the printing press and the growth and popularization of diverse types of knowledge, literacy expanded to include the skills needed to read more diverse materials. In the nineteenth century, when individuals were pressed to understand the world around them by reading the newly invented newspaper, they had to expand their literacy skills. As reading skills have expanded, literacy functions have become more differentiated. "Scientific", "mathematical," "esthetic," "technological," and "language" denote some of these literacy functions. They also symbolize bodies of knowledge that go substantially beyond those in Luther's day or, for that matter, in Horace Mann's time. Significantly, they imply high expectations for schools, and they help to explain the emergence of compulsory education.

The Distinctions

Computer literacy has already undergone considerable differentiation. Inherent in Previous descriptions of operational, instrumental, programmatic, and role-related concepts of literacy are such functions as word processing, computing; programming, information processing, and participation in teledemocratic arrangements. On the other hand, Marvin and Winther, through a study of computer specialists, have arrived at a different set of functions. Employing an electronic mail questionnaire sent to users of the Advanced Research Projects Agency Network (ARPANET), a large computer network, they obtained perceptual data from respondents about "thè major types of skills and levels of knowledge that organize computer users into major classes." After analyzing their data, Marvin and Winther posited five levels of users. These classes of users, along with pertinent functions and skills, are described here:

1. Many individuals each day come in contact with microwave ovens, candy machines, cash registers, and related devices; since they perform passive rather than active functions, they do not require particular skills.
2. Members of the next group are called "tourists" or casual end-users. Professors, who rely upon experts for data analysis, fall into this category. The skills "tourists" need are very limited.
3. Programmers constitute the next group. They range from those who have written one workable program to those who have written model programs. The skills required by programmers, as already noted, are specialized ones.
4. Near the top of the hierarchy is the fourth group, called "hackers," who deal effectively with computer "logiams" and "bottlenecks." Their skills, which they express inventively, are, highly technical.
5. At the top of the pyramid are "wizards." Noted for their capacity to perform "amazing feats," they can effect

> results seemingly by "passing their hands over circuit boards." Their skills are of the highest order.

Marvin and Winther concluded that "the definition of literacy and its proper objects is at any time not only a standard of skillful performance but also a social sorting procedure for labeling certain tasks and domains of knowledge as worthy of social attention and effort."

If computer users at IBM, the New York City public Schools, and the Pentagon had filled in the electronic questionnaire, their lists of functions and skills would likely have differed from one another and from those identified by ARPANET users. Given the diversity of their missions and "social sorting" procedures, they would, in other words, have arrived at different skills. Obviously, schools cannot prepare individuals to perform all computer functions; rather, they must concentrate on basic skills relevant to many differentiated functions.

If computer literacy skills are arrived at through processes of social construction which go on in highly specialized organizations such as ARPANET, the following question becomes pertinent: How are current definitions of literacy, as described above, likely to be reconstructed in the decades ahead? the expanded and interrelated uses of micro-technologies provided one context for examining this question. Since the microcomputer is the most visible of all microelectronic technologies, thinkers have understandably concentrated on computer literacy during the last decade. This approach to literacy has provided a useful focus for designing new learning experiences. However, "computer," as the modifier of literacy, may prove to be an impermanent concept. To be sure, microcomputers are pivotal points in the processing of information; however, they are only part of a much larger and more extended communication complex. The microcomputer is, to use concepts from gestalt psychology, a small "figure" against a more encompassing and expanding "ground."

3

Basic Aspects

Attempting to incorporate a significant amount of computing in any coursework in the School of Education at this time requires the use of batch processing on the mainframe system because of the limited availability of terminals. The only resident equipment within the School of Education was an ancient keypunch machine. The computing facility itself is approximately two miles distant. The first attempt to break out of the mainframe "mindset" began with a request for resident equipment for the school of education.

When looking up a synonym for the word "web," one is likely to run into the word mesh, which then leads to the word netting which in turn leads to words like concealment, camouflage, cover, and blind. "Blind" might accurately capture the way many people feel as they wander through the World Wide Web and surf the Internet. This wonderful, yet sometimes perplexing, new technology has a variety of properties such as nonlinearity induced by hyperlink connections that can lead individuals on an indirect path that branches out exponentially rather than the traditional straight and narrow road. Unfortunately, this maze-like trek through cyberspace has the potential to cause anxiety in numerous individuals. The general area of computer anxiety has been well documented and studied; however, the more specific form of anxiety, Internet anxiety, is still too new to have been fully explored and researched. The purpose of this study was to focus specifically on Internet anxiety and determine what instructional techniques and behaviors either reduced or exacerbated anxiety in an Internet class for novice adult students. The Internet, which allows people to communicate through their computers, no matter the location, has become and still is becoming a global phenomenon of impressive proportions. One of the most well known aspects of the Net is the World Wide Web which is defined as "a convergence of computational concept for presenting and linking information dispersed across the Internet in an easily accessible way". This linking is responsible for the non-sequential properties of the system that affords people a high degree of choice when traveling through it.

From its limited and covert beginnings as a cold war communica-tions system, the Internet has now grown to serve over twenty-one million households. It is thought that the numbers will grow as new technologies come into play such as a digital system, offering a new level of access, and Netscape, providing a new level of security which should entice individuals and business to conduct more and more transactions on the Net. Thus, the Internet is a technology that is becoming indelibly interwoven into society and unfortunately, one that will antiquate those individuals who do not learn to maneuver in cyberspace.

Although the cognitive aspects of Internet learning have been researched, the affective aspects of Internet learning such as feelings of anxiety have not been studied until know. Thus, the following definiiion and review of the literature will come from the body of work relating to the broader category of computer anxiety.

Knowing the Machine

Computer anxiety is a fear of interacting with computers that is disproportionate to the actual danger of the situation. Computer anxiety leaves the user in an uncomfortable mental state in which he/she experiences debilitating physical and/or emotional symptoms. The type of fear experienced by the computer user varies from one individual to another. For instance, a person might fear breaking the computer, loosing important data or experiencing embarrassment in situations that he/she feels might arise from lack of computer mastery. After failing to adequately cope in an anxiety-provoking situation, the computer user may experience learned helplessness, a feeling of incompetence, inadequacy, and powerlessness. Learned helplessness can become a problem, since individuals who feel helpless will tend to avoid the anxiety inducer. Besides anxiety's relationship to avoidance behavior, computer anxiety is also related to poor performance. Anderson found that college students who failed a computer test had significantly higher levels of computer anxiety. Causality cannot be determined in this case, yet whether anxiety played a part in causing students to fail the test or failing the test increased students' computer anxiety, those students reporting anxiety cannot be allowed to slip away and drop out of the computer age.

Principles and Basis

The area of study known as computer anxiety, in several cases, including Todman and Monaghan's work has links to Albert Bandura's social cognitive theory, particularly with regard to students' self-efficacy. Self-efficacy is defined as a person's judgment about his or her ability to perform a task within a specific domain. The tie between low self-efficacy and anxiety makes Bandura's concept significant to the study of computer and Internet anxiety. Students, with low self-efficacy are more likely to: attribute their failures to low ability; feel they are less in control of their environment; and avoid the activity in the future. Given the attributes of low self-efficacy, it comes as no surprise that anxiety is often inherent to it. Students who judge their ability to perform a task as being low tend to "experience stress, anxiety and depression when goals have not been met". Thus, when studying students' computer or Internet anxiety, it is important to look at instructional techniques and behaviors that either lower or raise students' self-efficacy so that instructors can learn what to avoid and focus on effective strategies to employ.

As the Internet has grown so has the need for effective approaches toward curriculum and instruction pertaining to the

Internet. Often articles present models for teaching and effective instructional techniques; however, they do not so often address Internet anxiety specifically. The following are some instructional approaches that have been used in Internet classes: teaching students about both the hardware and software components of the system and information skills simultaneously providing hands-on experience; giving one-on-one assistance; attempting to make the students' first experience a successful one; asking students what they expect out of the class; encouraging students to share "questions, problems and triumphs" with the whole class; using step by step work-sheets as a supplement to verbal lectures; and encouraging peers to help one another.

Several researchers have proposed instructional strategies that are intended to take the "byte" out of computer anxiety. For some of these strategies, there is a high degree of agreement among professionals, while the verdict on other strategies remains elusive. The following are just a few examples of some of the most talked about ways to reduce anxiety or stop it before it ever starts.

An antithetical relationship exists between playfulness and computer anxiety. It is thought that play might be of particular benefit for people who are in, what is called the inquiry frame, which is the self-directed stage; people enter when they become focused on expanding and deepening their computing-knowledge. Others however, have found play to be beneficial in the beginning stages of learning. Pina and Harris, who focused on anxiety-reducing and confidence building teaching strategies to be used in computer literacy courses with pre-serviced teachers, cited play, such as allowing students to press any button on the computer as one of their main strategies.

Learning through verbal lectures and learning by doing are certainly not synonymous experiences and should not be misconstrued as such by instructors. For instance, a student listening to a lecture about a process on the computer may not be able to translate those words into actions which could cause a fair amount of anxiety for the student hence, the need for hands; on practice. Several researchers studying computer anxiety have documented the benefits of hands-on experience. Castleman and

Pina and Harris promoted the hands-on approach in a non-threatening environment as well as Hunt and Bohlin, who also advocated providing demonstrations and ample hands-on time under the supervision of "tirelessly patient" instructors so that students can sharpen their skills.

Much of the literature in the area of computer anxiety focuses on unpressured instruction that increases self-efficacy and beliefs about the controllability of the situation. The notion of self-efficacy stems from Bandura's social cognitive theory, while the idea of locus of control comes out of attributional theory. Self-efficacy is defined as an individual's judgment of his or her ability to perform a specific task. Thus, a person with high computer self-efficacy would have confidence in his/her ability to master it. Locus of control, on the other hand, refers to a person's belief about the controllability of a situation. Those who view a situation as out of their control are frequently subject to anxiety and avoidance whereas those who believe they are in control tend to be more persistent and put forth more effort. In a qualitative study, Todman and Monaghan concluded that regardless of age, a relaxed, unpressured introduction to computers, in which the individual is encouraged to feel competent and in control, tends to result in a lower level of computer anxiety and a greater tendency to use computers subsequently as a student.

They define a relaxed environment as one in which stringent requirements and evaluation methods are avoided and methods to improve self-efficacy and controllability beliefs are sought.

The verdict is still not in with regard to self-regulated learning as a method for reducing computer anxiety. Pina and Harris advocated self-regulated learning and said it met with much success in their classrooms. However, in a different study that ran counter to the authors' expectations. It was found that a group of university students, who received computer training through direct teaching, exhibited less anxiety at the conclusion of the study than a group who received training through a combination of direct teaching and collaborative self-learning. The direct instructional model was considered a traditional model that included the presentation of new material, practice and review; where as self-regulated learning was thought to be consistent with a constructivist philosophy and a social cognitive perspective that emphasized students' employing appropriate strategies to achieve challenging goals which they have set for themselves thereby increasing self-efficacy. The researchers, in this case, utilized a quasi-experimental design together with qualitative methods such as interviews, adding depth to the study. Because of the relatively small sample size (group 1, $n = 16$, group 2, $n = 15$), caution should be exercised with regard to the generalisability of these results. Thus, it seems that more research needs to be done in this area to clarify the outcome.

It has been shown that because of the widespread and still growing use of the Internet, it is necessary to provide an Internet education to as many people as possible, in the best way possible, so that they will have the motivation to seek new computer knowledge and experiences in future. Part of providing this education in the best way possible is to acknowledge and attempt to alleviate computer anxiety in the classroom. Several of the instructional strategies used to deal with computer anxiety that have come out of the research, were discussed in this review. Although many of the strategies that are meant to reduce computer anxiety may be applicable to Internet anxiety, there is still a point where the two types of anxiety diverge. The one-of-a-kind virtual world of the Internet is a place without boundaries and a space without a core that will cause users to experience different kinds of emotions, some of which will be more negative than positive. For this reason, it will be important in future to address a more specific form of computer-anxiety-Internet anxiety.

In order to provide a vivid description of a particular site regarding a nascent concept-Internet anxiety—the decision to use qualitative research methods, supported by observational data, interviews and documents, was made. Qualitative research or field research beneficial are often used for detailed analysis of small group situations. In order to maintain confidentiality, all names presented in this study have been changed.

The subjects in this study were adult students in an Internet class designed for beginners at a suburban, mid-western community college. At the start of the class, there were twenty-one subjects whereas by the end there were seventeen. The purpose of the class was to have students acquire basic skills (i.e., using search engines, learning HTML format) and general theoretical knowledge about the Internet. Each individual's purpose for taking the class varied. Some individual reasons for choosing the course included: fulfilling college requirements; learning how to create a Web page; enhancing Internet and computer skills for career; and learning the Net for fun.

Generally, the students in the class varied in age, ethnicity, race, socioeconomic status, and educational background; the class included four and two-year college students, retired students, and students who were already well into their careers. The majority of the class was white however, two Chinese women, a Middle Eastern male and an African-American male added diversity to the class. There were close to an equal number of men and women. As far as computer background, all had some limited experience with computers and the Internet; although, some had much more computer experience than others. For instance, one young man used a personal computer everyday at his job. He stated, "I use Microsoft word and programs such as Excel regularly." Other students, however, had no regular access to computers and little experience with the Internet.

Several methods of data collection were employed to achieve triangulation: Observation, semi-structured interviews, unstructured interviews, and documents (syllabus, class handouts). The methods were used to identify instructor techniques and behaviors that were either alleviating or exacerbating the students' Internet anxiety. While observing the class and conducting interviews, the focus was signs of anxiety such as cues of non-verbal frustration and fear cues of verbal frustration and fear, and cues of learned helplessness along with avoidance behavior.

Miles and Huberman's three-part interactive model of data analysis was followed for this study. The first phase, called data reduction, includes choosing, focusing, consolidating, abstracting, transforming, and coding data gathered from observations and interviews. Part-II involves a data display which is concise, organized information such as in a graph or a chart. In essence, it is a summarizing image of the data. Lastly, part-III entails drawing conclusions and verification. It is at this phase that the triangulation of data is emphasized. Overall, Miles and Huberman's model is complete, detailed and well suited for the purposes of this study.

HTML (Hypertext Markup Language), SLIP (Serial Line Internet Protocol) connections and URLs (Uniform Resource Location) are just a few of the lexicons of the Internet/ computer world that are part of learning in a beginners Internet class. A majority of students in this class had feelings of anxiety as they were introduced to a host of new vocabulary words and acronyms. A black male in his thirties explained that it was like, "learning a new language where you only understand pieces of information."

Arriving at the intended location on the Internet is not an easy task. There are often problems in limiting and narrowing searches, problems with documents that have been closed or never existed in the first place, and various technical blocks to finding the desired site. An older white male commented, "The Internet is like a maze-you can't look over the top—you have to keep backtracking all the time. Sure it's very frustrating for some people." Several members in the class accepted the uncertainty of searches as a fact of life while others experienced moderate to extreme anxiety. During an interview, Diane, a thirtyish white female majoring in criminal justice, explained that, when she "gets stuck" and is not able to find the information she is looking for it, "eats me up". She said, "It sometimes gets to a point where I just don't want to go to class, I think I'm not going to make it through the day." In another interview, Newman, a young white electronic media major with a fair amount of computer experience stated that he felt extremely, "frustrated and betrayed" when he was not able to find the topic he was searching for on the Net. He added that it frequently caused him to avoid the Internet for a certain period of time.

Internet Boom

At this time, technology has not caught up with the demand of the millions of people who want to go online. The Internet is clogged with more and more people, causing more and more busy signals and time delays. The "anger" and "frustration" several students felt, especially under time pressures in their own lives and homework due dates, was apparent in this class.

The Comprehensions

A few students in the class expressed a diffuse fear of Internet failure. This was a generalized anxiety that they would not be able to negotiate the Internet, not be able to learn the content of the course if failed to complete the homework assignments and failed the tests. Jane, a young female education major with little computer experience and a dislike for technology, on her first day of class, repeatedly lamented, "Oh my God, I'm gonna fail this class." She dropped the class after a few weeks.

Low self-efficacy was the thread that ran through each of the four areas of Internet anxiety. A student who has low self-efficacy, as mentioned previously, judges his/her ability to perform a task as being low, feels less in control, and believes that low ability is internal. For each of the four areas of anxiety, there were examples of students in class blaming themselves for failing to perform. For instance, Diane exclaimed, "I think it's me. I think it's me. I think I'm not capable of getting where I want to get and when my friend Dana wasn't here today I felt lost... I got this panic feeling like, oh my God, he's gonna give us an assignment and I'm not gonna get to it in time." Even with Internet time delay anxiety which is basically a problem with the technology, Newman, felt it was his fault when he was stopped because of time delays. He explained that he felt, "stupid" and thought it must be his fault that he couldn't get to the information he wanted. In another instance, Diane's friend Dana, who did not seem to experience much anxiety in the class, was not exempt from blaming herself for not being good at book learning (as opposed to hands-on learning with the computer) even though most of the class seemed puzzled after a lecture imbued with a barrage of cryptic text. From these examples and others, it was clear that, in this class, low self-efficacy played a significant part in Internet anxiety.

The following section is a list of instructional techniques and behaviors, some of which mitigated the students' Internet anxiety in this particular class and some of which exacerbated the students' fears. All of the instructors' tactics related to one or more of the four areas of anxiety identified, in that he either addressed the concerns in these defined areas or failed to alleviate the students' anxieties as they related to the four categories of anxiety, including Internet terminology anxiety, Internet search anxiety, Internet time delay anxiety, and general fear of Internet failure. Additionally, many of the successful tactics used by the instructor addressed low self-efficacy concerns either directly or indirectly.

Grooming the Learners

The instructor emphasized the Internet as a "live Internet" which counteracted some of the false promises that people like Newman felt they had been bombarded with. The analogy of the Internet being like a living organism highlights the fact that it is not perfect, i.e., sites come and go so people may not be able to find what they are looking for. The instructor also warned students about time delays several times which Newman said helped him to be less anxious because he knew it wasn't he who was doing something, "wrong or stupid." The instructor devoted class time to a brainstorming session about the pros and cons of the Net.

4

Organised Literacy

Change in Technology

Programmed learning is one of the important invocations of the 20th century in the teaching-learning process. It is a self-instructional technique for providing individualized instruction or learning experience to the learner. In programmed learning, the subject matter or learning experience is logically sequenced into small segments. The learning experience is self-corrective.

The English writers prefer to use the term programmed learning and the American authors prefer the use of programmed instruction.

It is held by some educators that 'Gita' is the first example of programmed learning. They hold that the text of the 'Gita' has several ingredients of programming: initial behaviour, small steps, active participation of the learner, terminal behaviour, immediate feed-back and self-evaluation by the learner.

Several educators regard Socrates as the earliest programmer. Socrates used to guide his followers to gain knowledge by conducting them conversationally along a path from fact to fact and insight to insight.

Programmed learning emerged in the beginning of the 20th century from the efforts of American psychologists. E. L. Thorndike (1874-1949) was the first psychologist whose findings bear direct relevance to programming. Other important psychologists who have made significant contribution in the field are Sidney L. Pressy, Robert M. Gagne, Robert Mager and B. F. Skinner.

Programmed learning is related with the 'Law of Effect' as explained by Thorndike. Sidney L. Pressey, a psychologist of Ohio State University, is credited for developing in the middle 1920's practical machines which could teach as well as test. The teaching machines as developed by Pressey present a series of questions to a student and inform him immediately whether his response is right or wrong.

In 1943, Skinner and his two other colleagues started programming by teaching a pigeon to roll a small bowling ball by operant conditioning. By 1954, Skinner and James G. Holland devised the auto-instructional methods which have served the present generation as the basis for present work in programmed instruction. In Skinnerian programmed instruction, whether mechanised or otherwise, the learner is initially asked a question which he can easily answer correctly without any previous study of the particular lesson. The learner is taught by the sequence of questions. He is asked more and more as the lesson proceeds in very small steps.

In 1955, Norman A. Crowder developed what he calls "automatic tutoring by intrinsic programming" as against "extrinsic programming" developed by Skinner.

Robert Mager (1958) gave a new concept known as "Learner Controlled Instruction" which is a kind of Socratic dialogue in reverse, in which the learner led the instructor. The instructor remained silent until the learner himself stimulated the instructor with questions that suggested the needed illustrations, demonstrations, practice or some other help.

Stoluron, at Illionis, aimed at developing a process which should provide for greater individualization by measuring needs and developing programmes that require a computer to assist instruction.

In 1962, T. F. Gilbert gave formalized expression of his technology of education called Mathetics. Pennington and Slack expressed in 1962 further detailed methods of preparing lessons from mathetic principles.

Programmed learning is a process of arranging material to be learned in a series of small steps designed to lead a learner through self-instruction from what he knows to tne unknown of new and more complex knowledge and principles. A programme takes the place of a tutor and leads the learner through a set of frames of specified behaviour designed and sequenced to make it more probable that he will behave in a given derived way.

In programmed learning, it is said that the most efficient, pleasant and permanent learning takes place when the student proceeds through a course by a large number of small, easy-to-take steps. Wilbur L. Schramm (1962) lists the essential elements of programmed instruction as: (*a*) an ordered sequence of stimulus items, (*b*) to each of which a student responds in some specific way, (*c*) his responses being reinforced by immediate knowledge of results, (*d*) so that he moves by small steps, (*e*) therefore, making few errors and practicing mostly correct responses, (*f*) from what he knows by a process of successively closer approximation, toward what he is supposed to learn from the programme.

Following definitions provide a comprehensive view of programmed instruction.

Dale, Edgar (1962). Programmed learning is a systematic, step by step, self-instructional programme aimed to ensure the learning of stated behaviour.

Das, R. C (1993). Programmed instruction is a method of individualised instruction where each individual learns by himself at his own rate. Programmed learning consists of elements of new knowledge called 'steps' which are arranged in a sequence in such a way that a student can easily learn by himself.

Espich, James E. and William B (1965). Programmed instruction is a planned sequences of experiences, leading to proficiency in terms of stimulus response relationship.

Gulati and Gulati (1990). Programmed learning as popularly understood is a method of giving individual instruction in which the student is active and proceeds at his own pace and is provided with immediate knowledge of results. The teacher is not physically present. The programmer, while developing programmed material has to follow the laws of behaviour and validate his strategy in terms of student learning.

Jacobs and Others (1966). Self-instructional programmes are educational materials from which the students learn. These programmes can be used with many types of students and subject-matter either by themselves, hence the name "self-instruction" or its combination with instructional strategies.

Kampfer (1970). Programmed learning is a device which presents an exercise or a problem to a student, inducing him to respond; and revealing to him whether or not his response is correct.

Leith, G. O. M (1966). Programme is a sequence of small steps of instructional material (called frames), most of which require a response to be made by completing a blank space in a sentence. To ensure that expected responses are given, a system of cueing is applied, and each response is verified by the provision of immediate knowledge of results. Such a sequence is intended to be worked at the learner's own pace as individual self-instruction.

Luonsdaine Arthur, A (1964). An instructional programme is a vehicle which generates an essentially reproducible sequence of instructional events and accepts responsibility for efficiently accomplishing a specified change from a given range of initial competencies or behavioural tendencies to a specified or terminal range of competencies or behavioural tendencies.

Marke, Susan (1969). Programmed learning is a method of designing a reproducible sequence of instructional events to produce a measurable and consistent effect on the behaviours of each and every acceptable student.

Navi, N. S. (1984). Programmed instruction is a technique of converting the live instructional process into self-learning or auto-instructional readable material in the form of micro-sequence (the segments of subject-matter) which the learners are required to read, make some right or wrong response, correct wrong responses or confirm right responses and attain the complete mastery of the concept explained in the micro-sequences.

May, K. O. (1965). Educational programming is the scheduling and control of student behaviour in the learning process.

Smith and Moore (1962). Programmed instruction is the process of arranging the material to be learned into a series of sequential steps. Usually it moves the student from a familiar background into a complex and new set of concepts, principles and understandings.

Stolurow (1966). Programmed learning can be described as a process in which a teacher presents (*i.e.*, communicates), a subject matter to a learner so that he responds to it (i.e. communicates to the teacher) the next item of information to be presented.

From the above mentioned definitions of programmed learning, following characteristics may be derived:

1. It is a method of individualized instruction.
2. In this technique, instructional material is logically sequenced and broken into suitable small steps or segments of the subject matter called 'frames'.
3. For sequencing a particular unit of the instructional material, the programmer has to pay due consideration to the initial or entering behaviour of the learner.
4. In actual operation, the beginning is made by presenting a 'frame'. The learner is required to read or listen and then respond actively.
5. Programmed instruction system has an adequate provision for feed-back.
6. The interaction between the learner and the learning material or programme is very important.
7. Programmed learning provides self-pacing to the learner.
8. Programmed learning provides for continuous evaluation.

Devices for Teaching

There are three basic types of programmed instructional material—The teaching machines, the programmed textbook and scrambled textbook.

The teaching machine. A teaching machine is intended to function as a private tutor. It is simply a mechanical devise or piece of apparatus designed to present to the student a sequential programme of learning activities comprising instructional items which requires the student to make an overt response and which provides the student with immediate knowledge of the accuracy of his response. It represents the practical application of laboratory technique of education.

Programmed textbook. Each page of the programmed textbook consists of usually four or five panels. The student begins with the top panel on page one, responds to it, turns to page two to get his answers confirmed on the top panel, goes to the top panel on page three, responds to it, confirms the answer by turning the page, and so on.

The scrambled textbook. In a scrambled textbook, branching or intrinsic technique is used.

Principle of Small Steps. It is shown by experiments that even the dullest students can learn as effectively as the brightest students if the subject matter is presented to them in suitable small steps. When we divide the task to be learnt into very small steps, and ask the students to learn only one step at a time, then probably all the students will be able to learn one small step at a time and sequentially learn all the steps. It is a difficult task to climb a mountain but once steps are built even a child can climb the mountain very easily. This is known as the 'Principle of small steps'.

Principle of Active Responding. The second psychological principle is that the students learn better and faster when they are actively participating in the teaching-learning process. In our classroom teaching the teachers to ask a few questions and the students respond. But is not possible for the teachers to ask all the students to respond at each small step. A teaching machine text or a programmed text contains a large number of questions—one question at each small step and the students respond actively. The principle of active responding is used for the programmes. The teaching machines and programmes have proved to be superior because they provide opportunity to every learner to respond at every small step.

Principle of Reinforcement. Every response even approximately correct must be reinforced immediately. Delayed reinforcement fails to work. This is possible only when a teacher has to teach only one student at a time. The most ideal situation is when the teacher can cater to the needs of his students individually. But in classroom teaching this is hardly possible. No teacher, however efficient and sincere he may be, can reinforce each correct response of each of his students as soon as it is made in a classroom situation where he has to teach abut 40/50 students. The teaching machines and the programmes do the job more efficiently.

Principle of Self-Pacing. The programmed instruction is based on the basic assumption that learning takes place effectively if the learner is allowed to learn at his own pace. Therefore, a good programme of the material always takes care of the principle of self-pacing. A learner moves from one frame to another according to his own speed of learning.

Principle of Student-Evaluation or Student Testing. Continuous evaluation of the student and the learning process leads to better teaching-learning. In the programmed instruction, the learner has to leave the record of his responses because he is required to write a response for each frame on response sheet. This detailed record helps in revising the programme.

Important stages in the Development of the Programmed Instruction

Preparation. This is the first stage in the development of the programme. It includes:

(*i*) Selection of the topic.
(*ii*) Writing assumptions about learners.
(*iii*) Defining objective in behavioural terms.
(*iv*) Writing the entry behaviour (present status) of the learner.
(*v*) Developing specific outline of the content.
(*vi*) Preparing a criterion test.

Construction or writing of the programme. The programme is written under these heads (*i*) Writing draft frames in a sequence i.e. from simple to complex. (*ii*) Editing the draft frames by a team of experts usually comprising a subject-matter expert, a skilled writer and the programmer.

Try Out Revision. It includes (*i*) Trying out the programme on a few individual learners and finding out their reactions and making necessary changes in the light of reactions, (*ii*) Trying out the programme on a group of learners and making necessary changes on the basis of their reactions; and (*iii*) Trying out the programme in the field.

Evaluation. This implies finding the success or the failure after implementing a programme.

CIVICS-CLASS X

Introduction. This a programme meant for you for the study of salient features of the Constitution of India.

In this programme you will find paragraphs which are called frames. Study each frame carefully and write down what is required. Answers are given at the end. After stating you answers, check them. If your answer is wrong or you do not understand anything, you can again go back to the frame. It is not a test but instead it is a self-study programme.

Frame 1. The Constituent Assembly of India was set up under the provisions of the Cabinet Mission Plan to frame the Constitution of India which was formally adopted on 26th Nov. 1949 and came into force on 26th January 1950. It took nearly three years to complete the work.

(*i*) What was the work assigned to Constituent Assembly?

(*ii*) Under whose provision was it formed?

(*iii*) When did our Constitution come into force?

(*iv*) When was it adopted?

(*v*) How much time did Constituent Assembly take to complete its work?

Frame 2. The Preamble of the Constitution has a great significance but is not a part of the Constitution. The Constitution was framed by the people of India through their representations. It stresses the fact that the reign of the land lies with the people of India.

(*a*) Is the Preamble a part of the Constitution?

(*b*) By whom was the Constitution framed?

(*c*) In whose hands does the reign of law of India lie?

Frame 3. The Preamble of our Constitution is as under:

We the people of India having solemnly resolved to constitute India into a Sovereign Socialist Secular Democratic Republic and to secure to all its citizens:

Justice, social, economic and political;

Liberty of thought, expression, belief, faith and worship

Equality of status and of opportunity; and to promote them all;

Fraternity assuring the dignity of the individual and the unity and integrity of the Nation.

In our Constituent Assembly this twenty-sixth day of November, 1949, do hereby adopt, enact and give to ourselves this Constitution.

Note—Three new terms—Socialist, Secular and Integrity were added to the original text of the Preamble when it was amended in 1976 with the 42nd Amendment.

The Preamble stresses the democratic basis of the Constitution by stating that the People of India gave to themselves this Constitution. It also states objectives like justice, liberty, equality and fraternity.

(i) Who has given the Constitution of India?
(ii) What kind of justice has been ensured by the Preamble?
(iii) What type of Republic is to be constituted?
(iv) What kind of equality has been given to its citizen?
(v) How many types of liberty can a citizen enjoy?

Frame 4. Another important feature of the Preamble is that the people themselves adopted and enacted the Constitution. Thus, the representatives of the people frame the laws of the country and they have the power to change or amend the Constitution.

(*a*) Who frames the laws of the country?
(*b*) What has the power to amend the Constitution?

Frame 5. The Constitution of India has many unique features which distinguish it from Constitutions of other countries. The framers of the Constitution freely borrowed ideas but took care to adapt these to the needs of the country.

The Constitution makes India a Sovereign, Socialist Secular, Democratic Republic. The word Sovereign means that India is completely free from external control. No outside power has the right to interfere either in her internal administration or direct her in the conduct of her foreign policy.

This was emphasised to ensure that India was no longer 'dependent' on the British Empire as she had been before Indian Independence Act 1947 or 'dominion' as she had been from 15th August, 1947 to 26th January 1950.

(*a*) What kind of status did India enjoy during 15th August 1947 to 26th January 1950?

(*b*) Was India sovereign between 15th August 1947 to 26th January 1950?

(*c*) What is the meaning of the word 'sovereign'?

(*d*) Does the Constitution of India have unique features?

(*e*) Did the framers of the Constitution borrow ideas?

ANSWERS

1. (i) To frame the Constitution of India.
   (ii) Provision of the Cabinet Mission Plan.
   (iii) 26th January 1950.
   (iv) 26th November 1949.
   (v) Nearly 3 years.
2. (*a*) No.
   (*b*) People of India through their representatives.
   (*c*) People of India.
3. (i) People of India.
   (ii) Social, economic and political.
   (iii) Sovereign Socialist Secular Democratic.
   (iv) Equality of status.
   (v) Five.
4. (*a*) Representatives of the people.
   (*b*) Representatives of the people.
5. (*a*) Dominion.
   (*b*) No.
   (*c*) India is completely free from external control.
   (*d*) Yes.
   (*e*) Yes.

Process for Testing

Merits of programmed instruction. 1. A well-programmed instruction is a great thrust in the direction of individualised instruction, as it is tailored to the needs of the individual learner in the class. 2. It permits individual learner to progress at his own speed. An intelligent learner needs no longer to be bored or allowed to lose interest on account of his slow progress of other learners of the class. He can make progress as he is capable of. 3. Since a programme requires continuous response from the learner, it overcomes the inertia and passivity on the part of the learner. 4. The teacher can give explanation in the classroom if the error is common or he may arrange individual conferences on specific points. 5. Learning material in a programmed instruction is presented in such a way that learning becomes an interesting game and the learner is motivated to meet the challenges set by his own capabilities. 6. Programmes are developed by experts. They are empirically tested and modified till they are standarised. A number of learners can use a single good programme and thus evade textbooks. 7. In programmed instruction the learner is immediately reinforced to correct his response and this reinforcement sustains the motivation of the learner. 8. The self-instructional technique presents material in which its complexity is simplified through the analysis of the subject-matter into small and more easily assimilated segments of information. 9. The introduction of programmed instruction is of great significance for developing countries which are set on the path of educating millions of learners and are short of teachers. 10. Good teachers are freed from the boredom of routine classroom teaching and they are in a position to devote more time to more creative activities. 11. The programmed instruction has been used more successfully in teaching the discernment of the logic of various disciplines and inspiring students to creative thinking and judgement. 12. Certain motor skills and intellectual abilities normally taught by frequent drills and rote memorisation can be very efficiently taught by self-instructional devices. 13. Self-instructional materials have been found to be very useful in the West in revolutionisng the social setting of the classroom. Problems of discipline have been solved and a new hope for eliminating emotional and social problems has been generated. 14. Programmed instruction enables the teacher to diagnose the problems of the individual learner. 15. The introduction of programmed instruction is very helpful in certain situations where human instructors are not easily available in the required number, for instance small schools in the isolated or hill areas.

Programmed materials have been severely criticised as a threat to replacing the teacher.

It is also argued that there is too much emphasis in learning facts and very little emphasis on the mastery of principles and concepts.

Some critics of programmed instruction maintain that the user of a programme does not now where he is headed to.

They also point out that the learners are not aware of the organisation and programmed instruction is unrelated to other aspects of instruction.

It is also argued that the programmed instruction material is very costly and only rich nations can afford it.

It is also stated that the development and use of programmed instructional material require expert knowledge and training. An average teacher finds it very difficult to make use of this device.

As a result of experimental studies and research, following types of programmed instruction have emerged.

1. Linear or Extrinsic Programming
2. Branching or Intrinsic Programming
3. Mathetics Programming
4. Rules System of Programming
5. Computer Assisted Instruction (CAS)
6. Learner Controlled Instruction. (LCS)

The first three styles—linear, branching and mathetics are the basic formats. The rules system represents the deductive and inductive approach to teaching. The other two types, Computer Assisted Instruction (CAI) and Learner Controlled Instruction (LCI) are not the basic format of Programming. They are, infact, the ways and means of providing instruction. Here we have taken up only the basic type of programming.

Linear Procedure

B. F. Skinner is the originator of linear programming. It is also called a single tract programme. According to Skinner, a creature, a bird or a human being can be led to a desired behaviour by means of a carefully constructed programme consisting of small steps leading logically through the subject-matter from topic to topic, provided each step is reinforced by some kind of favourable experience or reward. The increments in information which the learner is expected to absorb are small. The favourable experience or response increases the probability of the same response to occur again in the future. The process of rewarding the correct response to a stimulus increases the general tendency to give a response.

The sequence of frames and path of learning in programmed learning is systematic and linear. That is why, this type of programming is referred to as linear programming. Hence all the learners have to proceed through the same frames and in the same order.

In a linear programme, learner's responses are controlled externally by the programmer sitting at a distant place. Hence linear programming is also termed as extrinsic programming. In branching programming, learner's response is controlled by the learner himself internally. It is, therefore, also called intrinsic programming.

Merits. 1. Immediate knowledge of results acts as a great motivator and releases anxiety and tension. 2. The smallness of the frames brings the sub-goals within the reach of the learner and thereby facilitates secondary reinforcement. 3. Repetition strengthens the responses and ensures learning. 4. Easy nature of the programme provides 'success experience' to the learner.

Limitations. 1. In linear programming, the learning process becomes quite dull on account of the following reasons (*a*) Subject matter is broken into very small pieces, (*b*) Responding is quite mechanical and restrictive, and (*c*) The learning process is quite slow. 2. The use of linear programming is limited to some subjects and topics. 3. Linear programming cramps the imagination of the learner and initiative for creative, integrative and judgement learning. 4. Linear programming encourages guessing. 5. Linear programming does not develop the discriminating power of the students.

Intrinsic Procedure

Branching or intrinsic programming was developed by Norman A. Crowder (1954) an American technician. According to Crowder, branching or intrinsic programme is one which adopts to the needs of the learners without the medium of any extrinsic device such as a computer. It is not controlled extrinsically by the programmer.

Norman A. Crowder was a technician who was working in the United States Air Force. He was faced with the problem of efficiency of vocational training. His programme is based on intuition. His approach at the most is practical. This type of programme employs multiple choice response patterns. The learner is required to select one right answer out of several responses presented to him.

Merits. 1. Big size of a frame as well as the branching minimises unnecessary repetitions and responding, thus reducing the amount of learning time and fatigue. 2. The pitfalls and consequences of erroneous logic are usually explained in the remedial frames so that the learner not only gets the correct responses but also understands why some other response is not correct. 3. Instead of simple response it provides alternatives in the form of multiple choice. 4. Through its broad frames, branching programme provides for more freedom to respond and scope of choosing one's path of learning according to one's need. Thus, it helps in maintaining the interest and initiative of the teacher. 5. Branching programme is helpful in the development of the power of discrimination of the learner. 6. Branching programme helps in the development of creativity and problem-solving ability. 7. Branching is most useful in the areas beyond facts, definitions and basic skills. 8. The frames being of a large size contain a good deal of information and this may enable the programmer to enrich the style and expand his ideas.

Limitations. 1. The multiple choice questions provided in this programming may lead to guess work on the part of the learner and he may not understand the subject matter of the frame. 2. The setting of appropriate multiple choice questions suiting to the entire material of the frames proves a difficult task. 3. No branching method can provide infinite branching to take care of all possible needs of every individual student. 4. The cost of branching programme is very high when compared with traditional teaching approaches. 5. The branching programme is not suitable for small children as they are unable to express symbolisation. 6. The programme needs revision after every five years. 7. It is difficult to cover the entire subject matter of the curriculum in the stipulated time. 8. The diagnostic questions framed by the programmer may or may not suit the needs of the individual learner. 9. The programme cannot shape the behaviour of the learner.

Teaching Instruction and Programmed Instruction. According to Edger Dale, "Teaching' is a broad, vague, ill-defined term and instruction' is a purposeful, orderly, controlled sequencing of experience to reach a specified goal. 'Programmed instruction' is a sub-head under instruction and represents a more rigorous attempt to develop a mastery, over specified goals to secure 'insured' learning."

Programmed Instruction	*Traditional Method*
1. It is an individualised technique of instruction.	1. It is a group technique.
2. It is based on the teaching principles that have been known for years.	2. It becomes difficult to apply teaching principles in crowded classrooms.
3. It presents the instructional matter step by step in logical order.	3. It presents the instructional matter as a whole.
4. The size of the unit of information presented to the pupils is a small bit of information.	4. The unit is a lengthy one. There is very little provision for response from the students in the form of answers to questions.
5. Immediate feedback is given to the learner.	5. The learner does not get immediate feedback.
6. Objectives are defined very clearly in operational terms.	6. Objectives are not well-defined and are usually vague.
7. The programmer prepares his programme with care and precision.	7. Very little preparation is made.
8. Programme is prepared in such a way that the student automatically participates actively by making responses continually.	8. The student usually remains a passive listener and the teacher himself does the summarising and reviewing.
9. A programme is developed empirically through a series of tryouts and refined gradually. Effective sequences students reaction of frames are retained and ineffective ones discarded.	9. It is usually found to be very difficult to modify traditional instruction.

Teacher's Role

Programme learning cannot replace the teacher. Any innovation in the school programmes and practices must remain in the hands of the teachers. The radio and T.V. did not displace the teacher. Similar is the case with programmed instruction. It is upto the enlightened teachers to take up the challenging task of preparing programmes. We have got a wide market. The programmes can be sold all over the country. A student who is convinced that he can learn better, achieve more with the help of this programme, will definitely prefer instead of buying this programme to buying a text book. By taking up this challenging task we will not only help the cause of education, help our fellow teachers by setting them free from the routine task of information, giving help to the students to achieve more, but we will be helping ourselves also.

It may also be remembered that these gadgets can be used mainly in the cognitive field and possibly in the psycho-motor field to develop certain abilities and skills of the students as an individual. A teacher is something more than all these gadgets put together. He has to bring about socialization of the individual; he has to promote socially desirable attitudes and interests and mould the personality of the students. The effective domain is almost reserved for his care. At present the teacher is not able to devote his energy and time to this important task as most of his time and energy is consumed by his routine job as an information giver. We always talk of education for three 'H's' – the head, the hand and the heart. But it has almost remained a mere slogan. Programmed learning, teaching machines and other gadgets will set teacher free from routine work. These are labour-saving devices for the teacher so that he may function more effectively in a field of his own choice.

Technique involved in programmed instruction can be used in teaching different subjects. Teaching of mathematics, science, social studies and elements of Indian languages can be done effectively with the help of this new technique. The teacher has to formulate objectives of teaching a particular subject, undertake content analysis of the subject matter in the light of objectives, frame a chain of questions which will lead the pupils in the direction of the objective and present the questions to his pupils who are expected to try their hand at answering the questions independently. The teacher will have to play the role of a friend, guide and philosopher in the class when the pupils are engaged in solving the riddle and at the same time acquiring knowledge or skill. The question of class discipline may not arise as the pupils will be found busy doing the task assigned to them by the teacher. The teacher will have to do remedial or corrective teaching as the weakness of his pupils will be located in the very act of learning. The pupil will also undergo a process of self-evaluation as he completes his work.

Role of the teacher in the changed context of Programmed Learning may be stated as under :

1. Teacher as an advisor in helping students in the selection of programme learning material.
2. Teacher as a discussion leader for focussing the attention of the learners on important points.
3. Teacher as a guide to clarify doubts and elaborate on various points asked by the learner.
4. Teacher as an evaluator of the learning outcomes.
5. Teacher as a consultant to the various agencies engaged in production of programmed material.

The programmed learning approach can be adopted in normal classroom teaching in the following ways:

1. A teacher can make use of the principles of programmed learning such as active responding, minimal errors and confirmation while teaching various subjects in the conventional manner.
2. A teacher can define behavioural objectives in advance of teaching.
3. A teacher can validate the instructional systems of a class in terms of the performance of learners immediately after teaching is over.
4. A teacher can regulate questions and answers. The answer of a learner can be immediately reinforced by informing or telling whether it is correct or incorrect.

5. A teacher can plan the entire instructional programme of a classroom and can treat the terminal behaviour, the pre-requisite skills and content analysis in advance.

Komoski (1960) an expert has observed "Two thousand years ago the world's first public administrator, a gentleman by the name Quintilian wrote what might be called a handbook for teachers." In it he has one bit of advice which will serve as an excellent starting point for a discussion of programmed learning and its potential uses. His advice is: "Do not neglect the individual student. He should be questioned and praised."

Organised Instruction

Programmed instruction is still in its infancy in India. Programmed instruction as an optional or elective paper has been included at the B. Ed./M.Ed. level in a few universities in India. It also forms a part of the paper of Educational Technology/ Educational Innovation. However, as regards its classroom use, it may be observed that it is almost nil. As far back in 1966, the Kothari Commission suggested to develop programmed material in different subjects to test the suitability of the technique in Indian conditions. An Association of Programmed Instruction has been formed to coordinate the research being done at different centres in the country. The association also disseminates the information on new studies through its journal issued from time to time. The National Council of Educational Research and Technology has also done some work in the field. In spite of all these efforts, it may be stated that the application of programmed instruction has not yet made an appreciable impact on our classroom teaching. Our methods of teaching still remain traditional, by and large.

5

Derived Value

Demand on Rise

The rapid changes that are taking place in computing in general and in educational computing and the increasing demand for courses and programmers in this area have resulted in several activities and events taking place in the School of Education. The faculties in elementary and secondary education both have approved the incorporation of a programme for an orientation to microcomputers in education for all undergraduate teacher educate students at the University. This programme is to commence in the fall of 1982 and will include approximately ten hours of instruction. The specifies of the content and scheduling of this programme are not yet firm, but will most likely include an overview of computers and their use in instruction, technology, features of hardware, machine operation and demonstrations of instructional software.

1. Within existing graduate degrees emphases in several areas related to educational computing are being considered. One emphasis is for those persons wishing to concentrate on instructional systems and computers. Many of these persons will likely find employment in educational settings in industry. A second emphasis would be for persons planning to remain in 'school classrooms but wish concentrated work on instructional

computing. A third emphasis would be for persons wishing to purse supervisory positions in instructional computing in school systems. Each of these emphases has somewhat unique needs for graduate work. Each of these emphasis could make use of coursework in computer science in addition to the coursework in education.

Coursework in computer science is available since their are existing graduate degrees in computer science on campus and two new undergraduate programmes in computing are being implemented on campus, one in Computer Science-Engineering and another in the College of Arts and Sciences.

The possibility of interested persons choosing one of these new emphases and the availability of supporting coursework in computer science will provide competent persons for positions in schools, school systems and industrial training.

2. The dean's committee will be addressing several questions of logistics and questions of future equipment needs and priorities. Logistical questions include the scheduling of laboratory time, instructional time and resulting machine use; financing expendable materials associated with the laboratory; the availability of materials and how to address increased faculty use in light of increased use instruction and by others.

   An important question that must be addressed concerns future purchases of equipment and what kind of equipment should be purchased. Up to now, all purchases were Apple machines, for the reasons cited above. It is anticipated that deviation from this will likely take place in the near future since we are approaching the minimally adequate number, of Apple machines for regular instruction. Pressure is already being felt to begin looking at other machines for various uses other than direct instruction.

3. Interactive video equipment has just newly arrived. Involvement in this field will begin soon but the direction

to be taken in this area has yet to be decided. The use of interactive video may prove to be an area of application of computer technology as exciting for education as many, say, the microcomputer will be.

The activities which have taken place in past years are the predecessors of many more activities in the future. These activities will involve many more persons, than before as more faculty become comfortable with the equipment. It is anticipated that this activity will accelerate, due in part to the faculty seminar and the increasing availability of equipment. This will necessitate greater co-ordination to minimize the duplication of activities. Without a broad base of faculty support and familiarity with the field little integration of educational computing into the programmes of the School of Education can be expected. Thus the philosophy to date has been to direct initial efforts for the incorporating microcomputers into the School of Education by the orientation of faculty and staff. We have succeeded in this thus far, however this has not been to the exclusion of other efforts, as can be seen by the above list of activities over the past three years.

Equipments at Disposal

Increasing availability of equipment has allowed greater numbers of persons to become involved with additional changes in technology, questions concerning the direction to be taken in the future will have to be addressed. Weighing these needs against a myriad of other demands on finances and personnel is a difficult process. The School of Education of the University of Colorado-Boulder is in much the same position as schools elsewhere. We do feel, however, that we are ahead of others in getting the total faculty and staff involved.

The nearly eighty percent participation in the faculty seminar will and has caused faculty who would otherwise not be involved to develop creative uses of these machines. In other ways we are experiencing the same technological growing pains that others experience. We are fortunate to have a supportive administration at both the School and University levels. The question of what to do for the pre-service teacher education students is being addressed and action will be taken soon. We force that the next few years in education will be challenging and exciting because of the pressure of technological change. We see greatly increased activity in computing in education and plan to be leaders in this field.

Computing will expand the focus of educators to include for more attention to process. Though end products such as the problem's solution or the finished essay will remain important, computing will sharpen attention usefully upon how such products are produced, helping the learner to become more self-sufficient by helping her or him to understand and improve the process that creates the products. Computing will raise graphics to a new level of importance, particularly when compared to text. Dynamic images and means to create, store and manipulate them will become as commonplace to future learners as parallel activities with text have been to preceding generations.

Computing will so permeate out lives that broad computing literacy will be absolutely essential. Those in education must help to develop that literacy, across the entire population. Computing will permeate and inform the entire curriculum, even as theology did in medieval universities. It will no longer be seen as something for mathematicians only but will be used integrally from one end of the curriculum to the other, even by people who see themselves as "non-scientific" or "non-mathematical".

Computing will be used in many different modes within education, and none of these modes should be neglected by those seeking to improve education. Though "tutee" or discovery or exploration computing may be exciting and fulfilling in the right situation, excellent tutorial software will always have available role to fulfil, as will other more tightly constrained software systems. Programming and being able to programme in several languages will remain a valuable background of anyone wishing to play a key role in the application of computing within education. Knowing what lies behind either a successful piece of software is critical in imagining the next step.

Evaluating and developing software are both essential skills for any one seriously applying computing to education. Extensive practice with each is indispensable. Broader human issues, the self-proclaimed expert in computing and education and the vendor have no interest in nor time for, must be constantly considered and debated. Institutions with some mass must be among those who continually press ahead with examining such issues.

Teachers, College is the graduate school of education associated with Columbia University. It enrolls more than 4000 students across three major divisions focusing respectively upon psychology, health and nursing, and instructional institutions and programmes. The activities of computing and education are housed within the division of instruction, a division which also houses the traditional instructional areas such as math education, science education, and music and art education, as well as such newer areas as TESOL and bilingual education. There are between forty and fifty students enrolled for degrees specifically in computing, mostly at the masters level.

Latest Provisions

Undergraduate and graduate students in computer science are in a completely different part of the university and utilize separate computing facilities from to se mentioned below as belonging to Teachers, College. During its near century of existence, Teachers, College has had a major influence on education, both in this country and around the world. If there is one thing that characterizes that influence more than anything else, it is its breadth. unlike other major private schools of education, Teachers, College has tended to aim its programmes, courses, and public proclamations at the mass of educators rather than the academically elite.

In computing, this is reflected in our attention to literacy, to broad programming skills, to a masters, level programme aimed at those without computer scientific skill, and to an attempt to develop materials and books that will be useful in educating a wide range of educators. It is also reflected in our attempts to incorporate computing into the entire curriculum, both in field projects and at the College itself. We believe the development of highly technical skills is best left to computer science colleagues; our job is to encourage them in the right directions, to creatively apply what they develop to education, and to make the mass of educators aware of the implications of the results. As the College reaches its centenary, computing will be an increasingly integral part of all its academic activities.

The new department was formed because faculty and students in the three programmes shared so many concerns and interest. They include, the effects of electronic mediation upon communication, the impact upon human communication of dynamic computer graphics, the meaning of the non-verbal forms of some computer activities such as arcade game playing, the implications for education of what MacCluhan dubbed the electronic "global village", and the relation between traditional skills in instructional design and programmed instruction and the development of computer-based software.

Since 1975, the college has offered a popular masters, degree in computing and education. It requires about 10 courses, five which must be from those listed in the section below subtitled courses, and two which in turn must be Programming I and II. Apart from Programming I and II, the course selected by and approved for the student depends significantly on her or his undergraduate major, work experience, and career interests. A course usually meets an hour and forty minutes, once a week, for a term. In this programme, it usually involves work on several computers, outside class, either independently or with partners in a lab. Most students are employed full-time somewhere in the New York metropolitan area, so all courses are scheduled in the evenings or on Saturdays. The typical load is two courses per term; so it usually takes two years to complete a masters, degree.

In the new department, students may also pursue a doctorate in either communication or technology, with a major in computing. In such programmes, students must complete 90 points and a dissertation. Though tailored to the individual, each doctoral student's programme would normally include most of the 10 courses listed below, several courses from communication and technology, courses on test construction and curriculum development psychology and other relevant areas, and from 10 to 20 points of independent study focussed on the dissertation. As with other Ed.D. programmes at Teachers, College, up to 45 points can be granted for comparable level work done at author institutions, provided the advisor, approves it as relevant.

The dissertation need not be primarily a document like a Ph.D. thesis; it can be software or other computer related materials, accompanied by a relevant justification and appropriate documentation. We expect, for example, that the new course in software development will naturally lead to dissertations for some students. Students are also expected to intern and assist, either in the Microcomputer Resource Centre, in courses, in various field projects, or in combination of several of these activities. The following are the ten computing courses now being offered in the department. The many offerings focussed more specifically on communication or instructional design are not shown, nor are seminars, colloquia, and internships common to the entire department.

- An overview of computers within society, particularly education. Demonstrations, readings, and hands-on participation introduce a wide range of computer applications and underlying concepts. Assumes no computing experience.
- Communicating with computers and humans through programmes. Uses FPL, a new language designed to clearly introduce fundamental programming concepts, and either BASIC or PASCAL or both. For beginners or experienced programmers.
- The use of computer text editing and processing systems in writing. Focuses on writing as a process, synthesizing psychological theory about writing with current computer capabilities. Assumes no computing experience
- Demonstrations, theoretical review and practical work with software for teaching reading, writing, grammar, and literature in English and other languages. Assumes no computing experience.
- A range of computers are used to explore specinc commercially available products and services that apply computing to instruction. Computer as tutor, tool, and tutee.
- Extension of Programming-I applies programming to significant problems through team programming projects.

- Teaching computing: Prerequisite: Programming-II. Explores and practices pedegogically sound ways to teach computing and especially programming to a range of students, including those outside math and science. Includes limited teaching activities.
- Computer graphics, Computing literacy, Programming-I, or comparable introduction. Introduces basic types and applications of computer graphics, particularly but not exclusively in education. Explores various hardware and software systems, provides some hands-on experience, but not programming.
- Permission required. Introduces a range of evaluative instruments and techniques and applies them, through student teams, to a number of representative, commercially-available instructional software programmes and packages.
- Permission required. Team approach to developing computer-based educational software in a variety of academic subjects. Complete modules and systems of software will be designed, programmed, tested and documented.

Since a major problem in integrating computer education into teacher training is the lack of models to emulate, methods to adopt, and materials to utilize; we have tried to make our work serve not only or immediate Programme needs but also the needs of other schools and departments of education as well. That is, we have tried to create materials that embody our developing methods and models, so that others may begin with more than we did.

The programme in computing and education and the various courses are models that embody methods which can easily be copied or adapted by the many students who graduate. Certainly they will make use of some or all of them, thus avoiding some of the initial efforts we had to make. But those who never study here will not benefit very directly from such adoption. We, therefore, have published some of our materials so that a wider audience may profit from them. Two examples will illustrate.

The language we use to teach teachers programming is FPL. The language and the material reflect our assumption that most people will learn more than one language, and that the first one learned should be well structured, graphic, and simple. Accordingly, FPL is taught first but is linked to the learning of both BASIC and PASCAL, in such a way that even the Basic programmes developed are well-structured and easy to read and maintain. FPL is simple, including only one graphic icon or image for each of the foundation elements of classical programming. The language is presented as we use it in Programming I and II, including our work in both BASIC and PASCAL, in the text Programming Primer. We have also developed a tutorial interpreter for FPL which greatly speeds of the learning of syntactic and definitional details of the language.

Both book and interpreter assume that learning occurs most consistently from copying and modifying models and that the best materials take seriously the learner's point of view, providing help and explanation in enough detail to be useful to the novice, but in a form and location where they can be conveniently skipped over by the learner who does not need them. Though only available under test status now, the interpreter will be made publicly available on several types of machines in due course.

To bring teachers more rapidly up to a position where they can wrestle with the educational implications of widespread integration of computing into education, we encourage them to use topologies, analogies, and other classificatory frameworks to categorize diverse examples of computer use in education. Such an example is used in The Computer in the School. That book represents the whole field of computing and education by a collection of nineteen pioneering articles, and suggests a three category framework to simplify coming to terms with that diverse field.

Various Kinds

By presenting several quite different types of educational computing and their implied presuppositions, this material makes it difficult for a student to easily maintain too narrow a perspective on what educational computing is. Act the same time, by the presentation of an appropriate framework, such material enables the students to superimpose enough order on the diversity to remain comfortable with its very breadth. Thus the learner can immediately assume a realistically broad outlook without feeling lost in the chaos.

Since by their general design, association conference leaves many relevant topics either totally unexplored or barely examined, we also sponsor specially focussed conferences from time to time. We hope these conferences, when they are any good, will also serve as models. The conference on Child Appropriate Computing which we held in 1981 is a good example. It was designed to make vendor products the focus of conferee evaluation and thus to determine the extent to which hardware and software marketed as appropriate for children was actually appropriate or inappropriate for them.

Ten vendors or developers came in and the one hundred conferees were divided into ten teams of ten members each. Each team spent one day evaluating four of the products, each in a one hour session. Each vendor made an identical presentation four times during the day, to four different teams. The presentation could take any forms the vendor or developer thought would best show off his or her products' child appropriateness. The evaluations were then written and pooled, and a closing discussion was held in which the evaluations and their import were summarized. By focussing on this topic and upon selected products, conferees and vendors alike got a deeper perspective on what was and what was not child appropriate about the products presented.

A good bit of effort goes into systematic evaluation of instructional software at Teachers, College. A funded project involving several micros and hundreds of hours of graduate student time continues to examine software and refine instruments and techniques for evaluating it. The EPIE project regularly publishes its findings through channels it earlier established for disseminating reviews of text books and other non-computer-based instructional materials. The knowledge of the evaluators and the presence of the software are rich sources of information and material for staff and students in the programme, not merely those few actually doing the EPIE evaluations. At Teachers, College, both inside and outside the department principally concerned with computing, considerable research dealing with computing and education is in process.

Some concerns how adults learn programming, how children learn both programming concepts and other ideas related to using computers, what teachers need to know beyond a language such as LOGO if they are to use it effectively in a normal classroom, and so on. By far the most extended research activity in computing and education here now, though concerns the use of computing in writing.

Under several separate grants, we have been both developing a more appropriate text editor/writing prompter for children and studying how the use of computers in writing affects the quantity and quality of their writing. We believe that a major impact of computing in schools will improve the learning of writing, and hope our work will provide useful materials too. Other departments at Teachers, College are also beginning to conduct research into various aspects of using computers in education and that work can only be expected to increase in the immediate future.

At this time considerable assistance is being given to a number of school districts, primarily in terms of short term training delivered by graduate students, going out to the districts requesting such help. The scope of this work varies widely, from one visit to arrangements that span several years. The latter kind are the most useful in terms of providing more solid help to the districts and some steady income to graduate students. Some of this work has been written up but most have not. We regard it as important not only for the help it offers districts but also for the research opportunities it may afford. Unfortunately, though some of our graduates are setting themselves up to do this sort of in-district training, there remains a shortage of people really qualified to do it here, just as in the rest of the country. Qualified people can make so much more money by applying their computing skills elsewhere, that few find this sort of work attractive for long.

The computing activities here utilize the DEC 20/60, the various micros in the Microcomputer Resource Centre, and indirectly, the many micros people now have access to at home or at work.

Approximately 20 of the terminals directly connected to the DEC 20/60 are available 24 hours a day, seven days a week on a first-come, first-serve basis to the several hundred students in various departments who make some consistent use of the computer. An additional 20 phone lines are also available, on the same terms, to those having access to a suitable, dialup terminal. In addition to FPL, BASIC, and PASCAL, several editors and a great variety of other software are available to students using this central time sharing system.

Students in the programme must use this system for some of their work even if they do most on one or more micros. We believe students should be familiar with both large and small systems.

The MRC includes both micros and helpful humans and together they play an important role in many of our activities. There are currently about 20 machines there of 6 different types and a vast array of instructional software. The staff include a director and 5 to 10 graduate students, each of whom puts in a few hours a week. Some staff double as instructors in orientation and training scheduled for the MRC; some double as software evaluators in the on-going EPIE software evaluation project. Most are familiar with several micros and a variety of software and thus can be usefully informative to students and teachers visiting the MRC.

The department has four professors, one of whom does nothing but computing and education, one of whom splins between instructional design and computing, one of whom spends a minor part of his time on computing, and one of whom spends full time in other areas of the department. In addition, the department has a full time instructor in computing and a number of part-time instructors who teach or assist with one course. There are two faculty members elsewhere in Teachers College who also spend most of their time on computing and education, one on the psychological implications of that computing, the other on administrative and management aspects of computing in schools and colleges. The department has a number of other adjuncts and instructors who are quite active in computing, typical examples being one in computing and writing and one software evaluation.

At this time, the future is only dimly and only the near future at that. So far as Teachers College is concerned, we think that eventually courses in computing and history, computing and music, and so on will spring up and become part of the curriculum in each separate subject area, so they will not be housed except temporarily in the department or programme of computing. At the same time, we think most schools and departments of education and teacher training will have separate programmes or sub-departments specializing in computing in education. While it may be true that computing should be integrated into other subjects, computing is and will continue to be a subject in its own right as well. It has emerged as a politically separate entity within the university curriculum and is emerging as a separate entity in the school curriculum as well, particularly in the form of courses on programming.

Resultant Factors

The implications of extensive computer usage in schools will be an important focus of study for some time to come, particularly in terms of graphics, interactivity, modelling, process, and problem solving. As the routine aspects of computing in education become normal parts of the traditional methods courses and as people arrive, already knowing how to programme as well as in necessary, our attention will increasingly be focused on what it all means. It many be that along with introducing artificial intelligence to schools, we may increase artificial ignorance. If some, we will have lots to think about.

Recall "The Saber Tooth Curriculum"- a satire on education, authored by Peddiwell with a foreword by Harold-Benjamin? This curriculum taught the students the fundamental of fish-grabbing-with-bare-hands and Saber-tooth-tiger-scaring-with-fire even after the tigers disappeared and fish nets were invented.

In teacher training, caught up in supporting a curriculum which, has been effective during the past five years but which may be totally inappropriate for the next five? The other day two professors from a school of engineering were discussing the merits of certain programmes within their department. One professor felt that the school's obligation was to put an engineer into the field who could function with the existing technology. The other professor felt that, since the technology would change before the student graduated, it didn't really matter what the student was taught as long as he/she possessed necessary learning skills. Five years hence, the student would still be an engineer only if he or she could keep up with fast changing developments in the field. To a certain degree, we who are in the profession of training classroom teachers are faced with a similar task.

The computer will have a dramatic impact on the classroom during the 80's. A current survey conducted the Oregon Department of Education has revealed that over 50 per cent of Oregon's schools are now using computers for instruction. Minnesota alone has 20,000 microcomputers in 1800 secondary and elementary public schools. The state of Alaska has adopted tele-computing as an integral part of their statewide educational system. Alaskan school systems consider the microcomputer a standard instructional tool and teachers have readily accepted its presence. Pitka's Point, a remote rural school district of 37 students provides eight APPLE microcomputers for general instructional use.

Anchorage, the largest district in the state, has well defined and articulated computer curriculum serving all 73 schools with computer-assisted learning. From Alaska to Florida, schools are budgeting for microcomputer equipment and supplies. By 1984, it is expected that over one million microcomputers will have found their way into the nation's schools. Today's freshman is tomorrow's beginning teacher. How can we prepare this teacher to cope with the existing technology and yet be equipped to face the demands of tomorrow's classroom? We have entered an era which will be known as the Communications Revolution. We must give the teacher entering this transition period the skills needed to survive the entering this transition period the skills needed to survive the first few years in the traditional classroom and yet build a foundation of knowledge needed to cope with the developing technology. Tomorrow's teacher must be an effective manager of learning rather than the principal source of knowledge. In tomorrow's classroom, through the use of telecommunications, the student will be able to call up information on almost any subject.

Many of the files accessible to the student could be learning episodes on various topics. Accessibility to information will not be a problem, but for learning to take place, some structure needs to be imposed on the sequence of accessing this information. The computer can keep records on students' interaction with episodes, but the teacher needs to interpret the record's meaning. It will be the teacher's responsibility to work with the student and the information system to help the student, maintain a reasonable learning pace.

More of the teacher's time in the future will be taken up with the task involved in assessing, diagnosing, prescribing, directing, and managing the instructional process. Ways will have to be found to help teachers manage the instructional environment more effectively if there is going to be time for the teacher to interact with students. The microcomputer presents the teacher with the opportunity to individualize instruction. No matter what delivery systems are created, there are certain aspects of learning which must be considered. Living in a society where we are interdependent, students will still need to gather together to foster social interactions and to learn how to live in a supporting manner.

Suitable Atmosphere

An educational environment will have to exist that will allow students to learn how to acquire and process information. Some areas such as mathematics, language, arts and reading can be assimilated at the student's learning pace independent of the state of the group to which they are attached. What kind of skills must our teachers possess? Every teacher, in addition to having a basic subject-matter competency, must be aware of subject-matter-resources and be trained in their evaluation. Every teacher must have some management training in order to effectively monitor students, learning.

The teacher must be able to organize and direct group activities. Finally, in order for the teacher to encourage students to progress on an independent basis, he/she must master the available technology to support the learning environments determined by student needs. To meet these needs, the pre-service and in-service training must:

1. Educate teachers to be managers of information..
2. Prepare teachers to be leaders of group process.

3. Train teachers to diagnose and place students within a learning system in which the student can make progress.
4. Instruct teachers to operate the equipment that will be used to help deliver the content.

All learning environments that permit student advancement on an independent basis require elaborate record keeping systems for tracking student's progress. Most future systems will be computer controlled so that record keeping does not impede a student's movement toward a defined goal. Within the next ten years students will no longer be dependent upon the teacher to begin a lesson. Students will be able to engage in a dialogue with the computer which will help them advance in fundamental skill development at a rate that is not possible within today's classroom.

The teacher should understand the technology of such systems in order to maximize his/her effectiveness. How should the teacher training curriculum reflect the needs of this learning manager? Future teachers need to be involved with computer based education throughout their college experience. Appropriate preparation includes a lower division computer literacy course and series of involvements with the microcomputers within other courses. The student is required to demonstrate an ability to interact with microcomputers and run application software. The student is expected to explore the impact of the computer on society. The student is required to write reports on the above activities and is expected to use the microcomputers as a tool to accomplish his task.

6

Learning by Instigation

The Fundamentals

Meaning of learning. Schools are set up for making children learn and all the efforts of the teachers are devoted to their learning. Learning implies a progressive change in behaviour. It involves new ways of doing things and it operates in an individual's attempt to overcome some barriers or to adjust themselves to new situations. Learning is the acquisition of knowledge, attitudes, habits and skills.

The Dictionary of Education by C.V. Good (1973) has given a very comprehensive definition of learning. The term 'learning' has been interpreted to mean, "change in response or behaviour (such as innovation, elimination or modification of responses, involving some degree of performance) caused partly or wholly by experience, such experience being in the main conscious, but sometimes including significant unconscious components, as is common in motor learning or in reaction to unrecognised or subliminal stimuli; includes behaviour changes in the emotional sphere, but more commonly refers to the acquisition of symbolic knowledge or motor skills, does not include psychological changes, such as fatigue or temporary sensory resistance or malfunctioning after continued stimulations."

In the words of Gates and others, "Learning may be thought of as the progressive change in behaviour which is associated on the one hand with successive presentation of a situation, and, on the other, with repeated efforts of the individual to react to it effectively."

According to most of the progressive educators, learning is a very personal experience. Carl Rogers says, "I have come to feel that the only learning which significantly influences behaviour is self-discovered, self-appropriated learning." Similarly Nathariel Cantor has very aptly said, "All genuine learning, in the final analysis, is self-education."

According to narrow view of learning, it takes place only in the classroom but according to wider view of learning it is not limited to classroom or even to school. It begins long before a child enters school and may continue long after school days.

Learning in the school is a tri-polar process in which the learner, the subject matter and the teachers are involved.

Learning may be multipolar process in which the learner, the learner's colleagues, the learner's teacher and the learner's parents and in fact the entire environment are involved.

Yoakman and Simpson have enumerated nine general characteristics of learning which we discuss below:

Learning is growth. The word growth is generally associated with the body which is growing, but through the mental growth of the learner. Although it is latent yet we can perceive its growth. Through his daily activities the child grows both mentally and physically. Therefore, we say that learning is growth through experience.

Learning is adjustment. Learning helps the individual to adjust himself adequately to the new situations. Children meet with new situations which demand solution. Repeated efforts are required to react to that effectively. Life is- full of experiences, and each experience leaves behind some effects in the mental structure. These effects modify our behaviour.

Learning is organising experience. Learning is not mere addition to knowledge. It is not mere acquisition of facts and skills through drill and 'repetition. It is the reorganisation of experience.

Learning is purposeful. All true learning is based on purpose. Purpose plays a big role in learning. According to Ryburn, "This purpose is always connected with the use of some instinctive power, with the use of the are energy with which we endowed with birth." We do not learn anything and everything that comes in our way, in a haphazard manner. All school activities should be purposeful so that the child should feel real urge for learning.

Learning is intelligent. Meaningless efforts do not produce permanent result. Any work done mechanically is without any soul. When a child learns something unintelligently, he is likely to forget it very soon. He does not assimilate but simply commits to memory. Only efforts made intelligently have lasting effects.

Learning is active. Learning does not take place without a purpose and self-activity. In the teaching-learning process; the activity of the learner counts more than the activity of the teacher. The principle of learning by doing is the main principle and it has been recommended by all modern educationists. It is the basis of all progressive methods of education such as the Dalton, the Project, the Montessori and the Basic.

Learning is both individual and social. Learning is not only an individual activity. It is a social activity also. Individual lad is affected by the group mind consciously as well asunconsciously. The individual is influenced by his friends, relatives, classmates, parents, etc., and learns their ideas, feelings and notions. Social agencies the family, church, film and gangs of playmates have a marvellous influence on the child and are always, moulding or remoulding him.

Learning is the product of the environment. Environment plays an important role in the growth and development of the individual. Environment should be healthy and rich in educative possibilities.

Learning affects the conduct of the learner. There is a change in the mental structure of the learner after every experience.

Other general characteristics of learning are:

Learning takes place through trial and error. Some learning is the outcome of trial and error.

Learning depends upon insight. Lastly leafning depends upon insight. Insight has sometimes been described as the 'flash of understanding:

Resultant Factors

Elements and implications in learning may be summarized as under:

Who is to learn? The child is to learn and therefore, his age, abilities, aptitudes and interests should be taken note of by all those who are charged with the learning of the child. The child must be allowed to play an active role in the learning process.

From whom to learn? Broadly speaking there are two most important elements from whom the learner teams i.e. the teacher and textbooks (including other teaching-learning materials). Therefore, a teacher must present good models of teaching-learning. Likewise textbooks and other instructional materials should be of good quality.

Why to learn? Learning goals must be very clear, should be broad based and should go beyond bookish knowledge.

What to learn? This aspect is concerned with the acquisition of knowledge, skills and attitudes.

Where to learn? Learning takes place in the classroom, on the play field, in the workshop, on the formal and in neighbourhood, etc. It may be stressed that school, thoug an important place of learning, is not.

How to learn? It involves various principles of learning, methods of learning, techniques of learning etc.

When to learn? This is concerned with motivational situations in learning.

Elements in learning may be presented in the following form:

Learning Elements

Who is to learn (Child)	From whom to learn 1. Teacher 2. Environment	Why to learn (Aims- of learning	What to learn (Acquisition of Knowledge, skills etc.)	How to learn (Methodology)	When to learn (Motivation)	Where to learn (Class-room, Playfield, etc.)

Process of Learning

Learning is as quite safe mental events to conditions leading to changes in the learner. The sequence of events, in the, learning process is as follows:

1. The individual has needs and is therefore in a state of readiness to respond.

2. He meets a learning situation problem. A new interpretation is required because previously learned responses are not adequate for reaching the goal and satisfying his need. He encounters something new or unexpected, and must search for a different response.
3. He interprets the situation with reference to his goals: He tries a response or responses, which seem to satisfy his need. The way he perceives the situation and the response he makes, depends both on readiness, and on external conditions of the situation.
4. If his response leads to desired goals or satisfaction, he will tend to interpret and respond to similar future situations in the same way. If not, he keeps on trying and reinterpreting until consequences are attained. The learning process is the whole sequence.

Learning is affected by the total situation. This total situation is dependent upon a number of factors. Some are external while others are internal. Among the external factors to the classroom situation, we may mention two important factors of heredity and the status of the home. A classroom teacher can neither change nor increase heredity. Of course, he can use it and develop it. Some children are very rich in hereditary endowment while others are very poor. The native intelligence is different in individuals. Children vary also in particular abilities. The intelligent children can establish and see relationship very easily and more quickly. Our ability to learn and the rate of learning are conditioned by our heredity. Maximum use should be made of the hereditary endowment.

Attempt should be made to see to it that children get opportunities to use and develop their hereditary endowment.

Physical conditions and home conditions also matter. Bodily weakness, chronic illness, malnutrition, fatigue and bad health are a great hindrance in learning. The home conditions-bad ventilation, unhygienic living, bad light, overcrowding, etc., affect the rate of learning and the general response of the child. Sometimes children have to walk long distances to and from the school and this also influences learning.

Internal classroom factors affecting learning are (1) Goals or Purposes (2) Motivation (3) Interest (4) Attention (5) Drill or Practice (6) Boredom or Fatigue (7) Aptitude (8) Attitude (9) Emotional factors Instincts (10) Speed, Accuracy and Retention (11) Age (12) Learning activities provided by the teacher (13) Testing (14) Guidance.

Different Strategies

Meaning, Definition and Significance of Motivation

It is well said, "Motivation arouses interest, interest is the mother of attention and attention is the mother of learning. Thus to secure learning you must first catch the mother, grand-mother and great grandmother." Motivation is the very heart of the learning process. It energises and accelerates the behaviour of the learner. No learning is possible without motivation. The intensity of motivation of the learner determines the effectiveness of his learning.

The word motivation is derived from a Latin word 'movers' which means to move. Thus, motivation is an internal force which accelerates a response or behaviour. At any given time, learners, other things remaining the same, vary in the extent to which they are willing to direct their energies in the attainment of goals, due to difference in motivation

With a view to having a comprehensive understanding of the term motivation, following definitions are given below:

Atkinson, T. We. (1966) states, "The term motivation refers to the arousal of tendency to act to produce one or more effects".

Bernard, H.W. (1965) writes, "Motivation is the stimulation of actions towards a particular objective where previously there was little or no attraction to that goal."

Blais. G.M. and others (1947) observe, "Motivation is a process in which the learner's internal energies or needs are directed towards various goal objects in the environment"

Crow, L.D. and Crow A. (1962) hold, "Motivation is considered with the arousal of the interest in learning and to that extent is basic to learning."

Good, C. We. (1973) regards motivation "as the process of arousing, sustaining and regulating activity."

Guilford. J.P. (1950) is of the view, "A motive is any particular internal factor of condition that tends to initiate and sustain activity."

Hebb, D.O. (1975) thinks that the, term motivation refers "(i) to existence of an organised phase sequence (ii) to its direction and content (iii) to its persistence in given direction or stability of content".

Kelly, W.A. (1955) refers to motivation as "The central factor in the effective management of the process of learning."

Lovell, K. (1964) is of the view that "Motivation in school learning involves arousing, persisting, sustaining and directing desirable behaviour."

Maslow, A.H. (1954) explains motivation as, 'The self-actualization tendency is growth motivation. Self-actualization is the development of personality which frees the person from the deficiency problems of growth. Motivation is constant, never ending, fluctuating and complex and that it is an almost universal characteristic of particularly every organismic state of affairs."

McDonald, F.G. (1972) considers motivation "as an energy change within the person characterized by effective arousal and anticipatory goal relations."

Monappll, Arrm and Saiyadain, Muza S., describe motivation "as the propensity or the level of desire of an individual to behave in a certain manner at a certain time and in a certain situation."

Skinner, C.F. (1947) states that "motivation in school learning involves. arousing, persisting, sustaining and directing desirable behaviour."

Functions of Motivation

1. To arouse interest of the stdents in learning.
2. To direct interest of the students in learning.
3. To initiate interest among the students in learning.
4. To sustain interest of the students. in learning.
5. To energise students in learning.
6. To arouse, accelerate, direct and sustain the behaviour of the learner.
7. To arouse the tendency and produce result by the learner.
8. To release the tension of the learner.

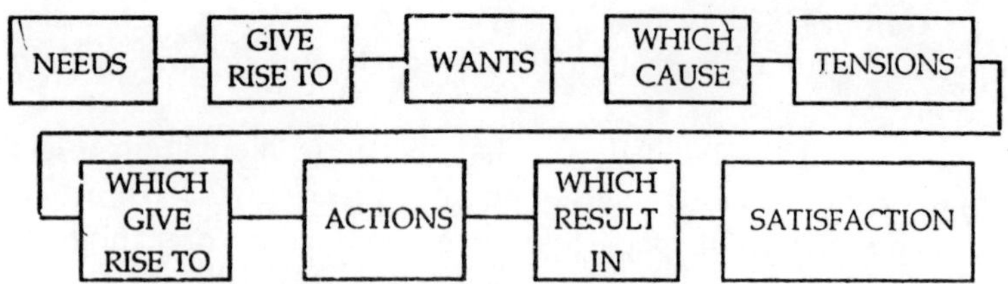

Fig. : Motivational Cycle: Needs-Wants-Satisfaction Chain.

Levels and Types of Motivation

Gourevitch and Feffer (1962) distinguish four stages/levels in the development of motivation, each level characterized by its own type of reinforcement. In the first stage, reinforcement is concrete and bodily. It is direct satisfaction of a physiological need. In the second stage, reinforcement is concrete but external involving tangible rewards such as prizes or intangible rewards like affection or belongingness to a group. The third level involves abstract but external reinforcement like esteem of others, being well-thought by others, etc. The final level involves active concern for self-actualization, reinforced by abstract and internal reinforces, such as self-respect.

Teachers are expected to keep in mind all these stages of development of motivation while dealing with children.

Extrinsic or external and instrinsic or internal are the two types of motivation. External motivation is based on the use of rewards and punishments. Intrinsic motivation is that which is aroused in the learning process itself. It arises out of interests of the students which are related to their attempts to solve their own problem. It is admitted that intrinsic motivation is by far the best type because it is accompanied by a pleasantness which flows out to other related activities and that is desirabale.

Students in the classroom learning need constant motivation from the teachers so that optimum use of their talent may be made for their development. The needs are the basis of motivation. Therefore, techniques that the teachers employ to arouse and maintain motivation will be successful only insofar as they make them perceive that progress is being made towards need-satisfaction. Since individual children differ in regard to their specific needs according to their personality patterns and socioeconomic background, the teachers will have to vary their motivational techniques and employ them judiciously. In other words, every individual pupil should be led towards goal that he is aware of and will want to attain. Secondly, goals should be within each pupil's reach, and should seem attainbale to him. Thirdly, he should be able to judge whether or not he is attaining his goals and how he is falling short. Fourthly, a teacher should not rigidly and strictly adhere to one technique of motivation but he should make use of all techniques judiciously and scientifically. Important techniques are given here:

Attractive physical and environmental conditions. First of all the teacher should attend to the physical conditions of the classroom. There should be no distracting factors in and, around the classroom. Noise, strong light and some undesirable scenes often distract the attention and do away with the interest. Abnormal temperature is also a disturbing element. Monotony results in boredom.

The rooms should, be ventilated and tastefully decorated. There must be flowery plants in the school compound. Cleanliness should be stressed adequately.

Sublimation of innate impulses. Most of the behaviour of small children is directed by their innate impulses. Curiosity, construction, self-assertion, submission, pugnacity and hoarding are some of their most powerful drives which form the basis of all kinds of their activities. Small children are very curious by nature. They like to do many things. Every new and strange things attract them. An efficient teacher will stimulate the impulse of curiosity . He will always start the lesson by exhibiting some very new and strange aspect of the same. Similarly, children like to construct things. .The teacher should encourage the children to learn by constructing and creating things.

Stimulus variation by the teacher. It has been generally observed that children are notable to attend to one thing for a very long period. The effectiveness of the teaching learning process in such a situation depends to a great extent on the stimulus variations used by the teacher behaviour. Some of the common teacher behaviours in the classroom which fall under variation are:

(i) Teacher movement
(ii) Teacher gestures
(iii) Changes in speech pattern
(iv) Changes in sensory focus
(v) Changes in postures.

Reinforcement. These may be classified as:

Positive Verbal Reinforcement. Following a pupil's answer, the teacher verbally indicates pleasures at the pupil's response by the use of words like 'Good', 'Fair', 'Excellent', 'Correct', etc.

Positive Non-Verbal Reinforcement. These include:

Nods and smiles.

Teacher's friendly movements towards pupils.

Teacher's friendly look.

Teacher writing student's response on the blackboard.

Negative Non-Verbal. This comprises gestures-sneering, frowning, expression of annoyance:, impatience, etc.

Negative Verbal. This includes comments like 'No', 'Wrong', 'No good', 'poor', 'of course not', etc.

Rewards and punishment. These are also termed as reinforcers, and the process of giving rewards and punishment is known as reinforcement. Rewards, whether material or symbolic and psychological, enhance and satisfy child's safety, belonging and esteem needs, and as such are capable of acting as incentives. Material rewards' seem to work better for poor children and symbolic rewards seem to work better for children from rich homes. Thus, a reward in order to act as an incentive must be perceived by the child as of some value. As extrinsic motivator, rewards may, however, become an end in themselves, and the child may not develop any intrinsic impulsion to identify himself with the learning activity. Therefore the students should be helped to perceive that successful performance is more important than any extrinsic incentive like prizes, marks and certificates. Intrinsic learning takes place when the individual is motivated without rewards, etc.

Pleasure and pain. According to the oldest theory of behaviour, pleasant experiences which give satisfaction are sought after and painful experiences are avoided by an individual. This theory has direct implication in classroom teaching-learning. The teacher must provide pleasant and satisfying experiences to the students so that they are motivated for further learning.

Attainable goal. There should be a goal to be reached in every lesson. Only then the students can endeavour to continue their efforts to a particular direction. The goal must be made known to students.

Experience of success. Experience of success motivates a child to continue. An activity. The teacher should, therefore, make school work, both curricular and co-curricular, sufficiently varied so that each pupil has a chance to experience success at his own level. He must ensure frequent and regular experience of success or reinforcement throughout all phases of learning but particularly during the earlier and more difficult phases.

Competition and co-operation. Competition is a spur to activity. But competition on individual basis is likely to be unequal and therefore threatening to some students. Competition between groups makes it possible to spread the share of success or failure.

Cooperation too provides motivation since it provides social situation to learners when they find satisfaction of their acceptance and belonging needs.

Knowledge of progress. Pupil's knowledge of their progress of how well they are moving towards their goal is a very effective form of motiovation. It also helps them put greater efforts. Individual progress charts not only inform a child as to how he is doing but also keeps the child involved in learning activity. Children are said to learn better through programmed learning because they get immediate information' of success or failure.

Novelty. The striving toward self-actualization makes pupils search for the new and the different. Field trips, excursions, dramatics, sports, literary activities, etc., satisfy the pupil's needs for self-actualization by providing them opportunities. But their safety needs require that they should know beforehand when and how the new experiences will be provided.

Individual differences of the children. Children have different interests and capabilities. All the children cannot be motivated alike for all the lessons at all time. It is the duty of the teacher to discover individual interests and capabilities of the children in his charge to motivate them accordingly.

Active involvement of the students. Students must be involved actively in the lesson.

Linking with environment. Examples from daily life should be given to illustrate the subject-matter.

Use of Aids. Relevant aids, if used judiciously are very helpful in the development of motivation among the students.

Teaching skills. Teaching skills of the teacher greatly influence motivation. It is not easy to give an exact number of teaching skills involved in motivating students in the class. Commonly identified skills in the teaching, learning process may be listed as under:

(1) Skill in introducing the topic
(2) Skill in putting questions
(3) Skill in dealing with pupil's answers
(4) Skill in stimulus variations
(5) Skill in the use of blackboard or the chalkboard
(6) Skill in handling teaching [illegible] and other equipments
(7) Skill in non-verbal cues
(8) Skill in reinforcement
(9) Skill in the use of illustrations and examples
(10) Skill in the exploition of sub-matter
(11) Skill in explanation
(12) Skill in encouraging group discussion
(13) Skill in planned repetition
(14) Skill in drawing out conclusions from students
(15) Skill in teacher liveliness
(16) Skill in the, closure of the lesson
(17) Skill in using appropriate methods of teaching

Teacher's own motivation and interest in teaching. The teacher must be interested in what he is teaching and in the children whom he is teaching. If he is not interested in the work himself, he can never motivate the class. It may be said that a teacher who has been teaching the same subjects to the same classes for years tends to lose interest. But this is not the fact. The subject-matter may be the same but the children are not the same. Even the subject-matter is changing and developing. Moreover, with experience the teacher will discover new approaches and methods of teaching the same subject.

7

Provisions in Software

Software programs which attempt to provide challenges to solve complex problems are (a) apt to require a longer a longer time for the student to complete, (b) difficult to integrate with the curriculum, (c) difficult for the teacher to master, and (d) difficult to evaluate. Nonetheless, there are computer programs and programming languages that, according to authors' claims, can improve problem-solving skills. Data assessing these claims, however, are scarce. Programming languages that allow the student to control the computer and provide an inherently rich problem-solving environment have attracted much attention. One such programming language is Logo, developed explicitly for young children. It includes an interactive component that allows students to give directions to the computer by informing a "turtle" what to draw. The computer draws what the child has directed. This process allows for immediate feedback. Part of the advocacy for teaching even young children how to direct or program a computer results from a belief that learning to think like a computer makes a better thinker. The argument is not that thinking like a computer is somehow better than human thought, but that the consideration of thinking makes humans more thoughtful.

Researchers have compared the problem-solving performance of subjects who used such programs with the performance of those who did not, but no conclusive results have emerged. Some data suggest that learning the Logo programming language is significantly different from learning other languages because of its interactive nature. Scattered and sparse evidence indicates that Logo instruction may have a positive influence on much things as fluency, originality, and divergent thinking. Some have hypothesized that increased facility with Logo provides the potential for improved thinking to the extent that it acts as a tool for expressing powerful ideas.

By using Logo, children have the opportunity to gain a personal understanding of abstract ideas they are unlikely to encounter until a much higher level of schooling, if at all. Evaluating claims about computer programs or language designed to improve higher-order thinking skills is a more complex process than evaluating knowledge-building programs. Definitions are not as precise and, as we have indicated, there are no agreed upon outcome measures. It is only recently that researchers have begun to prove the claims of developers for programs to improve higher-order thinking.

One of the ways in which computer programs may possibly help in developing the skills of higher-order thinking is through instruction in the use of heuristics, that is, instruction in particular strategies of problem solving. Before considering this matter, we found it useful to look into such questions as (a) Can heuristic strategies be taught and do they actually help students solve problems? and (b) Does training in such strategies transfer across various domains of content?

Select Techniques

One of the most popular views is that a way to teach higher-order thinking skills is to instruct students in particular strategies to solve problems. Simon has pointed out that "powerful general methods exist and... they can be taught in such a way that they can be used in new domains whether they are relevant." Perhaps the best known set of problem-solving heuristics is included in Polya's classic work *How to Solve it*. He developed four categories of heuristics: figuring out the problem, devising a plan, carrying out the plan and looking back. Feuerstein's instructional techniques to improve problem-solving skills include such activities as classifying and comparing attributes, recognizing relationships, planning, synthesizing, and logical reasoning.

It is important for students to monitor their own thinking by suing such strategies as identifying underlying assumptions, grasping whole-part and part-whole relationships, and applying principles to real-life situations. Newell, Shaw, and Simon argued in 1960 that "heuristics are...things that aid discovery. Heuristics seldom provide infallible guidance.... Often they 'work', but the results are variable and success is seldom guaranteed." Suydam, on the other hand, found that "research evidence strongly concurs that problem-solving performance is strongly enhanced by teaching students to use a wide variety of strategies of heuristics, both general and specific." The twenty years that separate these assessments account in part for the disagreement, but good data are still scarce, and the methods advocated for teaching heuristics are mainly based on common sense and intuitive understandings. As early as 1950, researchers explored the hypothesis that students who use explicit problem-solving strategies are better problem solvers than those who do not and that such strategies can be taught so that skills are improved.

Bloom and Broder investigated the problem-solving skills of college students across a variety of subject areas. They found that bright students who were poor problem solvers could be trained to improve their problem-solving skills using the strategies employed by peers who were successful problem solvers. These, who participated in the training tended to score 49 to 68 grade levels higher than matched groups with no training they also expressed confidence and optimism about their newly learned problem-solving abilities. More recently, Pet found that specific instruction that followed the four-step heuristics of Polya's model was effective in improving fifth graders' use of the strategies, but he did not find significant differences in success in solving problems between the experimental group and a control group that had no training.

Since the period of treatment was only four weeks; it is not surprising that problem-solving outcomes were not dramatically influenced. In another study, fourth graders who were taught to develop pictorial aids, such as tables and diagrams, could solve more problems than others who did not receive such instruction. Within the area of mathematics, instruction in problem solving heuristics is generally supplied to clearly structured problems. Schoenfeld successfully trained college-level students to use specific techniques to improve their strategic for solving work problems in algebra. In a follow-up project, Schoenfeld reported that not only did college level students increase their use of particular strategies, but those who used the heuristics effectively were also more successful at solving algebra problems. Perhaps as a result of this success, the students' self-reports of their problem-solving skills were more favourable. In another study on solving word problems in algebra, Mayer, and Bovenmeyer found that performance was predicted by ability to understand the problem and plan the solution.

Some researchers believe that effective problem-solving strategies are specific to particular domains. The argument is that a student gets deeper into a content domain the problem solving skills become more and more specific to that domain and therefore may not transfer to other domains. Studies of expert and novice problem solvers are particularly salient here. These studies have found that when novices and experts are faced with a problem in the experts' domain, they approach the problem in different ways. Novices tend to focus on the literal objects defined in the statement of the problem.

The possible strategies for solution seen by experts are expanded by their understanding of the relationships among concepts and procedures specific to that domain. How are we to reconcile the findings of these expert-novice studies with the views of those who see the value of generalized problem-solving heuristics across different subject matters? One line of argument is simply that increased knowledge of a content domain makes possible a more efficient and precise application of general heuristic procedures.

Greater knowledge of a domain should increase the chances for a person to define a problem accurately, allow on to decide more easily among possible strategies for solution and facilitate resting the validity of possible solutions. In this argument, procedural problem-solving skills interact with the knowledge base to increase the abilities of the student to solve the problem. We might imagine a model with three significant effects: two main effects and an interaction effect of the two.

Drawing from observational studies of students, recent researchers have considered this issue. In a detailed analysis of problem solving in geometry, Greeno argued that three kinds of knowledge are critical for success: (a) heuristic knowledge necessary for carrying out proofs, such as setting goals, forming plans, and generally organizing the problem-solving process; (b) knowledge of specific geometric facts, such as the definition of lines and angles; (c) geometric concepts essential to making inferences and proving theorems. Similarly, Glaser and Pellegrino concluded that two critical and inter-releated components are necessary for higher-order thinking to occur: (a) thoughtful consideration of procedural constraints of a particular problem area, such as inductive or analogical reasoning as problem-solving tools and (b) subject area knowledge.

Recent theoretical work in cognitive sciences has used the notion of knowledge structure or schema to help explain the way people remember, comprehend, and solve problems. Schema theory attempts to describe the relationships between knowledge previously acquired, the way it is organized in the mind, and the ease with which new knowledge is acquired and used. Experts re- viewed as having rich and complex schema that facilitate the acquisition of new information and the rapid solution of many problems.

The prior knowledge base and schema of the expert in physics is sufficiently rich so that many high school physics problems can be solved algorithmically. The expert "knows" the way to define the problem, "knows" the right strategy to solve it, and "knows" how to evaluate the solution. He may apply Polya's steps but he will do so unconsciously and rapidly; for him this is routine processing, not higher-order thinking. To a high school student with a less complete knowledge schema in physics, however, the same problem may pose a complex task requiring higher-order thinking. Although the student may have a solid base of facts and an understanding of the basic rules of physics, the problem may require combining the facts and rule in novel ways.

The student may have to examine multiple ways of representing the problem and explore a variety of possible will be engaged in higher-order thinking only when they are stretched beyond situations where they already know how to find the solution. It also implies that constant deepening of a subject area to include increasingly complex material is critical for either students of experts as they deal with tasks that require higher-order thinking. Psychologists investigating metacognition suggest that students who self-consciously consider their own cognitive processing can enhance their thinking. Much recent research indicates that the student is very active in selecting, interpreting, and even altering the content of instruction. The key processes seen as integral to effective monitoring of cognition are (a) planning activities prior to undertaking a problem (b) monitoring activities during learning and checking outcomes. These activities are remarkably similar to Polya's heuristics and they also reflect Papert's argument for teaching children to program computer.

Controlled use of Polya's heuristic strategies may be viewed as an example of the regulation of cognition. Brown postulated that individuals have a central processing unit, much like a computer, that controls heuristic routines for problem-solving, planning and scheduling appropriate strategies, and monitoring and evaluating the effects of strategies. The complex operations performed by the executive control component take one of two approaches automotive or controlled. Automatic strategies are quickly retrieved, make little demand on the cognitive system, require minimal conscious learner control, and are not dependent on short-term memory.

Controlled strategies are more slowly retrieved, executed in a deliberate, purposeful way, and thus require a great deal of learner effort and control. Controlled strategies can evolve into automatic operations. For example, if Polya's heuristics are practiced in a controlled, conscious way across a number of problem areas, there is reason to believe that their application will become automatic. This discussion has implications for school curricula intended to encourage higher-order thinking. First, for students to find new ways of interrelating knowledge and algorithms they must have a firm grasp of the knowledge needed to solve the problem. If they cannot retrieve this information automatically, they will be distracted from the problem-solving task. Second, if students are to be challenge with higher-order problems at various stages of their knowledge development in a field, then the curriculum should not be organized hierarchically to focus initially only on learning facts and formulas. Instead, students should be challenged to solve problems early, in their exposure to a field-problem based on the knowledge they have already acquired.

Considerable attention should be given early in the curriculum to the interrelationship among facts and rules in order to develop schema that are sufficiently rich to enable students to deal with problems that require organizing information in ways new to them. The selection of content for early problem-solving activities is therefore particularly important. In addition to depth in a single content area, repeated successful experience in using problem-solving strategies across a variety of content areas reinforces learners' use of them in new situations they recognize as resembling the ones in which they succeeded. Psychologists endorse training in multiple contexts because it "decreases the likelihood that a particular piece of information will be wedded to a particular context."

If students assume that solving a problem requires the use of a formula or algorithm applicable only in a single subject area, then they will use these strategies only within that domain. But, if they see problems requiring heuristic strategies and other substrative concepts across a number of domains, it is likely that they will become more fluid thinkers and, ultimately, more successful in solving problems. Our brief literature review suggests the importance of teaching heuristic strategies, that using these strategies in a rich context enhances their effectiveness, and that there is some evidence that strategies may be transferable across content domains. The analysis indicates that students can learn problems-solving heuristics and that, if they use these strategies, they are more effective problem solvers.

The instructional emphasis should be on the process of solving problems and not on the problem solution. One implication of this focus on process is the need for students to practice using heuristic strategies across a variety of content domains and with different types of problems. The depth of the content appears to be a critical component in improving higher-order thought. Research on expert and novice problem-solvers show the importance of a solid information base that is easily retrieved in a problem-solving environment. The problem-solver should be able to retrieve facts and algorithms automatically, but should also be able to perceive the interrelationships among various concepts within a domain.

There are conflicting opinions about the use in schools of computer programs which "only" provided drill and practice or tutorial instruction. One view is that these activities can be carried out by teachers or aids effectively and cheaply and that we use such programs limits students' and teachers' various on the power of computers and reinforces the already strong emphasis in schools on knowledge development to the exclusion of problem-solving activities.

Another view is that such programs can be easily integrated into the curriculum, that they can free the teacher for more demanding activities, that they have been shown to be effective, that they often command the attention of some students more than does conventional teaching and that they offer a convenient way to introduce computers into the classroom. We favor the latter view, though we quickly concede that many existing programs in these categories are not worth students' time and effort. Moreover, the attention in the early part of this chapter to the need for exposure to content depth and for facility of retrieval of knowledge and algorithms as prerequisites for solving complex problems reinforces our view that the knowledge development programs can serve a very useful purpose.

Drill and Practice Software: It focuses on previously learned factual knowledge and skills, in contrast, the other two types of knowledge development software focus on learning new knowledge or skills. Drill and practice software is used with greater frequency in schools than any other type of programs, other than programming languages. Over the past few years the aesthetic quality and the motivational attributes of these programs have improved greatly as program developers have acquired sophistication in the use of graphics and have learned something about how to design programs that sustain the attention of young people.

Properly constructed drill and practice programs should enhance cognitive processing by requiring students to increase speed in retrieving information and in carrying out skill activities to the point where these activities become automatic. This automatic processing, in turn, should assist higher-order thinking by reducing certain cognitive demands on students when they are faced with a problem- solving situation.

The goal is to get students to the point where they can focus on the dimensions of the problem rather than on the heuristics to solve it. One approach is to have the software deliberately focused on increasing student's speed in processing information. Unlike drill and practice activities that require only paper and pencil, a computer program can record the time it takes a student to carry out a problem or to remember or recognize certain information. In addition, it can adjust the amount of time required to present a problem, based on its record of how quickly similar tasks were complete. Finally, criterion levels can be developed experimentally to assess whether students have achieved the skills to carry out the task automatically.

A second approach would be to design programs to increase the student's capacity to chunk together related pieces of information. The ability to solve problems is partially constrained by the amount of information a person can manipulate in short-term or immediate memory. The capacity of human short-term memory is limited to a small and finite number of independent pieces of information-in the neighborhood of seven. If students could automatically chunk together pieces of information so that the pieces are no longer independent, they might be able to increase their ability to solve complicated problems. Based on some assumption about the structure and extent of students' knowledge schema, drill and practice programs might be designed to help them bring together or "chunk" related information.

Content Tutorial Programs: These differ from drill and practice programs by focusing on new facts and skills rather than on going over material already learned or partially learned. Typical software resembles some of the early teaching matching programs with dry presentation of desecrate information and only a limited branching capacity.

Many of the early tutorial programs developed by the Minnesota Education Computing Consortium are of this sort. More interesting tutorial performance could challenge the student to become involved through game-like situations. The tole of these programs in enhancing problem solving is to provide sufficient grounding in content and skill areas so that complex problems can be presented. The ETS-LAUSD study and other reports indicate that programs in this category can be very successful in teaching information and skills.

The quality and sophistication of this type of program have also increased dramatically over the years. Their demonstrated ability to engage students, particularly low-achieving students, is a good reason to make them available in more schools. Nonetheless, or earlier review of the literature suggests a variety of ways to improve the usefulness of content tutorial programs for preparing a student to solve complex problems. As in the case of drill and practice programs, the concept of chunking has been neglected and might be used to enhance effectiveness. Two strategies that could aid in chunking are (a) the use of mnemonic devices, and (b) semantic mapping. The first strategy is often used to facilitate the learning of lists of apparently unrelated objects. Pictures as well as key words can be useful. Semantic mapping is closer theoretically to the notions of cognitive scientists who perceive the ability to chunk as characteristic of "expert" thinking. It is designed to aid the individual to develop cognitive structures or schema, to organize new knowledge. In semantic mapping, new concepts are systematically related to already known concepts in order to place the new information into a familiar structure or context.

Using semantic mapping as a model for teaching new content would require that the computer program acquire information about .the prior knowledge of students in order to relate new information to familiar concepts. Here the computer is at a distance disadvantage when compared to a human teacher; not even the most powerful electronic brains comes close to the capacity of the human brain to make judgments about students' previous experience and to tailor information to meet special group and individual needs. Nonetheless, we can imagine tutorial programs that initially interrogate a student to determine a general level of prior knowledge and then use the results of the interrogation to tailor the tutorial to student needs. Where schools knowledge is ordinarily learned in a hierarchical manner as in mathematics, the computer could pretest and then use responses to place students at the appropriate level in the tutorial.

In areas where knowledge is not clearly hierarchical, the initial assessment would be complicated and require greater teacher involvement. A related way to improve tutorial programs is through the use of diagnostic routines that identify the type of errors that students make and then coach or instruct them in ways to avoid making such errors. This strategy appears to be particularly useful for learning skills such as arithmetic operations. The classing example of such a program is BUGGY, a diagnostic program to detect the nature of errors made by students doing subtraction problems. In its original form it identified a very large number of possible independent error patterns, though the actual errors that students made tended to cluster in far fewer patterns. This software was initially written for a large computer but it being modified for microcomputers.

The small amount of quickly accessed memory is still a general problem for developing effective instructional software for microcomputers. But the BUGGY experience suggests that programs containing a diagnostic and coaching component may need to include only the most frequently occurring errors. Ideally, the program would instruct a student to request teacher assistance if it could not determine the student's error. This would free teachers to focus on the most comply instructional problems. Cognitive scientists have recently observed the phenomenon of systematic misconceptions in the areas of science and mathematics. In the early grades these misconception have only minor consequences for "getting the answer right" and therefore persist into later education, where they could have considerable influence on the problem-solving abilities of students.

Heuristic Tutorial: These programs are specifically designed to teach problem-solving strategies. These computer programs use a well-structured and circumscribed, often game-lime environment for training and practice in the use of specific heuristics. The classic computer programs in this area is the game of "Wumpus", which was designed to teach basic knowledge of logic, probability, decision analysis, and geometry to a wide range of learners, from young children to adults. The game logic resolves around a set of five' basic rules of reasoning. The player is placed randomly in a connected web of waves and is told the neighbors of his current location. The goal is to locate the horrible Wumpus and kill it by shooting an arrow into its lair. Moving from one cave to another produces information on the new neighbors. Players can minimize dangers and make progress in finding the Wumpus by using the warning signals to make appropriate ligistc and probalistics inferences. If the players exhaust their supply of five arrows before killing the Wumpus, the game is lost.

We believe schools and most program-developers are missing major opportunity by not developing and using programs like "Wumpus". Properly developed programs could be used on a regular basis in schools with students of widely varying background to provide them with systematic exposure to problem-solving situations. For instance, the Sunburst Corporation has published a problem-solving skill matrix that is included with software packages designed to teach complex thinking skills such as discrimination, looking for a pattern, and information gathering. Generally, these computer programs are open-ended and create a fantasy environment. For instance, in "Memory Castle" students learn mnemonic systems by playing an adventure game that leads them through a castle, and they must use a special code to find the way out. In another program, "The pond", a small green fraog, lost in a pond of lily pads, teaches students to recognize an articulate patterns and generalize from raw data. The student chooses from six ponds, or levels of difficulty, in which lily pads are displayed in increasingly complex patterns.

The objective is to determine which pattern can get the frog across the pond. A second level of the game encourages students to collect points by directing frogs through as many points as possible in the fewest number of moves. There is little question in our minds that these programs areas successful in teaching students to use specific problem-solving heuristics within the limited program environments, but we know of no quantitative evaluations, and whether the strategies learned from these programs have effects that generalize to other settings, particularly those where the problems are more complex or less well-structured, in another matter. Improvements in these programs might proceed along some of the same lines that we have suggested for content tutorial and drill and practice programs.

The use of error diagnosis and coaching routines seems especially promising. Burton and Brown used this strategy in a modification of a well-known arithmetic game programs, "WEST", originally developed for the PLATO system. They included routines which contrast the player's moves with optional strategies and which occasionally suggest alternative moves to the player. Once again, however, we know of no systematic, controlled evaluation.

Practical Aspects

The task of problem-solving simulation programs is to pose complex problems for solution. Unlike knowledge-building programs, which provide practice in sing knowledge and skills and which teach students facts and how to use certain heuristics, simulation programs present situations where the problem itself needs to be identified, where there may be a large variety of possible heuristics to use, and where there may indeed be a number of acceptable solutions. To present such a situation, the computer simulation must assume or create an environment with a sufficiently rich knowledge base and structure so that complex problems can be posed. Paper has labelled this idea "microworld" and defended it as a subset of reality or constructed reality that allows learners to exercise powerful ideas and intellectual skills.

The use of a microworld is based on a learning theory that promotes active exploration in an environment that is sufficiently limited and thus conductive to constructure exploration and at the same time rich enough for discovery. Such a requirement creates a very difficult problem for computer programs because of the difficulties in assessing sufficient levels of students' prior knowledge and the limited memory of the microcomputer.

The limitation on memory, for example, reduces the computer's capacity to communicate easily with students, for only a small vocabulary and a simplified syntax can be stored in a microcomputer. One approach is for the program to build an environment based directly on the curriculum or the common real-life experiences of students, thereby reducing the effects of difference in prior knowledge. A second option is a computer-created artificial environment where the effects of the prior knowledge of the student are minimized. Both of these approaches are described here.

Content Simulation Programs: These are designed to provide environments as lifelike as possible for students to use in problem-solving activities. A substantial number of existing computer programs do this in a sophisticated way. Programs that pose diagnostic problems in medicine, automobile care, or business management are widely used outside precollegiate education.

Much of the content would be inappropriate for elementary and secondary schools, and many of these programs are on large computers rather than on microcomputers and therefore not generally accessible to schools. But they can serve as a vision of what is possible. One prototype is the "MYCIN" system, an interactive program that simulates a medical consultant who specializes in infectious diseases. For approximately twenty minutes, the program questions and responds to doctors seeking the help of a specialist. They may ask "MYCIN" for advice on identifying organisms and prescribing drugs and, further, to explain that advice. This program strikes us as particularly salient in at least three ways. First, it allows the physicians to learn more about the complexities of diseases and treatments outside their specialities. Second, the encyclopedic function embedded in explaining treatments in an option and not a necessary step in using the program. Third, it allows for improvements in the system as new information becomes available, it can always be current. It is not difficult to see how this model might be followed in training students in a variety of content domains.

There are, however, few good examples in education and little use of content simulation programs in schools. Two classic simulations for use in elementary schools have been developed by MECC: "Lemonade", where the students manage a lemonade stand and earn or lose money based on their decisions; and "Oregon

Trail," where a student acts as the head of a wagon train in the middle 1800s. These simulations are popular as demonstration devices but typically are not integrated into the curriculum. At the high school level there have been some interesting new programs, but they only scratch the surface. For instance, "Revolutions: Past, Present and Future," developed by Focus Media, was designed to teach high school students a model for understanding the development of revolutionary movements.

Students build their own model of events leading to a revolution following a computer comparison of the American, French, and Russian revolutions. This program is particularly appealing because the objectives include both process and content variables. Another example is "South Dakota", an economics simulation developed by Educational Activities. It is designed to give students an understanding of variables affecting a framer's success. As a grain farmer, the student has a farm of 150 acres on which to survive for ten years and, ideally, make a profit. The student must make decisions in choosing the kind of grain to plant, hiring help to plant and harvest the crop, providing for family needs, paying taxes, and keeping the bank satisfied. In attractive feature of this program is that it can be used individually or in groups. If used in groups, the program requires students to pool their information to succeed.

The limitation on memory is one reason for the lack of useful software in this area. The program needs to be fast and rich enough in content to overcome major differences in the prior knowledge of different students in the classroom. One approach to the memory limitation problem would be to build into the simulation itself tutorial software that could be interrogated by students seeking data or other information, such as the technical terms needed to solve some of the problems posed in the simulation.

Drill and practice programs could be embedded in the simulation program. Error detection and coaching routines could be part of the simulation programs and could, in face, trigger the programs to indicate to the student the need for a tutorial or for a drill and practice experience. These "helping" programs could be designed as part of the simulation "game" though every student need not use them. Designed in this way, they would not have to be carried permanently in immediate memory. This use should reduce the effects of students' prior knowledge. Other strategies to overcome school-based problems seem plausible. It is not entirely possible to control time demands, for the very task of solving a complex problem may require considerable time, but it is possible for the computer to save a simulation until later, and advantage that could help fit higher-order thinking tasks into fifty minutes, time slots.

The biggest problem is to integrate simulations into the curriculum; it's solution would require the acceptance and use of both the computer and problem-solving activities in the classroom. We actually feel quite pessimistic about whether this will occur to a substantial degree in the next ten to twenty years; the conservative nature of the major textbook publishers and the tremendous inertia inside classroom work directly against it. Nonetheless we have a number of suggestions about approaches that might be taken. One strategy would be to create first-class simulations that focus on content in areas outside the mainstream of academic life in schools.

The vocational education is a prime example; programs that pose problems in aircraft and automobile mechanics, in structural design, and in business management already exist and could be used in many schools. Art, music, health, and the chess club are other areas for which simulation programs are either already developed and used or easily could be. These areas may be able to respond to the new technology more creatively than academic areas in part because their knowledge domains are better defined and in part because they are less bound by tradition. This tactic might also enliven the curriculum in these areas.

If we continue the logic about well-defined knowledge domains, the first academic areas to tackle would be mathematics and science. In both of these areas the national concern over the quality of the curriculum, pedagogy, and the teachers could work in favor of using some high quality programs. Mathematics, for example, will be a fertile field for simulation programs that pose problems in statistics, probability, and data analysis, if the recommendation of a number of the national mathematics groups are adopted. In science, the potentially useful simulation situations seem limitless.

Wonderful Experiences

Artificial environment simulations generate a make-believe world with a sufficiently rich knowledge base and set of rules of that complex problems can be posed by the programs. Their capacity both to tutor and to pose problems in an integrated fashion allow them to control the influence of prior knowledge; this control enables the computer to provide successively deeper information and more complex problems. A wide variety of types of programs fits out general conception of this category. These include fantasy adventure games such as the "ZORK" series, science fiction games such as "World Builders", and complex artificial problem settings such as "Rocky's Boots". One such program, "Robot Odyssey I" is both a simulation and an adventure game.

Students can either construct a simulated robot or work through and adventure game that teaches the basic of digital electronic. Players design, build and test robots in a parts laboratory and tutorials assist students in all stages of the game. The problems posed by these programs, in our view, often are of equal or greater complexity and take more ingenuity and perseverance to solve than the most difficult problems posed in schools. Programs like these could present problems of varying complexity, designed to build on themselves in a regular fashion, and include systematic tutorial, diagnostic, and coaching systems to help students.

Real Impact

The task of designing effective programs, however, is probably minor compared to the challenge of convincing schools and the general public that problem-solving activities in artificial domains have merit and that time could be allocated for student use of these programs. The best of these programs are immensely popular in the home computing market and used almost not at all in schools. The reasons for the lack of use in schools are clear-they do not fit into the curriculum, they take a long time to run, and they seem frivolous since they are not based on real-life circumstances and are often advertised as games. In particular, adventure games seem most likely to be overlooked. We have observed student pursuing these progıams and we have little doubt that such games motivate students and engage them in sustained cognitive activity, whether they are working individually or cooperatively. We have seen students with serious reading difficulties, who rarely read printed material, spend extended periods working on adventure games that interact with users only in a narrative format.

The knowledge development and problem-solving simulation programs exert considerable control over the activities of the student using he program. Problem-solving aids, on the other hand, contain programs that require the student to use them in ways and will help solve problems which may be either self-defined or externally assigned. These programs, moreover, can be embedded in problem-simulation programs to help students to obtain information or to analyze data. We have included a large variety of programs in this category and have divided them into two general types: (a) tools for obtaining information or structural problems situations, and (b) programming languages.

Problem-solving aids are widely used in homes and schools, often for obtaining and structuring information for presentation or for aiding in solving relatively *ell-structured* problems. In our experience it is rare that tools are used in schools to aid in solving ill-defined problems. Thus, for example, a data management system will be used in a school setting to display some data on a chart rather analysis. Or students will be given very highly structured problems in a programming course rather than be asked to design and program solutions to problems of their own choosing or that are deliberately ill-defined. The exception may be when the aids are used deliberately to facilitate complex problem solving in advanced placement course for high school mathematics and computer programming.

Tools for Aiding Problem Solving: These include some of the most imaginative, interesting, and well-developed programs now available for the microcomputer. One reason is that many of them are simply elegant extensions on the microcomputer of tools that already exist in many schools, homes, and businesses; for example, world processing programs function as sophisticated typewriters.

Another reason is that these programs are usable over and over by the same person and therefore are cost-effective. In contrast, an adventure program, upon being solved, loses its usefulness to the solver. One class of these programs, which might deserve a separate category, is designed to facilitate writing. In terms of frequency of use in schools and homes, word processing programs, such as "Bank Street Writer", outstrip just about all other classes of programs.

The growing group of ideas or outline processors is also becoming very popular; they contain a variety of routines to help a writer organize and reorganize textual information. The use of these programs in schools parallels both the emerging literature on the close relationship between writing and higher-order thinking and the recent emphasis on the need to improve writing in the schools. As these programs become familiar to classroom teachers as writing aids, additional features can be added. For example, it should be possible in the future to combine the organizational aids of idea processes with routines which prompt students with question and information on topics related to he curriculum to encourage their writing.

Other tools in this category include dictionaries, information retrieval systems, and data management systems. In the context of our general discussion of software for problem solving, each of these tools could be viewed as standing along to provide information or assistance in carrying our analysis or could be embedded into problem-solving simulation programs. We might imagine a workstation of the future similar to "Dynabank" developed at 'Xerox Parc' several years ago. As student would sit at a computer terminal and have control over an information retrieval system containing as much information as the Library of Congress and the data-analysis power of any modern mainframe computer. It included capabilities for music composition and graphic arts.

The computer could pose a variety of types of problems for the student, provide diagnosis and coaching, encourage the student to enter into a drill and practice or tutorial mode, and keep continuous track of student progress. All of the components of such workstation exist.

Programming Languages: These are essential programs that require their operators to define and solve their own problems within the specific constraints of the language and the general constraints of a computer. Although we have classified programming languages as an aid for solving problems, learning to use the programming language is itself a form of problem solving. Without question, the act of solving programming problem often meets our definition of higher-programming problem often meets our definition of higher-order thinking. But, whether learning to program enhances a child's general facility in solving problems in other issues. Perhaps the view which links learning to programming with the development of higher-order thinking will wither away in the same way that the theories linking the leaning of Latin with complex reasoning have not survived. Computer programming languages, like playing chess, may be too highly stylized and structured to provide training that can be generalized to very different domains, especially those domains with more complex and ambiguous rules.

On the other hand, programming provides the opportunity for combining discrete elements to equal a whole concept, a gestalt. And this is a necessary skills for solving some problems. We indicated earlier that this literature is very thin and inconclusive. The most widespread use of programming languages in the content areas in mathematics, where languages such as FORTRAN aid students in learning how to formulate and solve problems. This is just the beginning of content-based programming languages.

8

The Network

What is Internet ?

A front-end analysis (FEA) was performed to ensure the course would meet training objectives that are validated against real job requirements. The approach was eclectic, based on the experiences of the team doing FEA. Initial contacts with domain experts (DEs) was by phone. Requests for documents, and clarifications over the phone, gave the team the first overview of the training requirements, target population description, and course objectives. Course materials for MDMP- training were gathered and evaluated. This evaluation guided the selection of instructional strategies, the media selection, and the advanced technology selection. The materials were considered up-to-date and suitable to create the interactive courseware for this project. New measurable objectives were created for the course based on the materials and discussions with the DEs.

The team travelled to Fort Knox and observed an ongoing class. This allowed the team to:

- observe the communication between the seven functional positions that the small groups (SG) of students role play;
- broaden our understanding of the tasks of the seven positions;

- observe students creating overlays/MDMP products;
- observe how the small group instructor (SGI) prompted and advised students;
- observe the Comrnander's briefing;
- gain a further understanding of the Armor School's expectations for the courseware;
- observe the creation of maps;
- observe the SGI prompting and advising students;
- observe the commander's briefing/ presentations of each position and meet with domain experts (DEs).

The Requirements

The team met with a contractor building courseware that is prerequisite to the MDMP course. The team:

- delineated responsibilities,
- reviewed flowchart; discussed standards and level of interactivity; viewed a demonstration of a small sample of the course; and
- discussed standards and level of interactivity and fidelity.

Area of Expertise

The team met with DEs to gather information. They:

- met with representatives of four of the seven positions the SG represents when doing the MDMP;
- discussed objectives previously defined with DEs and the Government PM;
- built a list of information students must reference to support the learning tasks;
- delivered a form to assist DEs to collect data for the courseware; and
- completed the information collection forms.

The meetings with the Army POCs and DEs were essential to determine the courseware design and development. The information helped to:

- create a user environment that simulates the work experience, allowing users to interact to solve a problem;
- develop a graphical interface to allow students td create and edit overlays/MDMP products efficiently;

- develop hints and feedback, possibly some intelligence to emulate the instructor;
- provide a technique to allow the seven staff positions to "look up" information; and
- develop ideas for how to make creating maps more efficient.

Select Field

The Armor Officer Advanced Course is a 20 week course composed of large group instruction, small group instruction, the JANUS command-level simulator exercises, SIMNET unit-level simulator exercises, and field exercises. Initially, the students attend large group instruction together. Then, the students disperse into groups of 15 for the small group portion; a small group instructor (SGI) is assigned to each group. The MDMP planning exercise reinforces the doctrine, planning, and decision making knowledge/ skills. The JANUS simulator is run at the battalion level, with all students divided into command and support functions. The SIMNET simulator is run at the company level, with all students manning specific tank operation positions. These exercises are planned and executed against an OPFOR composed of the instructor group. Field exercises are restricted to terrain appreciation and leader's reconnaissance of the battlefield.

Present Streams

In the current training, the SGI presents the small group with a situation and commander's guidance. The small group is required to exercise the decision making process and analysis tools detailed in the text, and produce intermediate "products" used as input to the next phase of the process. The final product is a recommended Coarse Of Action (COA) plan, which is briefed to the commander.

The Army has traditionally viewed military decision making as both science and art. Many aspects of combat operations, such as movement rates, fuel consumption, and weapon effects are quantifiable. Therefore, the Army considers them to be part of the "science" of war. However, the Army cannot quantify other aspects - the impact of leadership, the complexity of modern operations, and uncertainty regarding enemy intentions/ actions/ reactions.

Military Decision Making Process is a systematic approach to decision making, which fosters effective analysis by enhancing application of professional knowledge, logic, and judgment, and consists of six steps:

- Recognize and define problems.
- Gather facts and make assumptions to determine the scope of and the solution to problems.
- Develop possible solutions.
- Analyze each solution.
- Compare the outcome of each solution.
- Select the best solution available.

At the highest level, the actions done in the small group relate to:

- Gathering facts;
- Making assumptions;
- Analyzing higher mission and intent ; and
- Receiving commander's guidance.

The architecture for the application of technology to this training requirement will involve two major efforts:

1. the implementation of computer-based training activities. to provide mission guidance, provide detail data for analysis, and to capture small group intermediate and final products; and
2. the implementation of distance learning technology to link the SGIs with the small groups during and after the construction of the intermediate and final products.

Overlaying the automated instruction and DL technologies to the current course provides an interactive course that covers the same objectives as the current stand-up instruction course. The automated instruction functions provide situation details required for each phase of training action. The small group functions are still completed in small groups. The Distance Learning functions provide the organization and communication methods for the small groups to get help during the small group actions and to receive feedback on the small group products. Gates are closed until the student products are reviewed by the SGI. The

SGI grades the products and opens the gate before the group moves to the next MDMP phase.

The MDMP includes Mission analysis; Course of Action (COA) development; COA analysis and comparison, and decision and execution. The architecture was implemented as four major phases:

Phase one, Mission Analysis

Task description. Derive the essential tasks the unit must perform to accomplish the mission.

Input. Commanders guidance.

Methods. Follow the eleven step process for Mission analysis.

Approach. Using the automated instruction lessons, derive the necessary data to drive the small group interaction in the development of the MCOO, the SITTEMP, and the restated mission products.

Deliverables. The MCOO, the SITTEMP and the Restated mission products in a format for the SGI to access via distance learning technologies.

Phase two, COA Development

Task description. Develop multiple COA's that would accomplish the mission assigned by the Commander.

Input. Planning Guidance and Phase One products.

Methods Follow the six step process answering the what/ when /where /why/how of a possible plan open to the commander that would accomplish the mission assigned.

Approach. Using the automated instruction lessons, derive the necessary data to drive the small group interaction in the development of the COA plans.

Deliverables. Several significantly different COA products in a format for the SGI to access via distance learning technologies.

Phase three, COA Analysis

Task description. Utilize appropriate analysis methods to identify the COA with the greatest probability of success.

Input. Multiple COAs from phase two.

Methods. Utilize the appropriate analysis methods, such as feasibility checks, war gaming, risk assessment, and comparison of war game results, to identify the best COA. Note that several different analysis techniques can be applied based on the situation.

Approach. Using the automated instruction lessons, derive the necessary data to drive the small group interaction in the development of the COA plans.

Deliverables. The brief for the Commander on the selected COA.

Phase four, Execute

Task description. Review the COA with the SGI to determine the probable outcome of the recommended COA.

Input. Recommended COA from phase three.

Methods. The group will provide the SGI with a written analysis of the probable outcome of the recommended COA. The SGI will review, analyze, and comment on the recommended COA, and the small group's analysis of the recommended COA, in a small group session. Alternately, the SGI can interact with the small group in a conference call.

Approach. SGI and small group interaction on the recommended COA.

Deliverables. Analysis of the recommended COA's probable outcome.

Needs for Functioning

Successful completion of the final product for each phase.

Primary operational environment

The Fort Knox Campus is the primary operational environment. The campus environment is the local- area network, the available networked computer systems, and the client and server software.

Secondary operational environment

Distribution via the world wide web, WWW, is the secondary operational environment. This will be used to service Reserve and Active Duty forces for refresher and preparatory training.

From a standard SVGA PC connected to the ATM LAN at Ft. Knox, the student will download the Mission Analysis TOOLBOOK automated instruction activity which will be executed locally. Because the courseware is much more than page turner courseware, the courseware was deemed too large and therefore slow to do completely over the Internet, hence the hybrid solution. The TOOLBOOK activity will provide a simulated environment for the request for information by the small group; the feedback of the information; and for the control of simulated time to accomplish the discovery of the information requested. A team of four AOAC students will use Microsoft Word to provide a written text and graphic to communicate the intermediate products in a format for the SGI to review. The Word documents will be filed to a server, organized by an email notes file package. The instructor will comment on the Word document using the Word annotating features, which allows comments to be made without including the comments into the main document. The instructor will annotate the drawings; these comments are included in the original drawing.

Mapping Editor

Using a modified version of TIEPAINT from TIE, (Training Icon Environment,) Global demonstrated the abilities needed to display and edit the "layered" map scheme needed for the Army TDMP project. The modified product, called MAPEDIT, consists of the original TIEPAINT and added pop-up menu, labeled ViewLayers and EditLayers. The ViewLayer menu has eight items, numbered 1 through 8. A student can check any or all of these items, and the corresponding layer(s) will be displayed. The EditLayer menu item allows a student to select which layer he wants to currently edit. The editor is basically the standard TIEPAINT "vector" editor. Each vector object has an extra "tag" on it, which indicates which layer it belongs to. When items are displayed, only those items which are part of the active layer(s) are displayed. The scheme is simple, and works very nicely.

MAPEDIT is a 32 bit Windows application developed using Microsoft Visual C/C++ version 4.0. The source code consists of various c, h, dlg, ico,.bmp, all of which comprise the actual "project" file. There is also a "help" file, which uses Microsoft WordView to display hypertext style help.

Data flow

· Student and instructor workstations exchange data via a shared directory on a network server. We do not want to hard code the path to the shared directory. Instead, the directory path is stored in an INI file on each workstation: $WINDOWS \TDMP.INI. The section is "*Server*" and the entry is "Root."

In keeping with Windows convention, the INI file is stored in the Windows directory of each computer. All programs that refer to this file should use the GetWindowsDirectory function to get the name of the Windows directory rather than hard coding the usual path.

The group file serves as the main repository of information about the group's progress through the TDMP lesson. In a production version of the system, group information would be stored in a full-featured relational database with Internet capability. However, the proof of concept version will use a simple Windows initialization file ("INI" file). The INI file contains a section for each step in the TDMP lesson. The group file contains a summary of the group's progress. Large items, such as justification statements, COA sketches, the Sync Matrix, and the DECMAT, are stored in separate files.

The Assessment

One instructor leads a typical class consisting of 64 students broken up into 16 groups of 4 students each. The primary role of the instructor is to facilitate the tactical decision making process as students try to formulate effective course of actions (COAs). During the decision making process, students are assigned one or two functional roles in which to analyze the information. A total of seven roles are divided among the four students in each group. Students must submit two interim products and one final product. The instructors will review, score, and provide feedback to the group for each submitted product.

Independent Measures

The independent variables to be manipulated include instruction and on-line help. The dependent variables that will be measured include: 1. achievement and efficiency as scored by instructor ratings of the three submitted COA products and the time it took to reach the COA products, 2. subjective workload, 3. the mental model developed during the tactical decision making process as measured by paired concepts, 4. the rate and quality of communications across teams and, 5. affective preferences. Covariates will include individual differences in subject-matter knowledge as scored on a pretest and prior field experience.

Achievement and Instructional Efficiency

Two interim products and one final product will be scored and used as a measure of student achievement. The instructors for the course will grade these products. Each instructor will be responsible for scoring half of the products produced by each treatment group. In addition, the products will be submitted to the instructors using codes so that they will be blind as to the source of the product. These methods will be used to prevent bias toward a particular treatment condition.

The amount of time the students took to submit each COA will also be recorded automatically by the system. In the traditional classroom treatments, the instructors will log the time of each lesson taught. Any additional help by the instructor to various students outside the classroom will also be logged.

Collaborative Learning

The issue of collaborative learning is relevant for this project as students in both learning environments will be working together in four person teams. In addition to these four team members collaborating together to meet a mission objective, these teams are encouraged to seek advice and information from the other teams formed within the class.

Interaction Frequencies

Computer mediated learning involves many, sometimes radical changes in communication patterns. Rather than numerous verbal and nonverbal cues available in face to face encounters, distance learning environments constrain contact to primarily text. Typically, user acceptance of distance technology requires changes in how one thinks, composes materials, and communicates. Researchers point out that often new learners appear to experience some form of "culture shock" which dissipates with additional practice and experience with the system. In an attempt to quantify these reactions to the medium of communication, learner discussions will be audiotaped and transcribed verbatim, From these transcripts, independent raters will classify each recorded learner interaction into one of four categories suggested by Dalton in the measurement of computer-supported collaborative work: management, social, task, or content.

Attitudes Toward Instruction and Content

Learner attitudes toward distance learning can be grouped into four categories: 1. Attitude toward the technology, 2. attitude toward distance education teaching methods, 3. attitude toward student and teacher interaction, and 4. attitude toward being a remote student. Of the research reviewed, only one affective survey has been found that adequately samples learners on all four of these dimensions.

The Teleconference Evaluation Questionnaire was developed by Ball State University to assess students attitudes toward their telecourses. It consists of 33 items by which students rate their degree of satisfaction with various facets of their telecourse on a five point Likert scale ranging from "Very Poor" to "Very Good." Although developed to assist in the evaluation of telecourses, it will be adapted to survey learners' attitudes toward the current TDMP multimedia distance learning course.

9

Surfing on Net

Narrowing choices and searching out alternative sites were some of the most anxiety provoking situations for this class. A young man stated, "The most frustrating aspect of the Net involves obtaining the information that I am looking for. If I want to find information about caring for houseplants and use a search engine, I could bet information about anything from flower shops to power plants." He went on to say, "The professor told the means for narrowing searches on particular search engines... the professor has been very helpful with correcting information or suggesting alternative sites if something could not be accessed." The instructor also acknowledged the importance of helping students to search and narrow choices to reduce their anxiety. He stated, "They don't always get where they want to go and they find it frustrating... I try to provide examples and a variety of items to search for requiring different methods."

Time at Disposal

The instructor provided from a half hour to an hour and forty minutes of class time (out of a class that lasted for 2 hours and 40 minutes) for supervised practicing. Many times he stayed after class as students continued to work on their homework assignments. This was especially important for students who otherwise did not have access to the Internet and worried that they would not be able to finish their homework.

Fundamental Queries

The instructor welcomed questions and addressed concerns at any point during lectures, by calling on people right away and giving detailed answers. Moreover, he recognized and acknowledged the students' anxiety with statements such as: "People are probably nervous about the paper because it has to be in HTML. Don't let that stress you. Just do it like a regular paper. It's not that hard to transfer"; "I'm going to give you time to work on your papers now, since I know that's your major stress point... the latest stress point"; and "Your midterm results aren't that bad and you have time to recover."

The instructor allowed peers to help each other, which they did continuously, during class and practicums. Diane stated, "It's good to find people suffering with you, 'cause sometimes you think it can't only be you."

Game on Net

During class, the instructor allowed students to follow their curiosities and see where it led them on the Net. It seemed to help Jane who did something personally useful for herself by doing a search in the real estate section; although, she did diminish her accomplishment by saying, "Oh, I was just playing'."

Practical Aspects

Students who had problems with homework assignments were able to turn them in late for credit. Additionally, if it seemed he constructed a test question poorly, the instructor was willing to throw it out. In general, the leeway was built into the course.

Plain Attitude

Consistently, the instructor projected an easygoing manner and did not display anxious behavior. He modeled calmness by his even tone of voice, relaxed posture, smiles and humor, even in the face of problems on the Internet such as difficulty accessing particular sites.

The Other Side

During the second class session, the instructor used an abundance of acronyms and new vocabulary words including:

Web server, JAVA, STP, case sensitive, file path, VAX, FFP, HTTP, HTCP/IP Packets, Telnet connection, domain, and host just to name a few. Some of these words he defined, some he did not. The instructor also passed out several handouts with most of the words undefined. One-by-one the students seemed to drop out of the lecture as they were being presented with loads indiscernible text in a short time span. The students rolled their eyes, shrugged their shoulders, and eventually put down their pencils and began tinkering with the computers. This was even more of a problem for two Chinese students who soon after dropped the class.

Automatic Training

In this class it seemed that the students who had more anxiety tended to want direct learning from the instructor, whereas those who had little anxiety were comfortable with the fact that this class focused on collaborative, self-regulated learning. For instance, Diane, who experienced high anxiety in this class, explained that she preferred her last computer class to this one and felt less "panicky" because the instructor led the entire group through problems and processes: "Whatever he had on his computer [her last instructor] he would bring up on all of us screening the classroom. And then he would say now this is what you need to do and he would take us like step by step and I found that very useful. But it's more so him just telling us about these different sites and different things and we're just going there and doing it and that's why I guess I get a little panicky." The instructor himself acknowledged the importance of "working examples in class" to help decrease anxiety. On the other hand, Dana who didn't experience much anxiety liked the idea of being able to do a lot on her own.

The only possibility of use of existing computing facilities was batch processing or timeshare terminals on a large mainframe system and with little involvement in true instructional computing. The submission of requests for computing equipment for the School of Education was a twice yearly exercise which coincided with the cycle used by the university for equipment requests. Each request was slightly different from the one previous, reflecting progressive changes in technology. The physical size of the machines decreased the capabilities increased and costs dropped steadily. Each request was, for all practical purposes, disregarded. This cycle continued until the fall of 1978 when an administrative change within the School coincided with the marketing of the first of the microcomputers.

The first microcomputer for the School of Education was purchased in the summer of 1979. Some faculty feel that this machine was purchased mainly to see what would result as a consequence, with little expectation that it would have a significant impact. Since the receipt of this first microcomputer the School of Education at CU has seen considerable activity with respect to microcomputers and within the last year there are indicators of an acceleration of activity. In the three years since the first microcomputer arrived in the School of Education:

1. Twenty microcomputers are now housed in the School of Education. All of these machines are Apple II+machines with language cards. The decision to make all initial purchases Apple machines was based on at least two informal criteria. First, the primary focus of a school of education is education. It was felt that at the present time Apple machines have the greatest availability of educational software, and are the most common is schools. Secondly Apple machines were felt to be the most flexible. Therefore initial purchases, at least up to a number, which could support standard university course instruction, should be Apples. Once the minimal number of machines is reached then some purchases of other brands would be considered depending on their intended use.

   The most recent fifteen machines are housed in a "Microcomputer Laboratory". These fifteen machines are used in regular instruction in courses in the School of Education, laboratory work associated with these classes, courses in continuing education and "open" laboratory time for any interested user. The micro lab is housed in a room which is about 15m by 7m. The room has a chalkboard on one end wall and is equipped with electrical outlets on the remaining three walls in sufficient numbers and capacity to accommodate up to twenty-five stations. The existing fifteen stations are situated so that when students are present they face the front of the room with the keyboards at their fingertips. There are two chairs at each station allowing up to thirty students for a scheduled class. This arrangement appears to be the most beneficial for instruction, given the equipment that is available. The lab is supervised by a student assistant during the open use hours. The specific schedule for use of the lab varies depending on the classes scheduled.

2. An NSF grant of $ 85,000 has been received to conduct a project titled "Personal computers and Cross-Aged Instruction". This is a school-based experimental study utilizing nine complete microcomputer systems, seven of which have become the property of the cooperating school district, St. Vrain Valley Schools, and the remaining two systems are part of the permanent facilities of the School of Education. There were four primary objectives of this project.
   A. Increase the level of basic mathematical skill of mathematically low-achieving sixth graders.
   B. Increase the number of students enrolling in high school mathematics and science courses.
   C. Evaluate the use of microcomputers as a unique instructional tool.
   D. Develop effective applications of microcomputers in education.

These objectives' were achieved by training high school students on the use of microcomputers and teaching then about the difficulties that sixth graders encounter in mathematics. Each of these students then tutored a sixth grade student every other school day for one semester. The project staff monitored both groups of students to determine the achievement of the objectives of the project. The experimental phase of the project was completed in May 1982. The interim report of this project is available through the ERIC system and the final report will be available in the spring of 1983.

3. The Centre for Management Information Technology in Education has been formed to provide services to school systems in the area of administrative uses of computers. Dr. James Rose is the director of this centre. This centre has provided on-site courses for school and school district administrators on the use of computers in education administration, consulting services to schools and school districts and provided other support for schools and school districts in the area of the administrative use of information technology.
4. Several graduate courses have been instituted:
   A. "Computers in Education" is a survey course about computers and their use in education. The content of this course includes the history, characteristics, capabilities and terminology of computers: past, present and future of educational computing, both administrative and instructional; an orientation to microcomputer hardware and software; and includes on-site visits and demonstrations of current educational uses of computers. This course is designed for graduate students in all fields of education, is offered at least once per academic year and attracts thirty students per offering from many fields within education as well as students from fields outside education. It is a popular course and provides the foundation for other courses in education computing as well as serving as a terminal course for those students wanting only an overview of the field. There are no prerequisites for this course.
   B. "Computer Assisted Instruction" covers in detail the theory, design, development, implementation and evaluation of computer assisted instruction materials. Work on both mainframe and microcomputers is done in this course. Typically this course attracts students

with some background in computing, some exposure to programming and some background in instructional design. This course is offered once per academic year and is designed for persons desiring in-depth work in the development of computer based instructional materials. It is anticipated that there will be increasing demand for this course.

C. "Microcomputers in the Classroom" is a hands-on course for educators wishing an overall orientation to microcomputers, their operation, software and rudimentary concepts of programming. This courses is offered three to four times per year including summer and attracts thirty students per section. Students from all areas in education as well as other disciplines are attracted to this course and about one half of the students are not degree candidates. The overall reaction to this course has been highly positive and it is likely to remain popular for some time.

D. An undergraduate course somewhat parallel to the Microcomputers in the Classroom course described above has been scheduled for the fall semester 1982. This course will allow undergraduates to accumulate a greater amount of background on microcomputers than is included in the ten hours of instruction all such students will receive.

E. Other courses are planned for the future, some of which will be developed in the 1982-83 academic year. Areas to be covered in additional courses will be the more technical aspects of computers, authoring languages, programming and development.

5. The use of microcomputers is being incorporated into the graduate course in School Finance. Computers are used in this course to model financial decisions and provide a base for projections for enrollments and finances within school districts. This course is taken primarily by persons seeking a school administration degree or certification and attracts about twenty-five students for each of one to two offerings per year.

6. Two sections of a semester long seminar on microcomputers for School of Education faculty and staff were conducted in the spring of 1982. This seminar dealt with the characteristics, capabilities, operation, machine commands, software and uses of microcomputers in instruction and research in education.

The development and implementation of, and instruction in this seminar was the work of the writer of this chapter.

Recruiting for the seminar was accomplished merely by sending a memo to each of the faculty and staff of the school, asking who would be interested in a weekly seminar on the use and operation of microcomputers. Before the memo was sent, it was expected that up to ten persons would reply. Thirty-nine persons indicated their interest and two sections were arranged at times which allowed the greatest number of participants. Only one person could not attend one of the two sections.

The seminar met once per week for a full semester each session lasting two hours. The content of the seminar included an overview of features and capabilities of micro-computers, rudimentary concepts of machine control through machine commands and programming in BASIC; demonstrations of word processing or text editing, data management software and spread sheet software; a demonstration of LOGO and demonstrations of commercial instructional software including drill and practice, tutorials, simulations and games. There were numerous handouts given in the seminar, all locally prepared and there were few demands made on the participants for outside work.

Most all outside work was self-imposed by those participants who found the time had sufficient interest and felt the need to have additional work on the machines. Five machines were available at almost anytime a participant desired to have machine time for "outside work." The primary desired outcomes for the seminar were machine familiarization, getting the concept of machine control through machine commands and programming, overcoming machine anxiety, exposure to the more common types of software and to foster a positive attitude toward this new technology and its use in education.

Since the completion of the seminar several faculty have become involved with microcomputers who were not involved previously. The general reaction to the seminar was highly positive based on a written evaluation. No tests, quizes or term-papers were required partially because the participants and I were all colleagues and friends and partially to maintain a relaxed atmosphere. All feedback thus far has been positive and the apparent general feeling is that the individual objectives of the participants were achieved. Even the instructor is positive.

7. Several in-service courses for both teachers, administrators and others have taken place. In the past one and a half years nearly ten courses relating to micro-computers have been conducted by faculty in the school or with the equipment in the school. These have been primarily orientation courses for school administrators and teachers. The content of these courses varies with the intended audience and with the specifics of the request for such a course, or something similar to the content of the faculty seminar is common except the depth of coverage depends on the amount of time available.

   The course credit has varied from zero to three semester hours and the courses have taken place both in the School of Education and in schools around Colorado, with participants providing their own equipment when the course is off-campus. Requests for courses in this area typically address the need to upgrade the background of school personnel in an area where little background exists. It is anticipated that this need on the part of school personnel will be present foe some time and more such sessions are expected.

   Coursework beyond first courses such as these are typically satisfied through regular course offerings or specially designed courses in response to specific requests. Such coursework may or may not fit into a degree programme.

8. A School of Education committee for the coordination of efforts in education computing within the school has been formed. This committee is a Dean's committee and consists of the five persons most directly involved in using computer technology in the School of Education. The committee addresses questions relating to the priorities on the use of and acquisition of equipment, advises the dean on policy decisions related to computers in the School of Education, oversees possible duplication of effort among existing and proposed courses involving computing and co-ordinates efforts for the entire school on matters involving computers.

   The committee was established by the dean as an alternative to the more traditional approach to the appearance of a new area which is to create a new programme of division. It was felt that a committee would allow more flexibility at least in the initial stages of activity, seemed to be the more appropriate arrangement in an area which is more inter-disciplinary than existing areas in education and better accommodates the rapidly changing nature of the field.

10

The Web

The design team begins by meeting with someone who is intimately familiar with the training needs and audience. Instructional designers spend time with that expert, analyzing the current training situation and looking carefully at the role online training might play in meeting long-term training needs. They will work to clarify the training requirements. During this part of the process, clients often become aware of training strategies and methods existing in their companies that were never recognized as such. The design team keeps those strategies in mind while developing the courseware. After the session, the team provides a *Training Assessment Report* containing its findings:

- Where your training is today and where it might go tomorrow.
- A list of "next-step" action items.
- Concrete options for course delivery.
- Price ranges for various platforms and audio/ visual treatments.

If your requirements are already clearly defined, a Needs Assessment may not be necessary. In that case, it can be replaced with a shorter meeting or series of conference calls designed to gather information and collect all existing training materials. This process usually occurs if you are ready to proceed with a specific project and are able to provide detailed information on all of the following:

- Project description.
- Project scope.
- Audience profile.
- Current platform deployment.
- Desired delivery environment.
- Desired treatment approach.
- High level content outline.

After the Needs Assessment or meeting/ conference calls, the final decisions are made on the delivery method and scope for the course. Armed with this information, the design team will provide a price for the Content and Design phase of the project.

Basic Structure

The Content and Design phase results in the delivery of a Course Architecture and Design Blueprint. Together they specify what will be taught and how it should be presented. The Course Architecture is a detailed outline of instructional material that has been sequenced and structured (for example: modules, lessons, and topics). It describes:

1. What you want to teach?
2. What teaching sequence should be used?. What is the best course structure?

The Functioning

Instructional Designers meet with the Subject Matter Experts (SMEs) to extract all of the course content, existing or new.

- The design team puts the information about job tasks and job knowledge gained from these meetings to work to help design the hierarchy of learning objectives.

Before proceeding to the Design Blueprint, it is necessary to be certain that the content is both thorough and accurate. The appropriate manager must provide approval, indicating acceptance of the Course Architecture "as is," or "with changes."

Paper Work

Once the Course Architecture determines what needs to be taught, the Design Blueprint specifies how it will be taught.

- Designers work with the artists and programmers to define the creative treatment (look and feel) and plan the instructional, presentational, and navigational strategies.
- The team prescribes the menu functionality and designs the viewer interface screens based on audience and content needs.

The team selects and define key components and their functionality (such as a mastery test, record keeping, index, and glossary). The team creates flowcharts detailing possible pathways through the course. All of this information is put together in the Design Blueprint. It, along with the Course Architecture, becomes the "blueprint" for the training project. After review and approval of the Design Blueprint, a price for the production and delivery of your product can be determined.

Actual Design

In addition to the instructional design blueprint, the Engineering Design phase specifies the hardware and software delivery systems that will be used to deliver the course.

The engineering team reviews the options of the playback systems for course delivery considering your organization's available multimedia computer systems and online connection speed.

The engineering team defines all the software development tools to be used on the project including specific authoring languages or systems, graphics packages, and audio editing tools.

The engineering team specifies how the course will work at a detailed level. Course navigation, required media elements, and any other technical issues are carefully considered.

All components of the engineering design are clearly articulated. The course is designed to be error free from the start, a much less costly alternative than finding errors later.

The Models

The development and delivery of a Rapid Prototype constitutes the third phase. The Rapid Prototype demonstrates the planned look and feel for the course along with expected course navigation functions and sample screens. It is implemented using the software to be used for the final course and is delivered on the actual hardware you plan to use.

The Rapid Prototype allows us to make any necessary changes to the production plans before launching into full-scale production.

In certain circumstances, a more extensive prototype may be needed to fully prove the course concept. In that event, we will story-board and implement in software a complete instructional unit exactly as it will appear in the final product, inclusive of actual, approved course content.

Following the Content and Design and Rapid Prototype phases, instructional designers begin story-boarding the course.

A story-board is a written plan for a discrete unit of instruction, usually referred to as a topic. Developed with a special template customized for your project, a story-board is typically 5 to 20 pages in length depending on the duration and complexity of the topic. A typical course may have 30 or more story-boards.

Story-boards include:

- A description of the overall scene and action for the topic.
- Narration scripts for spoken audio voiceover.
- Onscreen text that the viewer will read.
- Quiz/test questions with feedback.
- Descriptions of visuals to be displayed (video, animations, and graphics).
- Descriptions of music and sound effects.
- File names for all multimedia elements.

Story-boards are delivered to you for editing and approval. There are no surprises you will see only content and design treatments that you have previously approved One way to measure perfection is how closely the final product matches the approved storyboards.

The Outcome

A production pathway, based on the seven production phases, is a definable and repeatable process. With input from the entire project team, the Project Manager customizes this process for each project.

A Pathway Document is created that facilitates the accurate and timely completion of all production tasks. This document reflects adherence to Instructional Systems Development principles. Not coincidentally, this process parallels practices in the best manufacturing plants.

In Black and White

Specifies procedures and standards for each of the production phases relevant to your project. Defines the day-to-day logistics to be used by the team for producing, storing, transferring, archiving, and assembling all of the video and audio elements of the program into a finished product.

Using the Pathway Document, together with the approved storyboards, the project team gets to work. The artists and animators create the visuals; the video producer shoots and/or edits live action footage; the audio engineer records the narration; and the music and sound effects are identified and produced. As the components are finalized, programmers assemble them to create a "beta" or test version of the product.

Evaluation of Utility

The purpose of Usability Testing is to see how representative learners from the target audience interact with the Rapid Prototype.

Testing can be done formally, in a usability lab... or... informally, within your company or training deployment site.

Information from a usability test is invaluable in determining the effectiveness of the proposed training, including instructional strategies, ease of navigation, and user reaction to the overall look and functionality of the product. Usability testing, thought to be superfluous by some, is actually an essential "reality check."

Joy Mountford, interface guru, said it all in an interview in Interactivity Magazine:

"The most important thing to remember is that the user is never wrong. If they feel it's not good, if they feel it's uninteresting, if they feel it's difficult, then they're right."

Superb Level

Using the beta version to identify every possible interaction and pathway through the course, our Quality Assurance and Testing coordinator writes a testing plan for the product. Supervised by the coordinator, the testing team uses a database utility to record and prioritize any bugs they find while following the prescribed testing pathway. After two (2) passes through the program are completed, any bugs are repaired and the program is retested.

After Quality Assurance and Testing, the beta course is delivered for final review (and in some cases, further Usability Testing) and approval before replication takes place.

Sustained Development

The Basics of ISD: (Instructional Systems Development)

ISD is a systematic approach to designing, producing, and evaluating multimedia training programs using a series of logically sequenced steps.

1. Who is the learner? (audience profile)
2. What does the learner need to learn? (objectives)
3. What will enable that learning? (content analysis)
4. What is the best way to teach it? (instructional strategies)
5. How can we be sure it has been learned? (mastery testing)

Why use ISD principles as part of the courseware development process?

Practiced effectively, this systematic approach minimizes the time, effort, and money needed for development, and maximizes the usage of these resources. Training projects in trouble can inevitably trace their woes to skipping or shortchanging one of the five key steps listed above.

Programs are produced without using the Instructional Systems Development (ISD) approach (you've probably seen some). It's a sad fact because critical content is often omitted, while irrelevant content is included. When instructional strategies and delivery platforms are chosen by default, the outcome is haphazard at best.

It is not a pretty sight.

Without ISD, testing is general rather than measuring specified and needed outcomes. There is a lack of cohesiveness across training curriculums, training goals, and testing. Finally, there is little or no attention given to assessing the effectiveness of the program or providing the means to keep it current.

Positive Aspects

Multimedia training, according to Rockley L. Miller, founder of the Interactive Multimedia Association, is reported by corporate users to have the following benefits:

Reduced Learning Time-Multiple studies have found that interactive technologies reduce learning time by an average of 30 percent.

Reduced Cost - The primary costs of interactive instruction lie in design and production not replication, distribution, and delivery. With traditional instructional methods, the costs of training lie primarily in the delivery (instructor salaries, overhead, travel, etc.) and remain constant or even increase as more students place greater demands on fixed resources.

Instructional Consistency - Technology-based instructional systems do not have bad days or forget to cover key points, nor do they cover the same material differently from class to class.

Privacy - With one-on-one systems, students are free to ask questions and explore areas at their own speed, without embarrassment or slowing down an entire class.

Mastery of Learning - Unlike normal classroom situations, an interactive system will not move on to new material until the current material is mastered.

Increased Retention - The process of interaction with material being studied provides strong learning reinforcement that significantly increases content retention over time.

Increased Safety - With interactive systems, students can explore any subject from within the safety of the training environment.

Increased Motivation - Interactive systems provide a level of responsive feedback and individual involvement that has proven to be highly motivating in both individual and classroom learning environments.

Increased Access - Interactive systems can provide greater and more equal access to quality training. They can be used to simulate laboratory equipment that is typically too expensive to make available to each student.

Enjoyment of Interactive Learning-Interactive systems allow learners to take greater control of, and hence, responsibility for, their own learning process. Along the way, they discover that learning can still be enjoyable-even fun!

Facility for Training

The power of any courseware can be augmented by web based training management. A good web-based training management system launches and works with web-based and CD-ROM-based courses. This tool can be customized for your company to:

- Provide convenient program distribution to multiple locations.
- Accurately manage and measure each stage of the program's execution.
- Broadly support advanced multimedia technologies streaming audio and video, animations.

To be effective, the web based management system must provide fast, easy access to courses for students and accurate, timely reports at a click of the mouse. To be responsive, the web based gaining management system must allow customized curricula, as well as changes and updates to the database from one central location.

11

Broad Information

Initially, the communications techniques were concerned with centralised systems. Terminal networks are all built around a central computer; similarly remote job entry stations are usually connected to a single computer. In the remaining chapters some of the problems and techniques of a network of intercommunicating devices are discussed. The devices at present connected to networks are usually general-purpose computers, with their own terminal networks. One reason for networking multi-access computers, rather than terminals or smaller devices, is that these computer systems already existed when networking was proposed. A second reason is that the protocols used in computer networks are very complex so that only a large computer system would have sufficient spare computing power to implement them. However, terminals can be directly attached to a network, by using a dedicated computer. In the near future computer networks will become as widespread as the telephone network, and large scale integration will enable cheap processors to handle the protocols. The result will be the networking of every sort of computing device.

Working Bases

The current trends indicate that powerful, single user, workstations would replace terminals for network use. The workstations will be directly connected to a local area network and use the resources of larger computers via the network. This chapter is primarily concerned with the technology used to connect the computers and devices that make up a computer network. For the purposes of description the range of technology has been divided into three areas:

1. wide area networks
2. Radio and satellite broadcast networks
3. Local networks

The network technology includes the techniques used to interconnect the computing devices and physically transfer information from one computing device to another.

The term 'wide area network' is applied to a network that covers a large physical area, say a whole country or large area under one administration. Such an area may be worldwide where a multinational organisation owns the network. The basic communication media used are dedicated circuits, usually of about 50 kHz bandwidth. Where digital circuits are available the bandwidth would be 64K bps. The recent introduction of fiber optics in long distance trunks has make link bandwidth of 2-3M bps available. Wide area networks will be using these links over the next few years. Examples of such networks, are PSS, ARPANET, Tymnet, Telenet, etc.; details of some of these networks are given at the end of this section. For reasons explained in chapter 3, the physical circuits are usually provided by a PTT, although in the case of PSS the whole network is also run by the PTT. Although 50 kHz bandwidth seems to be a lot compared with the 3 kHz nominal bandwidth of the voice telephone line, it is not very much when high-speed or large-volume transfers of information are required. Even at these high speeds the channel capacity is a resource that needs to be used efficiently.

It is now necessary to see how information can be transferred from one computer to any other on the network. The problem falls into two parts. The first is that of transferring information via a medium, such as a wire. The second part is concerned with addressing and routing. If there were only two computers on a network, then they could be connected by two channels, one for each direction, and whatever one computer transmitted the other would be bound to receive. When more computers are added, the bidirectional connection solution can be extended by having each computer connected to every other computer by a full duplex connection. To send a message to a particular computer the appropriate connection is selected; thus the routing of a message is carried out by the sender.

Using a dedicated connection between every computer on the network is very expensive. If there are n computers on the network then n(n-1)/2 lines are needed, and have to be paid for! As a single computer would not normally be communicating with every other computer on the network at the same time, most of the lines would be unused in a fully connected network. Therefore to increase the utilisation of the connection circuits, their number is reduced, and switching is introduced within the network. There are three forms of switching that can be used in communications: circuit switching, message switching, and packet switching.

Circuit switching is used on the PSTN to connect telephone subscribers. To use it for a computer network each computer would have a private circuit to a local exchange, and the exchanges would be connected to form a network. Whenever two computers wish to exchange information, a physical path is established between them Via the exchanges. The path is then disconnected when the connection is closed. The circuit has been, switched by the exchanges. This method of connection is not used on established computer networks.

As high-speed connection using good-quality circuits is important for efficient computer networks; circuit switching is discounted in favour of the other methods. Circuit switching is used for some networks connecting computers, for instance, the Nordic Data Network.

To overcome problems in setting up and taking down physical circuits via exchanges, computer networks use permanent circuits and switch the data. A partially connected network is used in which each computer has a permanent circuit to a number of its neighbours, but not to all computers on the network. An example will illustrate the basic operation of information switching where the unit of information is a message. If the computer at A wishes to send a message to B, the message must pass through either D or C. The points on the network are called nodes. A will address the message to B by placing the address of B in the message header. The message and address are then sent on the circuit to D. At D the node inspects the address; if the address is 'D' the message is given to the computer; if the address is not D the message is forwarded on a circuit that the node believes will enable the message to be delivered, In this case D will forward the message to B. Thus the node at D has switched the message on to the appropriate output circuit.

The nodes have been introduced in the network to carry out the functions of outing and store and forward, so the host computer is separated from the network operation as much as possible The 'hosts' are the user computers which wish to use the network. Often a number of hosts will be attached to a single node. The node computers are usually minicomputers chosen for their ability to respond in real time to the communications devices. Each node receives incoming messages and stores them.

When a complete message has been received the destination address is inspected so that the message can be placed on the output queue of a circuit to forward the message. If the message is for a host attached to the node, the output circuit will be the one connected to the host. If the message is for a distant host the node must forward the message to another node on the route to the distant host. While the message is in the node store, waiting to be processed or waiting for output, it is, of course, being delayed. The link into any one node may be used to carry messages from several different computers, as may the connection between the node and host. The physical equipment involved is used more efficiently than in circuit switching as a result of this multiplexing. Message multiplexing is the most important advantage of message and packet switching computer networks.

To distinguish between message and packet switching it is necessary to understand what a message is. This has already been introduced in earlier chapters, but a more detailed discussion is given here. The easiest way of defining a message is to say that it is a unit of information which is exchanged by users of a network.

This means the characteristics of a message are only dependent on the user or the application. A message could be a few bits or a file, or even a whole database. In a message-switching network the whole message is passed from one node to another as a complete entity. Compared with circuit switching, a message-switching network has the following characteristics:

1. Any computer can communicate with any other computer without having a direct physical connection.
2. Any computer can communicate with several others using the same equipment by multiplexing messages.
3. There is no delay arising from circuit set up, but messages are delayed when they pass through a node en-route.

The messages can be transferred between nodes, and nodes and hosts, using an ARQ protocol. Characteristic 3 implies that there is no delay arising from the use of a network other than the store and forward operation of the nodes. This is true in some networks using pure datagram techniques. However, in most networks the internode protocol used within the network introduces some delays.

Any network using a virtual circuit protocol, at any level, will introduce a delay when the message or packet is given to the network. In many networks the local node negotiates for resources within the network before actually forwarding a message. This is true of an X.25 network when the call is first set up, and is true of every message on the ARPA network.

Sending the Message

A user of a message-switching network will pass the network a message, together with a destination address, and the user will receive messages as single units.

The disadvantages of message switching relate to the possible occurrence of large messages, where the exact value of 'large' will depend on the network. If a network could be certain of only handling small messages, the disadvantages would disappear. The transfer of messages is a user requirement, so a network that meets user needs must be able to handle very large messages as well as small messages. The solution to these two conflicting requirements is to break the user's message into small packets for transfer through the network and have the packets reassembled into the message by the receiver.

The message header is included as the data in the first packet and that each packet has its own header. This refinement produces packet switching, which is the most widely used switching technique for computer networks. The physical organisation of a packet-switching network is the same as for message switching. The network is a partially connected mesh of nodes. For practical reasons most wide area networks use special node computers to perform the switching, with the user computers being attached to the nodes. The term 'host' is now widely used to mean a user computer system attached to a network. The nodes are part of the network, so the hosts use a well-defined interface for accessing the node to enable data transfer across the network. By using a node separated from the host, all of the packet-switching functions, such as storage and routing, are removed from the host. However, the host still needs considerable software to handle the protocols used to access the node and to transfer data to other computers on the network.

Wide area networks have been in existence since the early 1970s. The best known example is the ARPA network in the United States. This network was established by a government research agency to link together computer centres that had contracts for government research so that research workers could share the available computing resources. The network itself also forms part of a research project to evaluate the feasibility of a large computer network, and to investigate techniques that could be used in such a network. The ARPA network has been very successful in showing that the concept of resource sharing by use of a network is feasible.

One of the most noticeable advantages that the network has introduced is a mail facility. This allows each user with access to a computer on the network to exchange mail with all the other network users. The mail facility is probably one of the main sources of traffic on the ARPA network and has certainly improved the amount of communication between researchers at different sites. The basic techniques used within the ARPA network have been influenced by the defence aspects of the research. particularly the need for a fast response and resilience to the failure of any part. The network consists of a mesh of partially connected nodes called Interface Message Processors (IMPS). Each IMP can have up to eight hosts connected to it and may be connected to up to eight other IMPs. Each IMP accepts messages from the hosts of up to 8K bits in length.

The IMP breaks the message into IK bit packets which are then forwarded through the network of IMPS to the IMP attached to the destination lost. This destination IMP reassembles the message before delivering it to the destination host. If a host wishes to send a message of more than 8K bits it must break the message up itself, into 8K packets, and the destination host must reassemble the message from the 8K packets. Thus the translation between messages and packets takes place at two levels. Within the network of IMPS, packets (1K) are sent individually along whichever route is best at the time, so that packets in a single message may use different routes and may arrive at the destination IMP out of sequence. The destination IMP has to reassemble the message from the packets as they arrive. However, messages passed from the host to the IMP are delivered in the same sequence to the destination host. The technology developed for the ARPANET is now used in a number of commercial wide area networks all over the world. The British Telecom network PSS (Packet Switching Stream) is an example of a network provided by a PTT as a public service. The design requirements for such a network are different from those of the ARPA network so they have resulted in a network with different characteristics. The network topology consists of a number of exchanges which are also partially connected. Each exchange is connected to a number of host computers in its area

Machine at Work

The exchanges contain the node computers, the number of node computers 'in each exchange depending on the number of hosts attached to the exchange. The hosts use an access protocol called X.25 to enable them to make virtual calls to other hosts. A host will give the local exchange the destination address of the host with which it wishes to communicate. The network will route the call to the destination exchange which will then complete the call to the destination host. The call is represented by information kept at all the exchanges on the route. The information is then used to forward the packets transferred on the call. Once the call has been established the hosts may exchange their own information. This is very similar to circuit switching on the PSTN although it is provided using packet-switching techniques.

The PSS network techniques are different from those on the ARPA network, where each message is addressed and transferred separately. The hosts can use a single link to the PSS exchange to carry a number of virtual calls to other hosts, thus the link is used to multiplex the calls.

Radio and satellite broadcast networks differ from wide area networks in the way in which the channel is used for communication between users. Broadcast networks use a channel to which all the users are connected, so all the users receive any transmission made on the channel. At present the two types of channel in use are local radio, covering up to a few hundred kilometres, and satellite channels which are used to span very large distances. Networks using radio and satellite channels have special problems because noise in the channel can cause errors. There is also the problem of allocating the channel for transmission.

The first operational broadcast computer network was built at the University of Hawaii using local radio transmission; many of the techniques and much of the terminology derive from this first network. Every node receives all packets transmitted on the broadcast channel. When the received packet is complete, the node checks the packet for errors and then checks the destination address. If the address of the receiver matches the packet destination address, it is accepted; otherwise it is discarded. The problems particular to a broadcast network occur in the allocation of the channel to a node for transmitting a packet.

Different solutions are used for radio and satellite links. Each node is only able to communicate with each other node via the common channel, so some scheme is needed to coordinate transmission. The schemes that have been proposed and used are discussed here in increasing complexity and are compared for channel efficiency. The simplest transmission technique is called pure aloha; when a node has a packet to transmit it does so immediately. Having transmitted the packet, the node waits for an acknowledgement. This is therefore a positive acknowledgement protocol. If an acknowledgement is not received within a time out period, the packet is assumed lost. Transmission collisions, which occur when two nodes transmit at the same time and thus interfere with each other's transmission, are detected by the time out mechanism. When a collision is detected, each node waits a period of time of random length before retransmitting the packet to of traffic increases, the rate of collision will increase and more re-transmissions will be needed. As the older packets are re-transmitted, more stations will have newer packets to transmit, causing more collisions, etc.

Analysis has shown that a pure aloha scheme can only use a maximum of about 18% of the channel bandwidth. A node may transmit at any time, thus the maximum length of time the channel is wasted as a result of a collision is 2t, where t is the transmission time for one packet. The 2t period is the worst case, where one node begins transmitting just before the previous transmission is complete. An improvement on pure aloha is slotted aloha in which the transmission channel time is divided into time slots of t. Each node is then only allowed to begin transmitting a packet at the start of a time slot. The nodes are kept in synchronisation by a time signal on the channel. Now if a collision occurs only one slot is wasted, so the maximum efficiency rises to about 34% of the channel capacity.

When a collision is detected, a transmitter must wait for a random number of time slots before retransmitting. When the traffic is light the wait can be quite short, but as the traffic load increases the waiting period should be increased. From the aloha schemes it can be seen that it is collisions that cause problems, so a collision avoidance mechanism should improve efficiency. In packet radio networks a scheme known as Carrier Sense Multiple Access (CSMA) is used. When a node is transmitting all other nodes can receive the transmission, so they can avoid a collision by not transmitting themselves until the channel is free. A transmission is detected by the presence of the carrier signal in the medium. When a node has a packet to transmit it looks for the carrier; if there is no carrier the packet is transmitted. If the carrier is detected the node waits for a random length delay and tries again.

Even in a radio broadcast the signal from a transmitter takes a finite amount of time to reach all the receivers in the network. When two nodes find the channel free, they may both begin transmission because neither has heard the other one. This case is most likely to happen when two stations are waiting for the channel to become free. The length of time it takes to propagate the signal to all receivers is the time band in which collisions may occur, but it is less than the total packet transmission time. As with the aloha technique, the CSMA technique can be improved by dividing the channel time into slots and only allowing the transmission of packets to begin at the start of a time slot. The slot length is set to the propagation delay, not the packet transmission time.

The CSMA technique has been further refined by modifying the action of the node when the channel is busy. When the node samples the channel again and finds it free, it transmits its packet with a probability p, or waits for a further delay of random length, with a probability (1-p). This is called persistent CSMA or p-persistent transmission. If p is high then the delay before transmission occurs is lower, but the possibility of collision increases if two stations are waiting for another station to finish. In persistent C-SMA a trade off is made between channel efficiency and delay with the value of p. Channel efficiencies of about 80% may be achieved using these techniques. Packet radio networks have a small delay between the start of a transmission and the detection of the transmission by all stations on the network. On a satellite broadcast network there is a very long delay between transmission and receiving, of the order of a quarter of a second.

A satellite network operates by each transmitter sending its signal to the satellite. The satellite then broadcasts the signal to all of the Earth stations, which may be spread over a very large area. One satellite system currently used for packet switching connects nodes in England, Norway and North America using a satellite in stationary orbit over the North Atlantic.

Particular Technique

A different channel allocation technique is used on satellite broadcast networks because of the long propagation delay. This satellite channel allocation technique involves making reservations for the future use of slots in the channel. The channel is divided into frames consisting of a number of reservation slots and a number of packet slots. Each reservation slot represents a packet slot in the second part of the frame. All ground stations are synchronised to the frame timing by the satellite transmission. During the first part of the frame the ground stations reserve slots for the packets they have ready by transmitting a marker during the reservation slot time.

When the reservation slot is heard on the satellite down channel, the ground station inspects the slot to see if it contains its own marker. If so it can transmit a packet in the corresponding packet slot in the second part of the frame. This scheme uses some of the channel capacity to avoid the collisions which could reduce the network to a pure aloha scheme. Obviously more than one ground station may attempt to reserve a particular packet slot by transmitting during the reservation slot time. There are a number of algorithms to overcome this, including allocating some slots to busy stations. Thus if a station successfully obtained a packet slot in the last frame, the same slot is allocated to that station in the next frame without competition. If an allocated slot is not used then the slot is open for competition in the following frame: Usually there are some slots that all stations can compete for in every frame. Another mechanism involves using a central allocation station to which each station sends its requirements and the central station allocates the slots.

A local, or private, network is a communication system connecting computers in a small geographical area, say less than a few kilometres between the furthest points. The network is wholly owned and run by one administration. There are currently two basic types of technology used on such a network, these are cable or bus, technology and ring technology. Whereas wide area networks and satellite networks use nodes to separate the internal network switching from the user hosts, local networks are meant to be as cheap as possible and so the separate node computer is omitted. In both local network technologies all the computers are directly attached to the transmission medium by a special interface, and all the interfaces receive all the packets.

The difference between a ring and a bus system is the way in which the channel is allocated. Local networks are designed for use in local computing by allowing the interconnection of very small computers, such as microprocessors, personal workstations and peripheral devices. If the local network is to be useful, the cost of the computer. interfaces into the network channel has to be low compared with the cost of the computer or peripheral, and microprocessors are very cheap in computer terms. A widely forecast use of local networks is connecting word processors within a set of offices for the exchange of information and electronic mail.

The cost constraints, the limited processing power of the small computers and the protocols used on a local network are different from those used in wide area networks. A local network usually has a very high bandwidth channel of between I and 10 MHz and a very low error rate say one bit in several million might be corrupted. These characteristics permit the use of simple protocols. The lowest level protocol for using the transmission medium is built into the computer interface.

Cable or bus networks usually use a length of coaxial cable, or an existing cable such as that used for closed circuit television (CCTV). The medium is used in a broadcast fashion, exactly as described in the previous section on broadcast networks. The channel allocation techniques vary slightly on the theme of the CSMA techniques, or on a centralised slot allocation. The most popular broadcast local network is the Ethernet system developed by Xerox. The Ethernet principles can be used on any broadcast medium: radio, telephone lines, coaxial cable and optical fibres have all been used successfully.

To obtain the maximum efficiency from the broadcast medium an Ethernet transmitter can listen to its own broadcast to detect a collision and abort the transmission. This extra complexity is known as CSMACD (CD = collision detection) or listen-while-talk. As with the other CSMA techniques a station does not begin transmitting until the broadcast medium is free. Two stations waiting for another station to finish a transmission will begin transmitting together, and thus interfere with each other. The collision is detected by the stations and they both abort the transmission immediately. To enforce the protocol a station that aborts a transfer then jams the ether. After a collision each station waits for a random time before trying again.

The CSMA-CD technique enables the Ethernet system to obtain up to 95% of the broadcast channel bandwidth. The improvement in performance over ordinary CSMA is due to the stopping of transmission as soon as a collision is detected. Note that no slots are used so a network-wide timing signal is not required. The transceiver handles all of the CSMACD access, including the retries and delay calculation which is varied with the traffic load. Thus only complete, and checked, packets are passed up to the station interface and only one request is made for a packet to be sent. The checksum generation and-checking are carried out within the hardware: bad packets are discarded. A time out mechanism is used to retransmit packets that may have been lost as a result of errors.

Another Technique

The ring technique originated in the USA. The idea was then developed in parallel at Cambridge University in the UK and at two research centres in the USA. The version developed at Cambridge is known as the Cambridge ring in the UK. The computer interface is divided into two parts -- the repeater and the interface proper. A ring uses a twisted pair of wires as the transmission medium. However, to improve reliability, the repeater is powered from the ring and electrically isolated from the computer interface, so four wires are used to connect the repeaters.

The four wires are used as two pairs for signaliing and carry sufficient power for the repeaters. In this way the computer can be switched off and removed from the ring without switching off the repeater. With the ring the medium is terminated at each station, whereas in the cable network it is not. Each station is represented by a repeater, several of which are then connected together into a ring. The repeater is a simple device containing a shift register and some logic to detect certain conditions in the information being passed around the ring. The repeater normally passes any information received on to the next repeater, so transmission only occurs in one direction. When a station transmits data, the repeater transmits the information from the station instead of the information received from the previous repeater.

There are slight differences in the channel allocation mechanism used in the Cambridge ring and in those rings developed in the USA. In the Cambridge ring a fixed-size mini-packet is used which constantly circulates in the ring, and a special station called a monitor is used to -generate and maintain the mini-packet and provide the power for the repeaters. In the American versions a variable-size packet is used which may be lost and regenerated as required by each repeater. Note that only 16 bits of information are carried in a ring mini-packet whereas the broadcast network packet may contain several hundred bytes. The assembly of information into a block has to be done by the computer. The monitor station also provides a buffer if the ring is not physically long enough to hold a complete mini-packet.

The monitor performs a check on the mini-packet each time it passes to ensure that it is intact, and to replace it if not. The monitor is an obvious weakness in the Cambridge ring design so far as reliability is concerned; however, experience so far has shown that monitor failures are rare. The advantage of the monitor is that the repeaters can be very simple as well as cheap, which is the purpose of a local network. To use the ring to send a packet of information, the station will wait until an empty mini-packet is detected by the repeater. When the full/empty bit in the mini-packet passes the repeater it is set to one. If the packet was already full no change has been made to the bit; if the packet was empty (full/ empty bit = 0) the mini-packet is now reserved by this station. The repeater will use this mini-packet if the full/ empty bit was received as 0. The addresses of the source and destination stations are placed in the address fields followed by the next 16 bits of the information that the station wishes to send; these are placed in the data field from the station buffer. The reserved mini-packet then travels round to all the other stations on the ring. Each station has a source select register in which an address is placed. If the source address in a mini-packet matches the contents of the source select register, and the destination address matches the station address, the data field is copied into the station receive buffer and the accept status is set at the end of the packet. If the packet is refused, or the destination station is busy, the destination repeater will set the appropriate value in the status bits at the end of the mini-packet. No other change is made by the receiving repeater, and all other repeaters will pass on the mini-packet unchanged.

Special values which can be used in the source select register are: all ones, which means accept any source station address, and all zeros, which means do not accept the data from any mini-packets. When the mini-packet returns to the sending station the full/empty bit is reset to 0 and the status bits are checked to see if the information was accepted. As an error check, the station also reads back the 16 data bits and checks them against the data in its buffer. Having reset the full/empty bit, the station must now wait for another empty mini-packet before it can send the next 16 bits of information. In this way the now empty packet becomes available to successive stations around the ring and the packet slot is allocated in a round robin fashion. The variable nature of packet traffic in a local network makes it difficult to design a system that will provide a very fast response, especially when there is little traffic, and yet not become overloaded or unfair when the traffic becomes heavy.

The broadcast techniques provide a low delay, especially in low-volume traffic, as the transmitter can usually send a packet as soon as one is available. However, as the volume of traffic increases, the broadcast system suffers from collisions and longer delays which can eventually lead to an unstable situation. In the slotted ring the channel is allocated by means of a round robin mechanism so collisions never occur, and during a burst of traffic each station is able to continue transmitting with only a larger delay. During periods of low traffic volume the ring does introduce a delay while a station waits for the empty packet to come round.

Proponents of both systems argue that because of the very high bandwidth available on the channel, and the low processing power of the computers attached to the local network, the volume of traffic is nearly always low in a broadcast network and the delay is negligible in a ring.

The Telematics

The school education experts, on one hand have been designing computer literacy programs, the French have coined the term "telematique". The concept, translated into English as "telematics," refers to the growing connections between and among computers and such telecommunication media as moderns, information utilities, microwave relays, satellites, and cable TV. As such, telematics reflects a new technological reality that transcends nations and cultures. Rooted in research and development breakthroughs, telematics carries special meanings. it draws attention to the unprecedented scope of current communication networks and to the invisibility of much of their operations. It highlights the connectedness of networks components and their collective and far-reaching potential for influencing local, national and global communication.

Telematics, as a new symbol of the power of modern communication media, may well foreshadow the need for new literacy concepts. More specifically, children born in the mid-1980s, upon graduation from high school may find that computer literacy is a receding concept and that "telematic literacy" or some similar concept is making its way onto the educational stage. Since the schools today are only beginning to link microcomputers to information utilities and thereby to provide students new sources of knowledge and ideas, the move away from computer literacy will surely be slow. However, even today we can see that the concept of computer literacy sharply constrains our perspective on the new technologies and on our capacities to comprehend their educational possibilities; since "computer literacy" misses many important meanings inherent in today's complex information environments, it is a provincial concept. If future citizens, workers, and thinkers are to come to grips with the needs created by the changing information society, today's ideas about literacy will need to become more telematic. Such an expanded meaning will enable students to confront both the ends and the means of the microelectronic revolution.

By using a telematic perspective, they can probe the promise of micro-technologies and contemplate the dangers that large-scale, rapidly proliferating and smoothly functioning telematic systems present to individuals and society. The acceptance of a broad ended concept of literacy will enable individuals to gain more than basic understandings of telematic systems and of their import for society. Given the remarkable progress already achieved in electronic information transmission, skilled individuals pursuing decision-making, work, educational, or other objectives can even today tap sources of information far beyond those immediately available in their homes and local libraries.

Tens of thousands of adults are already accessing data through CompuServe; The Source, and other information utilities, in addition, through electronic linkages, leading schools are providing some students with the skills needed to use these utilities. As individuals learn to use electronic networks, they will be able to acquire information from new sources related to the solution of self-defined problems; to define, with the aid of other computer network members, technical and social problems and to seek solutions to these problems, and to develop with others new knowledge, products, and proposals. Form today's perspective such projections may seem unrealistic; however, when 1985 enrollees in kindergarten graduate from high school in the twenty-first century, they will step into a society where information is richer, more varied, and more accessible than it is today. The power of computers and of their telematic companions to change society will surely have more far-reaching effects on the purposes of education than on the means of instructions since schools are now "in between" the descendant industrial and the ascendant information society, their purpose need to be reformulated.

Underlying the all significant concepts of literacy and educational purpose assumptions about desirable qualities of thought. Given the fact that the beliefs about desirable qualities differ, policy makers face a fundamental question: What types of thinking should the schools develop in students? Since the information industries have an insatiable appetite for newly created hardware and software products, their representatives tend to press for means-oriented thinking that can alleviate this appetite. Others, disturbed by the negative impacts of large-scale, computer-based systems on society, see the need for a diffeient type of thinking.

The qualitative and quantitative needs for effective software systems in the future will grow markedly. Programmers responding to this need, as already noted, will apply algorithmic thinking, many other specialists engaged in the development and use of information technologies will be applying similar modes of "instrumental" thinking-modes that are notable for their technical problem-solving capacities, their highly rational expressions, and their effectiveness in dealing with means-oriented questions in here-and-now contexts.

Proficient in procedural analysis, instrumental reasoning can add to an already astounding array of technical solutions and computer artifacts: Significantly, however, more and more critics argue that this type of reasoning cannot resolve the troublesome societal problems which microelectronic technologies are creating. Such reasoning they contend, is too uncritical of the status quo, tco constrained by machine requirements, and too blind and indifferent to the negative consequences of large-scale telematic systems to address overriding social problems. Although critics have argued that instrumental reasoning lacks the capacities to deal effectively with a "permanent underclass," structural unemployment, the loss of privacy, clarification of purpose, inequity of access, nuclear warfare, and other problems created or exacerbated by modern technologies, they have not yet provided a clearly defined alternatives. Unless well-defined alternatives are developed, today's literacy programs, which are linked largely to traditional modes of thought, cannot easily be redirected.

Culture of the New Millennium

One place to look for the salient features of an alternative is in the computer culture itself. Outlined in broad strokes here are features of a type of thought nourished by the problems computerization is creating. Features dealt with include the scope of its perspective, its capacities for critique, the class of problems it addresses, and the outcomes it seeks. How the features depicted are related to the computer culture is also addressed. The computer culture is encouraging thinkers to think more about the future than did members of previous cultures.

Most of the history of book-literacy transpired in rural contexts where tradition was a strong influence on thought. Since past patterns provided reliable standards for the future, rural thinking tended to be oriented toward the past. Those living in the dynamic computer culture, on the other hand, have found that past patterns are very reliable forecasters of, emergent ones; consequently, individuals are pressed to anticipate and to think about the future in uncertain, rapidly changing, and sometimes threatening situations. Masuda has noted that the "purposeful use of future time" is a critical value of the information society. The founding in 1964 of the World Future Society, about the time the integrated circuit began to alter technology radically, is only one of many developments symbolizing the shift towards future's thinking. This thinking has found its way into thousands of publications in many languages; in addition, implementers of future programs in schools are seeking to engender a type of thinking very different from that required to program computers. Another concept of thinking spawned by the computer culture is associated with the term "global." Thinking directed at the development, programming, and operation of computers takes place in relatively bounded environments.

Developers are not pressed to probe the impact of their projected products on society, even though technologies have generated an array of complicated and largely unanticipated societal problems; paradoxically, at the same time technologies have eliminated barriers to worldwide, instantaneous communications and, in the process, have pushed global thinking to the fore. As a result, recognizing that sharply bounded definitions of problems suffer from missing ingredients, leaders are now applying the concept of "world problematique" to such disparate problems as energy and human equity. Expanding international databases are nurturing the budding trend toward global thinking. However, those engaged in such thinking face deeply conflicting national and world interests, as they think within almost unbounded perspective and as they strive to understand the intricacies of global issues.

Instrumental reasoning, by definition, is effective in the logical clarification of steps to be followed and procedures to be used in the attainment of specified objectives. Its mission is limited largely to the elucidation and implementation of efficient means. Users of instrumental reasoning tend to accept uncritically ends specified for them and to ignore the long-range consequences of the developments they achieve.

Pursuing means in contexts where ends are determined by others, instrumental reasoners are not oriented toward larger issues of policy. This condition highlights another feature of needed thought, namely, a capacity to be critical about the ends sought in the information society and how these ends are related to the large-scale technological outcomes that instrumental reasoning helps produce. This feature of thinking transcends narrowly proscribed contexts and concentrates upon purposive issues, strategic questions, and problems that center in public interests.

Its target would not be the development and use of technology but the consequences of such development and use. Eschewing the procedural orientation of instrumentally oriented thinkers, it would be more intuitive and eclectic in its methods. Its bias would be toward holistic thinking and against narrower instrumental tendencies in thought.

To return to the "whither" question, even with its impressive accomplishments instrumental reasoning as a mode of thinking is an insufficient guide for those designing computer literacy programs. Thinking that would counter instrumental reasoning, as already implied, would be directed not at technologies but at the attainment of an effective society. Certainly, the ideal of self-realization of, in more specific terms, the fulfillment of the potential of individuals would become prominent in the design of computer literacy programs. To be sure, it is easier to develop machines than to nurture individuals and it is easier to generate information than to use it wisely. However, only developed individuals will be able to achieve an effective society and to fashion a positive story about life and achievements in the computer culture. Literacy programs directed at the self-realization of individuals in the unfolding computer culture will need a base in thinking that reaches beyond instrumental reasoning. Although the press for instrumental reasoning will continue in both society and schools, emergent signs suggest that a different type of thinking is now in the ascendancy—a thinking that is more futuristic, global, critical, holistic, and goal-oriented in its expression. Computer literacy programs based upon the emergency mode of thinking deserve priority; the complicity and the severity of the problems created by micro-electronic technologies require it.

Programs based upon simpler concepts of literacy, while more widespread, are not as well integrated into curricula as are programs based upon more complex concepts. Activities directed at operational literacy, for example, are typically tangential to, if not outside, established courses; on the other hand, more complex concepts such as citizen literacy can be taught in existing courses; since most literacy programs are not integrated into existing course.

Since most literacy programs are not integrated into existing curricula, institutional support for them is likely to be weak. Much controversy surrounds decisions about computer literacy. Computers, as increasingly powerful machines, activate deeply rooted cultural fears; changes now under way in human-machine relationships, the pessimists stress, will surely bring about a dehumanized society. On the other hand, computer also stimulate expansive new dreams for a more effective society in which humans, aided by machines, reach new levels of self-actualization. Leaders who address literacy decisions, then, are faced with two very different messages, one coloured by despair and the other by hope. These inharmonious views about the consequences of computers complicate literacy decisions.

Given the tender age of computer literacy concepts and the paucity of relevant research, the analogy of "book literacy" can shed light on the query: Whither computer literacy? The history of book literacy contains clues about future developments in computer literacy. Thus, if computer literacy follows the pattern of book literacy, it will become increasingly complex, more expansive in its meanings, and more differentiated in the functions it denotes. Advocates of computer literacy will struggle long to realize equal educational opportunities as have advocates of book literacy; for several reasons, the former may face even greater challenges in attaining equity than have the latter.

Paralleling the struggle to achieve equity will be another challenge, namely, that of ever redefining computer literacy objectives to make them consonant with changing standards of knowledge and with altered societal needs. Since the computer is only a small figure in the larger context of electronic communication, it is already a provincial modifier of "literacy." A more fruitful and encompassing concept could be "telematic literacy", the latter provides a larger window for viewing the understandings and skills needed to function in the developing information society.

With Presumptions

All concepts of literacy contain underlying assumptions about what qualities of thinking schools need to develop in students. The press in the computer culture towards the development and use of hardware and software has required instrumental or means-oriented thinking. The limitations of this emphasis are becoming increasingly apparent; future concepts of computer literacy will need to place greater emphasis upon defining and implementing futuristic, global, intuitive, critical, ends-oriented, and holistic thinking. Most countries have a government body to run the telephones. In the United States a number of private companies are given licences by the Federal Communications Commission (FCC) which oversees the arrangements. Such licensees are known as common carriers in the USA. The effect of the monopoly given to the licensees is that only the licensee can erect systems to carry signals such as telephone conversations or computer data. The licensees are usually called Ms and this reflects the arrangements more common in the rest of the world rather than those in the USA.

The major problem with the PSTN is that it was designed before anyone even thought of computers. The telephone system is ideally suited to carry speech where a human being can concentrate on decoding the received sounds and try to understand them. There are a number of factors contributing to the PSTN being a poor medium for the type of signals. Firstly, the equipment has a frequency range of 3003400 Hz, which is not very wide for high-speed data traffic. Secondly, the frequency range is not continuous; some frequencies may be used to operate equipment at exchanges, which explains how phone freaks in the USA can make calls by whistling into the telephone handset and causing the exchange to set up the call. If a data signal produces the wrong frequency the call may be disconnected. This problem is taken up in the section on modulation.

Finally, to protect the exchange equipment from damage, no DC (direct current) is allowed through the local exchange. By looking at the type of wave produced by speech against a data signal, in figure,. it can be seen that the speech signal never has the same voltage continuously, whereas the data signal consists almost entirely of a continuous voltage at one of two levels. The continuous voltage is the DC part which would be removed by the exchange. Removing the DC part would seriously distort a digital data signal.

The Ms provide four solutions to these problems –

1. Special equipment to convert digital data signals into audio signals which can easily be transmitted through the PSTN.
2. Private four-wire connections to the local exchange, then a fixed circuit to the remote site. This cuts out some parts of the PSTN that cause problems, but not all of them.
3. Direct links of high bandwidth most of the way between sites.
4. More recently, some PTTs now offer digital services directly to the customer, in multiples of 64K bps.

The introduction of digital telephone exchanges will enable the provision of digital circuits direct-to ordinary subscribers in the near future. The major piece of equipment needed to transfer data through the PSTN is the MODEM. Modulation is a technique that can enable information signals to be passed through a medium not really suited to them. The original, and still the major, use of modulation is in radio transmission. By using that analogy it is possible to see how modulation can be used to pass digital data signals, through a medium designed to carry voice signals. The human voice does not travel very far on its own, and if more than one person were to try broadcasting at the same time it would be very difficult to separate out the messages.

The frequency range of an original signal is called the *base band;* for the human voice a base band of 300 to 3300 Hz is used on the telephone though a wider range is possible. When two people talk at once close together, they confuse listeners because they are both using the same frequency range, the base band. To transmit speech over long distances very much higher frequencies have to be used, and care must be taken to ensure that different frequencies are used for each different transmission. The original base band frequencies have to be increased and no two transmissions should use the same frequency range. The only problems now are how to increase the frequency of the base band signal without losing any information in the signal, and then how to recover the original signal so that the transmission can be heard in the base band. The problems are solved by modulation. Modulation, very simply, involves superimposing the information signal on to a simple carrier signal in such a way that one, or more, components of the carrier are modified to carry the information.

In the technique known as 'differential phase modulation', there are four possible phase changes (0°, 90°, 180°, 270°) so each possibility represents two bits of data. A continuous frequency simple wave is used so that only the phase component changes; figure shows the phase changes. To be able to detect the phase changes a complete wave, or cycle, is used. In any one cycle there are four possible changes that could occur, so each cycle represents two bits of information. For instance, if we use a frequency of 1200 Hz we can have an information rate of 2400 bits per second.

Sometimes a faster rate of data transfer is required, say for printing messages, though the input may still be slow. The bandwidth available on the PSTN is not sufficient, given the noise, to allow a full duplex connection faster than 300 bps. However, research is continuing on modulation techniques to achieve faster data rates. A second type of MODEM is used to provide a higher speed in one direction, but a much lower speed in the other direction. Up to 600 bps can be guaranteed on the PSTN in the UK, passing through the exchange in one direction, whilst the return channel has only 75 bps. The return channel is called a 'supervisory channel' and is not expected to carry much data.

Up to 1200 bps may be obtained using a dial-up connection if the noise is very low, but a 'private circuit' will provide a guaranteed 1200 bps. If a connection of 600/1200 bps is needed in both directions, then two MODEMs are needed at each end. If the PSTN is used 'via a dial-up line only a half duplex connection is possible, because the circuit can only manage 600/1200 bps in one direction at a time. If a private four-wire circuit is used then a full duplex connection is possible. Because the direction of the main data transfer is fixed, one type of MODEM is used for sending on the fast channel (600/ 1200 bps) and receiving the supervisory channel (75 bps), whilst a different model performs the reverse operation at the other end.

The receiving MODEM can always tell if the sender is using 600 or 1200 bps as the idle frequency is different for the two data rates. Note that the frequency range 13002 100 Hz fills the middle of the available frequencies on the PSTN. This means that the supervisory channel is relegated to using the low frequencies, and therefore has a low data rate.

A popular speed for synchronous transfer is 2400 bps. This is provided by a group of MODEMS that use differential phase encoding to obtain the higher data rate within the frequency range of the PSTN. The connection pattern is the same as for the 600/ 1200 bps MODEM; a simplex connection is available on the two-wire circuit via the exchange with a sending and receiving MODEM. If sending and receiving MODEM are provided at each end, a half duplex connection can be made by sharing the two-wire circuit.

A full duplex connection can be obtained by using a private four-wire circuit. A 2400 bps MODEM is available for use over the PSTN using a dial-up line, but may be limited to 1200 bps by noise. The 2400 bps main data connection can be augmented by a 75 bps supervisory channel in the reverse direction, as in the 600/ 1200 MODEM. The differential phase encoding uses four possible phase changes on a 1200 Hz signal to obtain the 2400 bps data rate. MODEM speeds of 4800 bps and 9600 bps are also available, but only using private circuits.

For use in inter-computer communications, an arrangement is available for data rates between 40.8K bps and 50K bps over 48 kHz wide band circuits. Some of the larger exchanges in the PSTN are connected by very wide band circuits. These can be utilised for data transfer, although a private high-speed circuit may have bypassed several exchanges on the way to the large exchange. For the high-speed circuit four MODEMS are used, one pair to reach the large exchange, and another pair at the other end. Between the end pairs of MODEMs the data is passed in the base band frequency of the data signals on a special private circuit.

The main uses of MODEMs are listed below.

1. To connect a teletype or slow VDU (110/300 bps) to any computer in full duplex, by dialing through the PSTN.
2. To connect a faster terminal (600/1200 bps); but to get a full duplex connection a permanent private circuit is needed, so only one computer can be used.
3. To provide a synchronous connection using higher data rates (1200/2400, 4800, 9600 bps); but again a private circuit is needed for full duplex and full speed operation.
4. A very high data rate can be achieved, but at a higher cost, using base band signaling for part of the distance on a special circuit.

In terms of cost the acoustic coupler represents the cheapest modulation equipment. The cost then rises through the four types of MODEM described above. The higher the data rate, the higher the cost; however, the relationship is not linear. A 1200 bps service does not cost four times as much as a 300 bps service: it is more likely to cost only about twice as much to install, especially if a private wire is needed, but the rental may only be half as much again. Thus the problem of obtaining the optimum cost/service is not easy.

The PTTs from all over the world work through a body called the CCITT. The CCITT is a part of the United Nations. It is concerned with enabling the individual PTTs from all over the world to cooperate and provide an international service. The CCITT is one of the most authoritative standards organisations in communications, so any standard adopted by the CCITT is very important. All of the MODEMs discussed in this chapter conform to international, standards for their operation, so it is possible for a terminal user in the UK to use a timesharing computer in Germany by dialing the computer. The German computer uses a German MODEM, while the UK user has a UK MODEM, but because they conform to the same standards they will be able to operate together. The CCITT have had a tremendous impact on computer communications by standardising various interfaces between computing equipment.

The most important interface is that between the MODEM and the user's equipment. For instance, for asynchronous terminals the interface standard is called V24. The V24 standard defines all of the control and data signals used to enable the MODEM and the user's equipment to operate together and pass data, including the signal levels. The result of the standards and their widespread adoption by equipment manufacturers means that any terminal having a V24 interface can be plugged into any MODEM, anywhere. Furthermore computer manufacturers now use the V24 standard for connecting local terminals as well. This compatibility between equipment is very important in allowing various different types of equipment, from different manufacturers, to be interchangeable. Because the manufacturers in the United States dominate the computer industry the standards adopted by the United States often become the international standards of the CCITT.

One of the US standards called RS232C is in fact the same as the V24 recommendation and preceded it. RS232C was the name given to the standard in the US before it became an international recommendation..Many US manufacturers still refer to it as RS232C rather than V24. The CCITT have defined a standard interface for connecting communications equipment to a digital switched network; this standard is known as X.21. A second interface standard, known as X.21(bis), allows the same mechanisms but over the analogue PSTN, because there are still so few digital services available. The packet switched network access interface, X.25, is defined to used X.21 as its lowest level. However, X.21 (bis), or even V24, may be used where a digital network is not yet available.

12

Technology for Practice

Changes in teaching and learning with the new educational technologies indicate changes in design and development of instructional materials. The impact of educational technology and its effects on students learning become even more important issues. Researchers argue that changes of technology attributes may not affect learners' cognitive and information processing. Students may benefit from the new techniques of presenting learning content through current educational technology. The phenomenon of today's technology, especially Internet technology, has changed our daily life. Massive amounts of information can be reviewed through desktop computers. We are able to communicate with others through electronic mail, video conferences, and chat lines without leaving our offices or homes. Recently Deep Blue, a super computer, defeated the world chess champion for the first time in history. Altris, a file management company, stepped forward to build software on the premise that document files have intelligence of their own. It allows users to be recipients of information without requesting it. Can we completely separate what technology can provide to us from what we can do with technology? Compared to the web, limits of each technology, including videotape and CD-RCM, certainly restrain our creative abilities in the design and delivery of our learning materials. We, as humans, have tried very hard to improve modern technology to provide quick connections, materials access, and interaction without boundaries and time constraints. According to Schrage, "The key is to remember that even as we use technology to shape our environment, technology is shaping us. Technology rearranges our perceptual world and subtly redefines our relationship with our environment". In a study by Internet Commerce, it reports that there are 34.6 million web users. We see the fast growing trend of using the web as a vehicle to deliver on-line educational programs. Educators should examine the approaches they choose for enhancing the learning process and make it as good, if not better than conventional teaching methods in the classroom. This article discusses students perception on learning through Web technology, including class syllabus, professor notes, course-packs, projects, tests, and self-paced learning courses.

Different Approaches

The web technology permits us to represent the learning materials in any combination of media format, such as text, image, graphics, and animation (no sound and video clips were employed on the web pages during this study). This multimedia information environment can be accessed and displayed simultaneously.

The survey was administered to the students who were taking the self-paced web units as a trial run for the new media. Fortysix participants filled out an on-line survey when they finished the units. Eleven of them were interviewed at the end of their final test for the course. All interviews were recorded and transcribed by the researcher. The interview lasted from thirty minutes to fifty minutes. Qualitative data obtained in the interviews were analyzed using interpretive / descriptive analysis procedure. Both data were employed to assess how students' experience of using new media influenced their attitudes toward their learning performance.

Experiment Results

The questionnaire and interviews indicated that using web-based instruction was a positive learning experience for the participants. The study indicated educational technology could offer a rich learning environment if we were able to integrate collaborative on-line environments, proper pedagogical design, and flexible user's interface.

Web-based instruction was designed in such a way that learning materials were arranged into small modules, including presentation, examples, and exercises. Objectives were incorporated into each module so that learners could be aware of the learning expectation. Preview and post-view questions for the learning content allowed students to analyze and evaluate their learning through each module. Students were presented with examples and exercises following reading paragraphs. Once they believed that they mastered the materials, they could move onto the practice test. There were links to an interactive learning environment. For each stage, a student was able to click on a more detailed explanation if he/she had any problems before proceeding. Auto feedbacks and diagnosis messages were incorporated in all parts of exercises. Students could evaluate themselves before they were ready for tests. They were able to communicate with the professor through email, chat room, and/or telephone. Following is a summary of the results—

All survey questions were on a Liker scale except items one to three. A majority of students (87%) had prior experience in using the web, which made implementation of web-based instruction much easier than what we expected. One-third of students had access to the Internet at home while others still came to use the campus labs. Students spent slightly less time studying a unit on the web (3-6 hours) than they did for the regular class. In general, the students were very positive about their experiences in learning through the web. The results indicated that the web-course not only met their needs but also helped them use time more effectively. However, they were undecided when asked whether they preferred the electronic format or the traditional instructor lecture. Their hesitation and concerns were also echoed during the interview.

The interview data agreed with the results of the survey. The students valued alternative learning styles that technology offered.

They praised the potential of technology to establish a feasible learning environment in higher education. However, they also addressed their concerns and limitation of educational technology.

Controlling the System

The study indicated that the high level of interactively inherent on the web gave the users dynamic control of information. Interaction with linked information was very structured in terms of proficiency level and direction. The students preferred such full control over their learning situation.

"I enjoyed it for a number of reasons. I could do it in my own schedule.... I could get back to review it which you couldn't do in a classroom."

"I thought that it was helpful to have questions where you got immediate answers and you determined whether you're right or wrong. That helped me for a couple of incidents because I always tested myself and that kind of exercise reinforces what you are looking at."

"I was going more in depth in the stuff that I didn't know. In a class sometimes, the professor has to go over it again if some people don't understand. With a computer, you have the control. It made it more personal for me."

Students also felt that the experience in working with web-based instruction offered the opportunity not only to learn the content but to learn how to use a computer and how to access Internet. The students were encouraged to browse other resources by being provided with course related links. They suggested that such hands-on experience was really beneficial.

"Using the Internet - what a great learning tool! I had some computer experience before coming to this class but had never used the Internet. Having our reading on it made for a great experience for the entire class."

"...for some people in the class it was difficult but they finally caught on. I am lucky to have my fiancé teach me at home. We've had Internet access for some time but I've never been that interested in it until this semester. In another of my classes we get our notes and important material off the Internet. Some of my friends were jealous that we learned this in this class."

" Allowed the students to experience technology. It is a very ingenious way to get people involved with Internet and apply what we learn to technology. "

"It made me use a computer. It was nice not having to use pen and paper."

Fruitful Training

In traditional classroom teaching, we focused more on the students' performance based on the selected objectives. Web-based instruction permitted the meaningful learning which allowed students to choose self-exam exercises after the guided practice and to have an opportunity to construct their learning to provide openness to new information and multiple perspectives.

"I think that the program was effective. I like how there are questions throughout the reading because it tests how much I am retaining. The animation entertains me and the graphs help me to understand what is being presented. The test helped a lot because it helped me to feel more comfortable when taking the exam."

"It took me a lot longer than I thought it would because I took so many notes but it was worth it."

"The first thing I did was to take the practice assessment. That was a kind of pre-test for me, which showed me what I needed to study and which behavior objectives that I needed to concentrate on.... So I took extensive notes for the objectives that I needed to work on and I just scanned through the reading, and I did OK."

"I feel that using a computer program helped me have a better understanding of the Epsilon mini-unit. The questions that follow the text really helped me understand the material. It seemed to go into more depth than in the classroom."

Without Restrictions

As we have learned, the World Wide Web is a universal medium that everyone who has an Internet access can use. It doesn't have problems with different platforms and can be accessed from anywhere in the world. The web is an international information delivery tool. Students' feedback regarding the class syllabus, professor notes, coursepak, and projects was extremely positive. First, students liked to have the convenience in accessing their class information. They valued the opportunity to read and/ or download the syllabus, professor's notes, or coursepak. Deadlines and test schedules through the web could be checked at any time. Instead of worrying about misplacing their hard copy of the syllabus and buying the coursepak, now they could turn to the web. Second, the study showed that students strongly appreciated their capability to obtain actual learning materials from the web without time and location boundaries, especially for people who worked full time. It not only saved them time from traveling to the campus but also offered flexibility for them to choose their own time.

"I like it because I could do it any time I wanted to and it was easy to use."

"I really liked that fact that I could work at my own pace at home. I did not have to worry about my notes not being adequate."

"I work full time and I feel this gives me flexibility."

Wide Range of Info

The web-based course provided non-linear access to resources links on the web which could be obtained rapidly and easily through multiple links and paths. Students could flexibly move among related elements of information and explored many related data and ideas in a non-linear format. Students liked the related links which broadened their learning beyond the classroom and also helped them obtain more information or real data, especially links to professional journals and organizations. The only suggestion from students was to have more meaningful links. Some students actually went out and searched for the links that they would like to have. As one of the students described:

"Internet offers us opportunities for self-direction and exploration. The more varied the cybernetic environment, the more possibilities exist for us to make connections, access materials and develop their own theoretical and practical postures as achievers. We are given opportunities to experiment and grow. We learn not just a few tricks of the keyboard but thinking strategies for connecting with rapidly changing technological landscape."

The learning styles and learners' characteristics have been the central concerns of educators. Each individual has a, personality which affects his/her learning style. Some learning styles and personality needs can be particularly well addressed in a web-based learning environment.

Some students, who were not out-spoken, were more comfortable working on web-based courses while others may have felt less pressure in such a format. Web-based instruction may provide a learning environment which better meets learning needs. One student stated: "I thought the computer course took off a lot of stress because it could be done when we wanted."

However, several disadvantages were identified by students, such as Internet traffic - a long waiting time to log on and/or to load some information, a lack of audio, and no face-to-face communication.

Records of achievement (ROAs) and the use of portfolios as frameworks for the assessment of prior learning from work and other social and vocational experiences (AP(E)L) have become widespread over the past decade. Both potentially lay the basis for recognizing achievements previously beyond the reach of assessment. Both were intended to foster 'learning through success' not failure. Both emphasize the notion of students as active learners responsible for their own development. When first introduced to education, both also emphasized personal achievement and development and centred upon the production of documents which represented not just an end in themselves but also a philosophy of education. This philosophy aims to raise levels of achievement by broadening the range of what is recognized as valuable and emphasizes the value of experiential, student centred approaches to learning. In particular the introduction of both ROAs and AP(E)L initiatives challenged the notion of formal examinations as a useful measure of achievement.

The early focus was on the personal gain to the individual resulting from going through the process of recording achievement. While the main aim was the production of a record detailing a range of achievements and learning, at the same tune the process itself aimed to encourage individuals by building confidence in their achievements, helping them review their experiences, helping to plan and manage future learning, and by providing a basis for viewing learning as something they were a part of rather than something that was done to them. As the use of ROAs and AP(E)L grew more widespread, however, they began to change. In some cases the emphasis shifted from personal to public, from formative to summative. Instead of focusing on an individual's perceptions and personal achievements, some ROAs and AP(E)L portfolios began to contain ever more information about the skills, attainments and personal qualities in a form which aimed to be of use to prospective employers and admissions tutors. From a framework for promoting a developmental process they became almost an alternative 'qualification'.

This shift in emphasis from formative to summative resulted in a confusing (and confused) variety of attitudes towards the production of records and portfolios. In early initiatives the formative process was justification in itself. The shift in emphasis to the summative, however, posed the questions of what was being assessed and how and also potentially devalued the process underpinning the document. Today the development of AP(E)L systems in higher education goes alongside moves towards assisting students to reflect on their learning experiences to enable them to gain formal credit for informal learning experiences. As the process gains recognition nationally and opportunities for crediting a wide range of learning increase, there is also increasing concern that such processes should have a degree of parity. The result has been a requirement that ROAs and AP(E)L portfolios conform to national quality standards. This sounds reasonable but marks a shift in emphasis, indicating that now the benefits of ROAs are for an audience outside the student not for the student themselves.

This paper outlines the background to recording achievement initiatives, summarizes the tension between the benefits of formative assessment and the requirements of summative assessment and identifies the issues which must be addressed if the tension is to be resolved.

The Recording Achievement initiative developed at the same time as the introduction of the assessment and accreditation of prior experiential learning (AP(E)L) to formal education. Both were a response to the social and political context of the 1970s and 1980s. At the time the primary political emphasis in education and training was the reskilling of the workforce in the face of foreign competition and the need to adjust to changes in the way work is organized. The demand for more skilled labour and for skills which are often informally learned, such as personal skills, resulted in an education and training strategy which sought to recognize and accredit the widest possible range of educational achievement in the attempt to raise levels of attainment as a basis for a more highly qualified labour force.

The education system which existed in Britain in the 1970s had been designed to qualify only between 20 and 30% of the population and was equally ill fitted to providing either qualifications or routes to further training for those who had traditionally left school with no qualifications at all. Against this setting, practitioners with a philosophical interest in promoting experiential learning and student centred assessment were able to develop a number of local initiatives. Records of Achievement provided the opportunity to recognize the achievements of young people who had traditionally been out of reach of educational assessment. AP(E)L enabled a similar process for mature learners to progress to further and higher education. Both provided a basis for a fuller account of the range of learner achievement as well as a way to recognize achievement which cannot be assessed with conventional methods of assessment. For a time, at least, policy objectives appeared to accord with the concerns of educationalists who wanted to broaden opportunity and promote experiential learning.

Recognizing a broad range of achievement was, however, only the first step to the policy objective of achieving a more highly qualified workforce. A tension soon developed between the aims of educationalists and the aims of policy makers as individual achievements summarized in ROAs and AP(E)L portfolios were looked at from the standpoint of providing evidence of ability to progress to further education or training, or as a basis for accreditation and formal qualifications. The need to accord with the public, externally defined criteria of higher education gatekeepers and employers was at odds with a focus on personally defined achievement.

The tension between the personal arid the public in recording achievement was played out in the development of the National Record of Achievement (NRA). Local ROA initiatives emphasized formative processes and student centredness. Once local initiatives were officially brought together in the NRA, launched in 1991, the emphasis was on summative documents. The drive to recognize and qualify achievement for a public audience also affected AP(E)L developments. At the same time as ROAs were changing to summative documents, moves to give prior experiential learning a semi-formal status as a basis for progression to higher education began to overshadow formative processes in AP(E)L in favour of satisfying criteria for public recognition and assessment.

The NRA was designed to coordinate, and publicly document, student achievement through school, college, higher education and employment. In 1992 action planning was incorporated into the process. Although inclusion of action plans in the NRA is not mandatory, failure to do so may be interpreted in a negative way, a development which clearly indicates the move towards an emphasis in individual accountability rather than personal discovery.

The NRA is presented as a framework for managing the teaming process. It requires learners to summarize the outcomes of their formal and informal learning and identify actions taken as a result. The underpinning process requires reflecting on past experiences ' reviewing progress and action planning. This ostensibly represents an active learning process in which the young person takes responsibility for their own personal development - but if the document is really about personal development per se why does it have to be public and follow a nationally dictated format? A prescribed format could be seen as being at odds with Kolb's notions of individual learning style.

Producing an ROA, it is argued, provides a framework for developing skills beyond the academic -personal skills and transferable skills can all be included. Such transferable skills are common to all areas of academic study and include outcomes of learning and competences which in the past have been left unrecorded. They include skills associated with both individual and group working and range from the ability to make presentations to the application of computerized materials. In all cases the students are encouraged to focus and reflect on their individual learning experiences in whatever settings they may occur. In doing this, however, and in requiring learner achievement to be summarized in forms which have employer currency, explicitly naming certain 'core' or 'transferable' skills for example, ROAs raise a number of methodological problems. Not only do they pose a tension between the benefits of the formative and the summative processes in ZOAs, they also raise questions about the nature of transferable skills.

The concept of core or transferable skill is a problem. It has dogged developments in the post-16 field for nearly a decade and remains unresolved. There is a continuing debate about the transferability of skills from one situation to another, particularly about problem-solving skills at higher levels. Findings on comparative studies between novices and experts in several fields appear to suggest that many cognitive abilities used in the conscious processing stage are domain specific and not generally transferable.

A related debate about issues in assessing core skills focuses on the problem of level as well as context. Wolf attempts to show that it is not possible to give meaning to a concept independent of the context in which it is practised. She further argues that it is difficult to give any general meaning to levels of problem solving or communication. From this we could argue that attempts to name and assess core skills independently of context, as in the NRA, may be meaningless.

Education at College Level

By 1995 a growing number of young people entering higher education had completed an NRA or ROA. Over the last five years increasing numbers of mature students have also gained entry to higher education through AP(E)L and the submission of portfolios summarizing their prior achievements. The idea of a common format for recording achievements for higher education is gaining ground.

The Record of Achievement is also potentially useful for professionals as a framework for Continuous Professional Development. In this case it might be referred to as a portfolio of professional practice rather than a Record of Achievement, but it is still engaged in promoting the same reflective process.

An ROA for higher education could be viewed simply as a logical step to extend what already exists. Some higher education courses have used such frameworks for managing learning for many years -largely BTEC awards and vocational courses such as initial teacher training, occupational therapy or physiotherapy. On such courses the demonstration of active learning takes various forms and may include a daily log or diary of work with school children, patients or clients and includes the assessment of progress made by the individual in their relationship with these groups. In completing the record for assessment the student has the opportunity to demonstrate their 'transferable' skills appropriate to a possible future career.

The establishment of the national Record of Achievement in schools means there is already a proportion of students entering higher education who are used to reflecting on their past learning experiences, whether formal academic studies or informal activities. Such students are able to assess their learning by reviewing their progress over all aspects of their course. They are also able to identify tasks and plan future study. This involvement in decision making enables students to gain confidence and carry over transferable skills gained through recording achievement to future learning. It also builds an expectation that the process will continue. If the student progresses to a vocational course this expectation is usually met in the production of professional portfolios or similar documents. For students embarking on non-vocational degree courses, however, the process may not be available. A range of personal and transferable skills may be lost unless recording achievement can be incorporated, either by integrating recording achievement into the framework for personal tutor systems or subject-based monitoring procedures, or by introducing institution-wide profiling schemes available to all students.

Alternatively the initiative to extend ROAs to higher education can be viewed as inevitably increasing the tensions between the educational aims of student centredness and the normative requirements of policy makers and employers. It has already been noted that the introduction of portfolios and profiling systems as frameworks for assessment in higher education should be based on a clearly identified purpose and the interests and involvement of all parties should be specified. True, a framework for recording achievement in higher education could have many benefits: providing a basis for tutorial work, enhancing student autonomy, promoting learner centredness, and providing a basis for the student to identify and present informally learned skills as well as academic learning to a future employer but the tension between these various aims should be recognised. A formative process-driven document is not necessarily the same as one which presents outcomes in a way that employers can recognize. Moreover, a personal formative document is almost by definition not the same as a summary of achievement which accords with nationally recognized criteria. This contradiction must be consciously managed if an ROA for higher education is, to be either useful or effective.

A number of formats for a higher education Record of Achievement have been proposed. The attached Summary Record of Achievement is based on papers already published by BTEC and UDACE which identify learning outcomes. Many of the learning outcomes are common to more than one subject area and echo the core or transferable skills identified by bodies such as the CBI, FEU and the NCVQ in the debate about developing core skills in the Post- 16 curriculum during the late 1980s and early 1990s. Learning outcomes proposed for higher education include the ability to manage and process information, to work cooperatively, to analyse and develop one's personal skills as well as act ethically and possess basic computer skills. BTEC have identified common skills relating to these outcomes which should be developed and assessed at each level in relation to their own qualifications.

The proposed record includes a summary-sheet outlining the student's achievements in a range of skills which all higher education students would be expected to achieve during the course of their studies. This poses problems. First the methodology of recording such information is proving difficult, which is not surprising given the difficulties in defining what we mean by core or transferable skills, or more recently 'key skills'. Second the initiative must be clear about the aims of the record -are they formative or summative? These purposes should be clearly defined and stated in advance. If the aims are summative how do we counter growing criticisms that portfolios and records of achievements are not a basis for rigorous assessment? If the aims are formative how do we justify them?

Prerequisites for Evaluation

One solution is to ensure that the credibility of any assessment is seen to be rigorous. Rigorous assessment systems need primarily to be reliable; results need to be replicable irrespective of the assessor or the context. Much of this depends on ensuring there is a focus on moderation, both internal and external, to agree standards and appropriateness of submissions. It also requires internal and external reviews and clearly stated outcomes against which achievement can be measured and assessed by both the students and their assessors. Above all it requires 'socialization' of assessors so that standards and procedures become common currency. Exemplars can assist the moderation process and enable discussion to focus on issues such as the acquisition of personal skills and their summary in reflective diaries or logs. Matching of evidence to outcomes is not an exact science and assessors need to agree on what they see as appropriate and inappropriate forms of evidence of achieving given outcomes.

The SEEC guidelines (SEEC, 1995) are a relevant development. These guidelines are an attempt to ensure that everybody involved in recording prior achievements for assessment and accreditation in a higher education institution is working to similar quality standards. The guidelines have developed to promote rigour and accountability in AP(E)L procedures but, because of the similarity between them, are also equally appropriate for the summative recording of achievement in ROAs. The guidelines require the assessment process to be transparent, with information available at all stages and levels of recording and assessment.

While the guidelines clearly have relevance for the practice of accrediting prior learning and achievement, what the guidelines cannot tackle is the context in which ROAs (and AP(E)L) are developed and used. It. could also be argued that the very emphasis on quality is, by implication, a contradiction of the original aims of AP(E)L. The emphasis on credit and academic quality negates personal development issues and student empowerment. The attempt to get our practices recognized means we conform with the very regulations and assumptions which AP(E)L once sought to challenge.

New Prospects

At present there is debate and concern about the notion of 'graduateness' and about the competence of graduates leaving higher education with degrees or other graduate qualifications. The HEQC is currently preparing its thoughts on the concept of 'graduateness' and how the meaning 'of the idea of a graduate has changed in relation to current employment patterns and policy initiatives. In addition to subject-specific knowledge and skills, new' graduates are also expected to acquire a range of transferable skills which will enable flexibility in a rapidly changing work environment. Such skills, especially at high levels, can only be recognized, recorded and presented when reflection has taken place. There have been fierce criticisms that this is purely an employer-oriented notion of 'graduateness'. On the other hand, it can be argued that the move towards profiling in higher education is a way of providing more effective support to individuals and enabling personal development for students who access HE from a variety of different routes.

Many vocational HE courses such as initial teacher training, occupational therapy, physiotherapy and social work courses already use this approach for assessing skills; although sometimes under a different name. In a number of cases the subject-specific criteria or competences are stipulated by relevant professional bodies, although significant staff development may be needed to enable education staff to understand, recognize and assess them.

Within the current trend towards an emphasis on lifelong teaming and continuous professional development, the recording of personal and professional skills will undoubtedly increasingly extend to all vocational HE courses and across education and training in general. ROAs will become increasingly important. The forms of assessment and the focus on particular skills may change as local and regional employment initiatives vary, but an increasing emphasis is developing on enabling the recording of evidence of an individual's 'employability'.

13

Databases at Work

Specifically, interesting is the effect of the existence of databases on the process of instruction itself. When information was difficult to access, there was a strong tendency to prepare all the materials that students would use in a course of institution. These would be written up in a 'set book' or collected together as a set of 'required readings'. Students would seldom branch out beyond this prepared material. With easy access to a much wider range of resources, it is possible to design course activities around problem-statements, leaving the students responsible for the identification and selection of appropriate learning resource. This seems a natural approach at the higher level of education, as it accustoms students to do their own library research. But there is increasing evidence that it is both possible and desirable to structure instruction this way at all levels of education.

Given an appropriately structured database, even elementary school children can discover for themselves, not only the facts about a subject, but also its structure and integral relationships. A database of geographical facts has been found in different regions. But in searching the database for this factual information, they are led to discover the relationships that exist between climate, feeding habits, physical attributes such as colour, size, speed, living habits such as migration and hibernation, etc. A few hours of guided searching of the database develops an understanding of a body of geography as a related whole, rather than as a set of individual facts.

Database with expert guidance systems is only a small step further to develop computer-based guidance in the searching of the database, in order to create a different form of computer-assisted instruction. This approach has not received the attention that it deserves. Its potential for the promotion of student autonomy in learning is obvious. Perhaps not so obvious are the benefits of developing one package on a given subject area in such a way that many different levels of student may find it useful for many different objectives. After all, the content of the subject is comprehensively covered, if the database is to be at all useful. But the 'level of discourse' about the subject may not suit all users, unless some form of adapting this to the needs of the user were to be devised. Some may need more and simpler examples in order to understand basic concepts. Others may wish to go much deeper into practical applications of the content. Yet others may wish to engage in a philosophical analysis of the importance / implications of a given topic.

A database can be structured to deal with any number of such aspects of a subject at several different levels of difficulty, so that, in theory, any user might find the information required, presented in understandable language. Of course, in order to find the appropriate content and level of discourse, the user will need help. This help function can be performed by a computer-based form of 'expert guide' that is capable of interacting with any user in order to diagnose individual needs in relation to the specific databases in question. With the advent of large databases accessible from anywhere by telecommunications links, such 'intelligent' databases are beginning to generate a lot of research interest. They have even earned their own jargon name-HYPERTEXT. Like intelligent CAI, they are as yet at the stage of laboratory research, but are showing much promise.

Coming now to the 'computer as tutee' as shall restrict ourselves to examining the research on the use of LOGO in education. The topic of how useful, in general educational terms, it is to learn to programme a computer is a fascinating question, but one which is not directly related to our interest here in the use of computers as instructional media. It is worth devoting a little space to the use of LOGO particularly, as so many claims have been made for its value in developing 'powerful ideas' which are generalizable to situations and content other than that used in the LOGO exercises themselves.

It should be stressed here, that LOGO is a general programming language, based on LISP and capable of being used for a variety of programming tasks. I have seen excellent examples of databases, and CAI courseware set up in LOGO. But its use in schools has generally been limited to the 'turtle geometry' aspects which are unique to this language and which were popularized so effectively by Papert and his followers. We illustrated earlier in this chapter how LOGO uses recursion, by a very simple turtle graphics programming exercises. The arguments of LOGO's supporters is that such generalizable concepts, once grasped in the context of playing with the turtle, are generalized to other branches of mathematics and indeed beyond. Paradoxically, however, there has been very little scientifically controlled research on such a theoretically interesting topic.

The enthusiasts say that classical research is not appropriate, as we are witnessing highly personal learning experiences which can only adequately described by detailed case studies. The doubters argue that little research has been published because the claims made for LOGO have generally not been substantiated when research was attempted. These two viewpoints are well illustrated by one of the earliest and most intensive and controlled studies of the use of LOGO-the Edinburgh project.

Edinburgh project findings involved a small group of some 11 students who attended the LOGO laboratory at Edinburgh University, regularly over a period of two years. When compared with their colleagues who had followed the same school maths studies but had not attended the LOGO experiences in the laboratory, the experimental group scored somewhat better on tests that measured comprehension of mathematical concepts, but worse on tests of mathematical procedures. The major finding reported was not measured by standardized tests, but was the observation that the experimental group were 'more willing to argue sensibly about mathematical issues' and were able to explain their mathematical difficulties more clearly.

Yet the widest reviews of the research literature have failed to show any very significant or systematic benefits to learning occurring from experience with LOGO. Perhaps the 'religion' syndrome is due to the Piagetian roots of Papert's philosophy. Those who believe in Piaget's view of the way that learners mature through a series of stages and progress from being 'concrete operational' learners to higher and more abstract ways of thinking, have tended to accept the LOGO approach on faith. But they forget that Piaget argues that the process is one of personal development which cannot be hurried on by instruction. Perhaps the theoretical under pinnings of the LOGO approach are not as sound as they appeared at first sight. But perhaps the approach suffers from the incapacity of untrained teachers to get the best out of it, as Michalyuk suggest.

Computer-assisted learning, like other self-instructional media, can be selected as the basis of a complete, automated instructional system. Alternatively, teachers may select specific CAL, exercises as components in their overall course or lesson, deign, just as they select a set of slides on film. In the first case the CAL system becomes the principal medium of instruction, replacing classroom teaching entirely or at least in a large part. It implies investment in a complex system of computer-based delivers of instructional and an infrastructure of courseware development /modification updating, hardware maintenance and repairs, etc. In the second case, the computer becomes just another instructional aid, which supplements the teacher at certain points in a course, but the teacher still remains the principal planner of each lesson and delivery medium of most parts of the lesson.

Although it is difficult to pinpoint exactly when the area of database management began, there is good reason to place its beginning with the APOLLO project of the 1960s, which was launched in response to President John F. Kennedy's stated goal of landing a man on the moon by the end of the decade. This project was certainly a vast and complex undertaking. Since, at the time, no available systems were capable of handling the coordination of the vast amounts of data required, North American Rockwell, the prime contractor for the project, asked IBM to develop one. In response, IBM developed the Generalized Update Access Method (GUAM), which went into production in 1964. It soon became clear to IBM that this product was useful in other environments and, in 1966, the company made the product available to the general public under the name Data Language/I (DL/I). This product is really the data management component of the Information Management System (IMS), which was certainly one of the most important of the early database management systems. IMS has been enhanced over the years and is still offered by IBM.

Data Bank

Another development was taking place in the mid-1960s. A system called Integrated Data Store (I-D-S) was developed at General Electric by a team headed by Charles Bachman. This system led to a whole class of database management systems, the CODASYL systems, which are still popular and influential today. In the late 1960s, the Conference on Data Systems Languages (CODASYL), the group responsible for COBOL, tackled the problem of providing a standard for database management systems. CODASYL charged a task group, the Data Base Task Group (DBTG) with the job of developing specifications for database management systems. The DBTG did this and in 1971, CODASYL presented these specifications to the American National Standards Institute (ANSI) for adoption as a national standard. Although these specifications were not accepted as a standard by ANSI, a number of systems were developed following the CODASYL guidelines. These systems are usually called CODASYL systems or DBTG systems.

In 1970, Dr. E.F. Codd presented a paper that was to have profound impact on the database community. In it, he proposed a new and, at the time, radically different approach to the management of data—the relational model. Throughout the decade of the 1970s, the relational model was the subject of intense research activity. In addition to purely theoretical research, prototype systems were developed, the most important being a system called System R, which was developed by IBM. It was not until the 1980s, however, that commercial relational DBMS's began to appear. Systems that are at least partly relational now exist in abundance on computers ranging from the smallest micro to the largest mainframe. The 1970s and 1980s have seen the development of a number of support products to go along with DBMS's. Data dictionaries, report generators, query facilities, and non-procedural languages have all been developed and, along with the DBMS, they are now a part of an entire environment, the so-called fourth generation environment.

We speak of systems that contain all of these facilities as Fourth Generation Languages (4GLs) or as application generators. They represent a tremendous increase in productivity. In addition, the 1980s have seen the development of microcomputer DBMS's. As the decade has progressed, these systems have increased greatly in functionally, to the point where they rival their mainframe counterparts in a number of areas. For an excellent account of the early history of database management, see the March 1976 issue of the ACM Computing Surveys in this issue, gives the history of database management and an overview of the various models; discusses the relational model; discusses the CODASYL approach; examines the hierarchical model; and presents a comparison between the relational and CODASYL approaches. There are a number of advantages to the database approach to processing, particularly when a powerful, full-functioned DBMS is used. The advantages are following:

1. Economy of scale
2. Getting more information from the same amount of data
3. Sharing of data
4. Balancing conflicting requirements
5. Enforcement of standards
6. Controlled redundancy
7. Consistency
8. Integrity
9. Security

10. Flexibility and responsiveness
11. Increased programmer productivity
12. Improved program maintenance
13. Data independence

The concentration of applications in one location allows for the possibility of smaller numbers of larger and more powerful computers, which usually results in an economy of scale. The same economy of scale may be realized by the concentration of technical expertise. Furthermore, since many users are sharing the database, any improvement in the database will potentially benefit many different users. In general, economy of scale refers to the fact that the collective cost of several combined operations may be less than the sum of the cost of the individual operations. Database processing makes this type of combination possible.

The primary goal of a computer system is to turn data into information. Even though all the data that Joan needed for a requested report was in computer files, she could not easily access it and thus could not obtain the desired information. If, however, that data were in a common database, she would be able to access it. Thus, this added information would now be available even though the database might not contain additional data not already present in the files.

The data can be shared among authorized users, allowing users access to more of the data. Several users might have access to the same piece of data, e.g., a faculty member's address is changed, the change is immediately relayed to all users. In addition, new applications can be developed using the existing data in the database without the added burden of creating separate collections of files.

In order for the database approach to function adequately, there must be a person or group within the organization in-charge of the database itself. This body is often called Database Administration (DBA). By keeping the overall needs of the organisation in mind, DBA can structure the database to the benefit of the entire organization, not just a single user group. While this may potentially mean that an individual user group is served less well than it might have been if it had its own isolated system, the overall organization will benefit. If the organization benefits, then, ultimately, so do the individual user groups.

With the central control mentioned in the previous paragraph, DBA can ensure that standards for such things as data names, usages, and formats are followed uniformly throughout the organization..

Since data that was kept separate in a file oriented system is now integrated into a single database, we no longer have multiple copies of the same data. Each of the four programmers at Marvel had his or her own FACULTY file containing, among other things, a faculty member's' address. Thus the address of each faculty member appeared in at least four different places. In the database approach, since there will be only one occurrence of each faculty member, this redundancy will be eliminated. In practice, there are places where we might actually introduce some limited amount of redundancy into a database for performance reasons. But, even in these cases, we are able to keep it under tight control. This is why it is better to say that we control redundancy rather than eliminate it.

Consistency follows from the control of elimination of redundancy. If a faculty member's address appears in only one place, there is no possibility that faculty member will have the address 123 MAINST at one spot within our data and 466 WTLLOW RD in another, for example.

An integrity constraint is a rule that data in the database must follow. Here is an example of an integrity constraint: the department number given for a faculty member must be that of a department that actually exists. A database has integrity of data in the database satisfies all integrity constraints that have been established. In the database approach, DBA can define validation procedures that will ensure the integrity of the database.

Checking Approaches

Security is the prevention of access to the database by unauthorized users. Since DBA has control over the operational data, it can define authorization procedures to ensure that only legitimate users access the data. DBA can further allow different users to have different types of access to the same data. The payroll department at Marvel College may be able to view and change the salary of a faculty member. The insurance department may be able to view the salary of a faculty member but not change it. The speaker's bureau may not even be able to view a salary. One way DBA achieves this security is through user views. Any data items not included in the user view for a given user will not be accessible to that user. Another means of achieving security is through the use of sophisticated password schemes.

Since the data that was previously kept in several different files by several different user areas is now in the same database, it is possible to respond to request for data from multiple areas in a much easier and more flexible way. Even within a single user area, the flexibility furnished by the DBMS to locate and access data in a number of different ways aids programmers in developing new programs to satisfy user requests. The use of high-level languages allows users to do some of their own programming in a very easy way.

Since programmers accessing a database do not have to worry about the mundane data manipulation activities, as they would when accessing files, they will be more productive. Studies have shown that on the average they will be two to four times more productive; i.e., a new application can be developed in one-quarter to one-half of the time it would take if it were a straight file-oriented application. In addition, with the advent of fourth-generation languages built around database management systems, the productivity increase can be much more dramatic. Ten to twenty fold increase in productivity are not uncommon.

When interacting with a DBMS, programs are relatively independent of the actual data in the database. This means that many changes to the structure of the data itself may not require maintenance to existing application programs. In a straight file environment this is not true. Even simple changes to file layouts can require substantial changes in every program that access the file. In addition, since the low-level data manipulation is handled by the DBMS, details concerning this manipulation do not appear in programs. Thus, the complexity of maintaining such logic is not a concern in a DBMS environment.

While improving program maintenance is one important advantage of having programs independent of the structure of the database; this independence has other advantages as well. Without such independence, changes to the database structure to improve performance and to meet changing corporate requirements become very difficult. The fact that all of the programs in the system need maintenance every time a change is made to the database structure would be strong incentive not to make any of these changes. Data independence removes this obstacle to changing the structure.

Data independence occurs when the structure of the database can change without requiring the programs that access the database to change. Data independence is achieved in the database environment through the use of external views or sub-schemas. Each program accesses data through an external view. The underlying structure of the database would not have to change. The conceptual schema is the overall global organizational view of data. Finally the internal schema is the view of the database as seen by the computer. It is the responsibility of the DBMS to map one view to another.

The only requirement imposed on the external schemas is that they can be derived from what is in the conceptual schema. Certainly, if there is no salary field within an external schema. If there is no relationship between customers and employees in a conceptual schema, for example, there can be no relationship between them in any external schema. The important point is that the conceptual schema could change without affecting the external schemas.

Obviously, an external schema would need to be changed if some field that it required were deleted from the conceptual schema. Similarly, an internal schema can be changed without affecting the conceptual schema. Storage details or access strategies could change, for example. Where a given field was stored as zoned decimal, we may now wish to store it as packed decimal or, perhaps, in a binary format. Where direct access to a faculty member had previously been accomplished through one scheme, say hashing, we may now wish to use another scheme, perhaps some kind of index, for this purpose.

DBA could thus make changes to the internal schema to improve the performance of the database. DBA could also make changes to the conceptual schema to respond to new requirements within the organization. In both cases, the external schemas could remain the same. In this way the independence described earlier is achieved. Any decent DBMS support the external schemas of the ANSI/ SPARC model. CODASYL systems call them sub-schemas. Many relational model systems call them views. In any case, the idea is the same: users can have their own views of what the database looks like.

Likewise, any decent DBMS support, in general the conceptual and internal schemas. In this case, however, the support is often not as complete as we would like. In the ANSI/SPARC model, logical details about the structure of the database belong in the conceptual schema, and physical details about such things as the actual storage and access methods for the database belong in the internal schema. Many DBMS products do not have this clear breakdown. Their designers may not have attempted to separate the logical from the physical at all or, if they have, the separation may not be nearly as complete as the ANSI/SPARC model requires. This is the direction in which systems are moving, however, and we have already discussed why it is a worthy goal. As you would expect, if there are advantages to doing something a certain way, there are also disadvantages. The database areas is no exception. There are several disadvantages regarding database processing, and they are follows:

1. Size
2. Complexity
3. Cost
4. Additional hardware requirements
5. Higher impact or a failure
6. Recovery more difficult

To support all the complex functions that it must provide to users, a database management system must, by its nature, be a large program occupying megabytes of disk space as well as a substantial amount of internal memory.

Again, the complexity and breadth of the functions furnished by a DBMS make it a complex product. Programmers and analysts must understand the features of the system in order to take full advantage of it. There is a great deal for them to learn. In addition, with many choices to make when designing and implementing a new system using a DBMS, it is possible to make these choices incorrectly, especially if the understanding of the system is not thorough enough. Unfortunately, a few incorrect choices can spell disaster for the whole project.

A good DBMS is an expensive product. By the time all the appropriate components related to the DBMS are purchased for a major mainframe system, the total price can easily into the $ 100,000 to $ 400,000 range.

Because of the size and complexity of a DBMS, greater hardware resources are required that would be necessary without the DBMS. This means that if the hardware resources are not increased when a DBMS is purchased, users of the system may very well notice a severe degradation in performance. Purchasing additional hardware resources represents yet another added cost.

Since many of the data processing resources are now concentrated in the database, a failure of any component has much more far-reaching effect than in a non-database environment.

Because of the added complexity, the process of recovering the database in the event of a catastrophe is a more complicated one, particularly if the database is being updated by a large number of users concurrently. In the early 1800's Charles Babbage, a man ahead of his time, designed the first mechanical calculating machine which had all of the components of a modern computer, including data storage areas, an output mechanism, a control unit for directing the machine's operations, and an arithmetic logic unit for performing additions at the "lightning" rate of one per second. Babbage did not call the components of his difference and analytical engines by these names of course, but his design paved the way for later development of these concepts. Babbage's *Reflections on the Decline of Science in England and on Some of its Causes* led to the foundation of the British Association for the Advancement of Science. His concern was that science not be pursued only by the aristocracy but that it really should be a profession of those who could apply it in business and manufacturing.

After 1842, Babbage's collaborator in computer design was Ada Byron, Countess of Lovelace, the daughter of the poet, Lord Byron. Ada developed the concept of programming loop and earned the reputation of the first computer programmer. Unfortunately, Ada and Babbage were frustrated in their designs because the technology was not capable of building a full-scale difference engine. Babbage's son after the turn of the 20th century, did have the machine built, and proved that it really worked, unfortunately long after cancer had claimed Ada's life at age 36. Virtually all computers before 1950 were calculating machines. When the Electronic Numerical Integrator and Calculator was built in the early 1940's by John Mauchley and J. Presper Eckert; it could perform 3000 multiplications per second.

The ENIAC contained several thousand vacuum tubes. Since the mean lifetime before failure of a vacuum tube was about 300 hours, one could expect to run the ENIAC for approximately 14 minutes before a breakdown. In those days, backup of data was already very important. The computer would be run for 10 minutes, then the contents of memory would be dumped onto a secondary storage medium so that a relatively smooth startup could be achieved when the computer did go down. Often, hours were spent diagnosing the source of the failure before the defective tube was found and replaced. In those early days programming a computer was a very different task from now.

Rather than having the program stored in memory, the computer had to be rewired or instructions entered by switches for each program change. Though slow and ponderous, the machines still represented a tremendous breakthrough, even with hours of downtime and hours of programming, calculations were performed much more rapidly and accurately than could be done by hand.

John von Neumann is given credit for developing the concept of storing programs in the computer, along with the data, in the late 1940's. Thereafter, changing a program simply meant changing the contents of the memory locations where the program was stored. The development of codes for storing instructions and distinguishing them from data was major accomplishment of this period. By the mid 1950's most programmers began to tire of writing their own routines for driving auxiliary memory and input/ output devices each time a new program was written. For each other, they were borrowing stacks of cards which contained prewritten program to handle I/O operations. Ultimately, a number of general purpose I/O subroutines were written which could be loaded with appropriate interpreters each time a program was run.

By the late 1950's FORTRAN compile-and-go routines had been composed. The programmer needed only to load program and data into the computer; the routines for compilation and I/O were already within the computer's memory or readily accessible to the computer from magnetic tape or another card-reader. By the early 1960's Input/Output Management Programs and routines to control the flow of jobs through the machine were built into most computers. These programs were stored as operating systems on tape, drum, or disk auxiliary storage known as the "system residence" devices.

Organs at Work

Operating Systems are a set of programs stored more or less permanently within the computer's memory for handling tasks that have to be done for most jobs. They made it easier for programmers and began to open entirely new possibilities for using computers. Until the 1960's most computers had been run in an "open shop"; when programmers wanted to run their jobs, they signed up on the schedule for a block of time when they could use the computer. It was their responsibility to learn how to operate the computer, much as personal microcomputer owners now do. The programmers would load whatever decks of cards they needed, including compilers and I/O handlers, if necessary, into the card reader, punch the button and wait to see what happened. Much of their time was spent looking at lights on the console and flipping switches to correct errors.

The computer was idle much of the time while the programmer/ operators were trying to figure out why their programmers were not working. Often they performed a core dump, listing out the contents of primary memory, and took the listings home to study before their next turn at the machine. It was apparent that the "open shop" was a tremendous waste of programmer talent, computer time, and money. Computers were so expensive that only the elite in science and engineering could afford them, and time was scarce. It was too expensive to buy more machines.

The next obvious step was to overlap operations. Why couldn't the Operating System handle Input/ Output operations on the peripheral devices while the central processing unit was processing another program or another segment of the same program? This could further reduce equipment time, improve turnaround, and make more efficient use of the machines.

By the early 1970's operating systems had been developed which would even allow concurrent processing, two or more users on the same machine, sharing the facilities at small intervals of time. Jobs could be swapped on an event-driven basis; when on job ended a particular task, the status of the job could be saved, and another task could be performed. By allowing more than one job at a time on the computer, greater interchangeability of data between programs was possible, and the process of turning raw data into useful information was speeded up even more. The next obvious step was the time sharing. Without sophisticated operating systems, stored permanently within each computer, this process was impossible. Now many users can sit at remote terminals, all believing they have complete control of the machine. Their jobs are switched in and out of the CPU at such rates, that by the time they get control after each break, only a few milliseconds have elapsed, often in time periods shorter than the persistence of vision. Time-sharing is time-driven; that is, each user gets a fixed block of time, usually a millisecond or two, in order.

Another major benefit of Operating Systems is that errors are reduced when the machines is under program control rather than operator control. The user's program is separated from the computer system. Either can be modified without changing the other.

The tasks performed by an operating system must include:

Job Scheduling. Of all the jobs entered into the computer, whether in an event-driven environment or in a time-sharing situation, whose job gets run when? Ideally, a good operating would be able to distinguish between high and low priority jobs and also schedule tasks for the most efficient use of the CPU and peripherals. The scheduler part of a control program is responsible for these tasks.

Supervision. How is the core memory allocated to the jobs which need it? Are entire programs loaded into core at one time, or are they divided into segments or pages and an alogrithm applied to determine which pages or segments swapped out when new ones are needed? The operating system keeps track of what locations in memory are used for which tasks. The user need to be concerned about memory allocation. What if the program page swapped out happens to be the next one needed? Such a situation results in program segments being swapped in and out vigorously with no processing being done, the computer is said to be "thrashing." A good operating system will be capable of recognizing this situation and correcting it by choosing another swapping alogrithm, at least temporarily.

Resource Allocation. If two users need the same tape drive at the same time, the operating system must be capable of allocating and deallocating, temporarily suspending operation of one program until the other releases the device. If program 1 is using Drive A and program 2 is using Drive B, what happens when program 1 requests drive B and program 2 requests drive A? Both programs would normally stop and wait for the other to release the requested drive. Such situation is called deadlock or "deadly embrace." The operating system must be aware of such problems and be written to avoid situations when the computer is doing nothing.

Communication with the Operator and Recovery from Failures. An operating system must communicate with the operator, providing messages about I/O devices, machine status, which jobs are running, which tapes or disks need to be loaded or unloaded, etc. Also, should there be a failure-whether it be with the building power, a problem in memory, or of any other type-a good operating system should be able to store and then find and restart on the status at some time before failure.

The operator must be given the status information and instructions by the operating system on how restart is to proceed. Ideally, data and status will be stored automatically by the operating system at short intervals so that it can be easily retrieved and updated, not just during failure but also on demand from the user.

Accounting. Most computer systems require detailed statistics on who uses the machine and its peripherals for what periods of time so that appropriate billing can be done. It is a fact of life that someone must pay for the computers and their operations.. Unless a machine is entirely dedicated to one department or operation, the costs must be divided. For the computer to stop each time a new user signs on or off, so that the operator can record the time from the clock on the wall, would not only be wastage of computer and operator's time, but also would not give a true picture of how much CPU time was used, how much peripheral time of what type was used, etc.

Operator error would be inevitably lead to arguments and problems regarding who gets charged how much. Therefore, these functions are now usually written into the operating system. If you have used a large computer you are aware that at log off you are usually told how much time you have used.

I/O Handling. Historically, the I/O handler part of operating systems is the justification for their development. Now I/O handlers are just one part of a comprehensive system on most machines. I/O handler programs tell the computer exactly how to write or read data to or from specific peripheral devices. Generally, each device is different, they use different data formats and have different data transfer rates, different buffer size and different methods of data transfer. Programs are stored within the operating system to handle these differences.

Even if you are using a microcomputer, you will have some I/O handling operations built into the system, such as how to print onto your printer, how to write on the CRT, how to read information from the keyboard, and how to store information on and read from a disk or cassette. The I/O handler allocates devices and auxiliary storage space to your programs and data. It control how the devices operate, organize, and close data files; maintain catalogs, and store and retrieve data. It should be noted that I/O handlers are machine dependent. They must be written for a specific computer and a specific peripheral attached to a machine. Also, they are not entirely self-sufficient; the user must tell the computer the parameters to be used by the data handler when information is to be transferred.

Efficiency. A perfect operating system should operate as efficiently as possible. It should be apparent that instructions for moving data from one point to another in the system are probably by far the most heavily used instructions in an operating system. These must be quickly accessed and executed. Providing status in an easily stored and retrievable form to recover from *interrupts,* whether anticipated in the form of time-driven swapping in a time sharing environment or unexpected error conditions, is critical. Testing a newly written operating system is a difficult task at best. It is impossible to predict the uses to which the programmers will put it. Inevitably, someone wants to do something that the system was not designed to do or performs a procedure in an unexpected fashion that causes the system to fail.

Normally, because of the myriad of situations encountered that could not be anticipated by the system designer, it takes months of operation on a large machine to get the bugs out of an operating system. Also, until a system is installed at its permanent location, the designer does not know what devices the operating system should be designed to support. Everybody wants something different, and operating systems must be written as generally as possible with the realization that changes and additions will be inevitable.

Before beginning a discussion of types of data storages and modes of computer operation, it is important to understand the basic concepts of how data is organized. All information in a digital computer is written in binary form. That is, in terms of binary digits, 0 or 1, called *bits.* A binary sequence of 8 bits is called a byte: e.g., 10110011 would be a byte. Normally, one byte is required to represent an alphabetic or numeric character, using one of the common codes to be discussed in the next chapter.

A computer word consists of a small number of bytes. For example, a small microcomputer may have an 8-bit word, whereas a large scientific mainframe may have as many as 8 bytes per word. The computer word is a physical concept, having reference to the computer itself and how it stores information. The word is usually the smallest amount of information that can be stored or retrieved at one time.

Logically, the way we like to see our data, a character is generally the smallest unit of data. Remember, usually a character is physically one byte long. Characters are grouped logically into fields. A *field* would be a string of characters representing an employee identification number, a name, etc. Fields are collected in *records*. A record might contain, for example, all of the information for a given student, such as student number, year in schools, age, address, courses enrolled in, etc. A collection of records, such as all of the records for the students in a given course, would be called a *data file*, or simply a *file*.

Data and programs are stored in two main locations in a computer. Ideally everything would be stored in high-speed main memory within the Central Processor. This memory is called *primary memory* or core storage. Before 1970 most primary memory was made of magnetic beads or "cores" approximately one millimeter in diameter, threaded on wires. Each core was capable of holding a binary bit, 0 or 1, depending upon the direction in which it was magnetized. Core memory was bulky as well as difficult and expensive to build. Now primary memory is almost always "semiconductor" memory, integrated circuits in which, roughly speaking, a current flowing past a point represents a binary 1 and no current is a binary 0. Semiconductor memory has advantages over core; it is much easier to build; thousands of binary bits can be packed into one small integrated circuit ship, and it is relatively cheap. Its major disadvantage is that it is "volatile"; that is, when the power goes off, no more current flows, and the memory has been lost.

Core memory was permanent; a loss of current did not affect its contents. Primary memory is often still called "core" memory, even though it may not consist of magnetic cores at all. The other location for storing data is in *auxiliary memory*. Secondary memory is always a peripheral medium such as cards, magnetic tape, disks, drums, etc. Two things make auxiliary memory more attractive than primary memory for large storage capacity. First, for keeping large amounts of data, auxiliary storage media are cheaper than main memory. More information can be stored per unit cost. Second, and perhaps more important, on machines with a small number of bits per computer word, if only one or two words are reserved for addressing, the amount of primary memory which can be directly addressed is quite small. For example, if an address is limited to 16 binary bits, then the maximum number of directly addressable memory cells is 2 = 65,536. This is the situation in many small microcomputers where the address registers are indeed two bytes long.

The properties of auxiliary storage media and devices will be discussed in considerable detail through this text.

The methods of storing and processing data can be categorized in many different ways. It is especially informative to consider the operating modes of the computer which is handling the data.

In *batch* processing mode, jobs are entered into the computer and processed one at a time sequentially. Indeed, there may be at any one time a number of different tasks waiting at the gate, for the computer to process. However, each job is completed before the next job is started. In batch mode, data is collected and sorted before being entered into the computer memory. When the data is recorded in auxiliary memory a master file is created; that is, the permanent file of data is recorded in sequential order.

The order of the information in the file is determined by one field, called a key, in each record. Updating a master file, inserting new information or deleting some records, generally requires a complete rewrite of the file. New information is collected and sorted into order by keys in a transaction or detail file. Updating is performed by a merge sort. The first records are read from the master file and from the transaction file and compared. The one which comes first is written to a new master file. Then the next records are compared, and so forth until the entire file has been rewritten. By this time a new master file has been created which contains all of the changes.

The old master and transaction files are kept as backup at least until the next update of the file, so that information can be retrieved in case something happens to the new master file. Assume that a master file contains record with information about types of small computers: their cost, memory size, peripherals, dealers, etc. The key by which each record is identified is the name of the company which makes the computer. The master file contains records for–

1. Apre, 2. Ather, 3. Crab, 4. JCN, 5. Olson, 6. Tarpen 7. Tinbox, 8. Unvar

We wish to update from a transaction file which contains names of records to be added, changed, or deleted. A separate field indicates which action is to be taken. The transaction file contains

1. Brown (NEW), 2. Homer (NEW), 3. JCN (CHANGE), 4. Tinbox (DLTE)-Delete

Batch processing mode allows considerable flexibility in scheduling jobs. They can be done in priority order or in an order which can be most efficiently handled by the central processor. Resource use of peripheral devices and human resources can be efficiently scheduled; accounting and rerunning of jobs are facilitated. This operating made is especially useful when producing lengthy printed reports of items in key sequential order.

In 1960 IBM built a computer for the Los Alamos Scientific Laboratory which was called STRETCH. This was the first example of a multiprogramming machine. In a multiprogramming machine, two or more jobs can be run concurrently with a single central processing unit. It is important to distinguish between the words concurrent and simultaneous. If two events happen simultaneously, they take up exactly the same place in time.

Events which are happening concurrently occur at different times, but the time intervals between the events are so short that they may appear to be occurring simultaneously. On the STRETCH, computer and most subsequent large machines, two or more jobs can run in the computer together, with the CPU performing the tasks alternately for each job in such short time intervals that it appears that the job are executing at the same time.

Computers periodically shut down, usually of their own volition and at the worst possible time. The occurs with such regularity that machines appear to have a diabolical nature of their own, running perfectly when routine work is being done, but inevitably shutting down when their use is most urgently needed. This problem was much more serious in the past than now, because microminiaturization has made circuits not only smaller but more reliable. However, an urgent need has been felt and is still felt in most critical situations to provide a standby backup system.

Buying two identical computers is one solution to the problem, available unfortunately only to affluent corporations or laboratories, rarely to the individual. An alternative to having two identical computers is to have a single computer with more than one CPU, a *multiprocessing system*. If the CPUs are *symmetric*, they can be used interchangeably for doing a number of jobs. Alternatively, the CPUs can be used for doing different jobs at the same time. For example, one CPU might be controlling an I/O operation while the other is sorting data, or one might be searching a file for the desired data while the second is performing arithmetic operations.

CPUs in a multiprocessing system may even be *asymmetric*, if the standby characteristics is not critical. For example, one CPU may be designed specifically to handle only I/O; all operations involving input and output are courted through that unit, allowing the other to continue its tasks without ever having to be involved in I/O operations.

In a time-sharing environment, whether with one or more CPUs, each user is "on-line" with the computer from a remote terminal. The time-sharer interacts directly with the computer. Processing a RETURN or ENTER key causes some action in the computer. The response is so rapid that the users feel like they are the only users of the machine. We have become spoiled, and if we have to wait more than a second for response to our requests, we complain about degradation of the response time. Programs are swapped in and out of primary memory from an auxiliary storage system as needed. Programs can be interchanged either in their entirety or in pieces, called pages or segments. In the latter case, the computer appears to have essentially unlimited core memory for programming, because the user need not worry about what pieces of a program are in the memory. It used to be that programmers had to handle program overlays themselves when programs were larger than the computer memory could handle all at once.

Programmers had to decide how best to divide their programs up into small segments and then load and run the pieces one at a time, performing the required processing before the next overlay was loaded. Now on a large computer an operating system does all of that. The computer is said to have virtual memory, as much memory as is needed to run any job. The limit to be number of users who can use a large machine at any one time is usually determined not by the size of memory but by the number of lines attaching I/O devices to the computer and by the degradation in response time which the users are willing to tolerate.

Virtual memory tends to make large computers cheaper because a smaller core is required. Data is processed as it is received, the time between runs is reduced, and computer programmers can concentrate on making their programs do the job they wish rather than on the details of how the program will run in the computer. Another important consideration is that a large capacity direct access auxiliary storage device where tens or hundreds of megabytes are available is quite different from a tape library where hundreds of tapes are stored. With a tape library, operator intervention is constantly required to find, mount, demount, and return tapes. Errors happen often. Data is easily lost or misplaced for long periods of time. With a large capacity direct access storage device, operator intervention is minimized and data is much more secure.

Closely related to the concepts of time sharing and virtual memory is the *remote job entry* operating mode. In this case, many users are connected to the machine, just as in time-sharing.

However, instead of providing a response as soon as a RETURN or ENTER key is pushed at the end of each line or record, the computer generally waits until the entire job has been transmitted before it begins any program execution or data processing operations.

With the exception of batch sequential processing, all the modes of operation discussed above require some kind of direct processing. In direct processing mode, the data and programs can be used and stored as they are needed. It is most necessary to collect data and sort it before placing it into memory. Access to the required data or programs is "instantaneous," or at least much more rapid than having to look at all the contents of auxiliary memory in order to retrieve the particular records desired.

Direct processing has been made possible by *Direct Access Storage Devices* represented by disk and drum type auxiliary memory. You can see that direct access to data would be very difficult to achieve if that data were stored on cards or magnetic tape. In general, direct processing mode allows more effective management of data and better controls on its security than batch mode; however, this may be at the expense of wasted space in secondary memory. As time progress, and DASD's become larger and faster, batch mode processing is being replaced more and more by direct modes of operation. Time-sharing is the accepted way of handling users on mainframe computers and on many intermediate-sized minicomputers. Even some larger microcomputers, especially those used in educational institutions, are capable of handling timesharing, direct access mode processing.

Here are more specific examples of programming which are possible only with direct mode devices and operating systems.

1. Data files which require large amounts of storage and fast access are now feasible. For example, assume you have an inventory requirement for an automobile parts store. There are more than 8000 items in your inventory, and you need to be able not only to print out the inventory periodically but also to keep a running total of parts on hands, so that when supplies are low you can order more immediately. Thus, you can avoid having

overstocks of items which tie up your capital. With direct access storage, when a part is sold or a shipment arrives, the inventory of that part can be updated immediately, without rewriting the entire inventory file. You can demand reports of items which are low in number, you can have the computer automatically warn you when an items is in short supply, and you can get your complete inventory- reports when they are due.

2. We would all be very upset if we had to wait for hours for a response to a request. How many of us would visit the office of a travel agent more than once if we were told to come back tomorrow or next week to find out if our airline reservations had been made? Virtually all airline reservations are now made on-line. A computer terminal shows flights available, a punch of a button confirms your reservation or puts you on a waiting list. Access to flight times and bookings is immediate. There is no waiting for long distance telephone calls or for a clerk to go through a file of thousands of cards or to read a magnetic tape.
3. In a bank it is impossible to predict which accounts will be active on any given day. Customer accounts must be retrievable rapidly and randomly. If there are 30,000 accounts at the bank, and the average rate of activity is 400 accounts per day, it would be absurd to have to read all accounts sequentially to find the balance for each customer who asks. In such a *low activity* situation direct access processing ideal and could not be done efficiently at all without direct access devices.
4. Suppose the management of a company wishes to expand the plant and change the way billings and payroll are handled. If that happens rarely, the files can be searched sequentially and updated by rewriting the master file. The programs can be rewritten, and the entire processing procedure can be changed. Suppose, however, you are building computers or some other high technology product, and daily changes are necessary in your

programs or accounting methods. Then you want to be able to get at the exact data and the exact program segments which you wish to change, without having to change the entire package.

5. Each evening all salespersons on your force report their daily sales, what items were sold, how many, and to whom. Your records must store this information for each salesperson, temporarily, in the order in which it is reported. Then, at the end of the pay period, the computer takes the information stored temporarily on the DASD's sorts it, updates the master payroll records, and calculates the commissions. This intermediate storage of information saves untold hours of processing time, which would be necessary if the information had to be sorted and processed piece by piece as it was collected.
6. Suppose you have 40 terminals in a student computer lab, and only one high-speed printer, if each student wrote directly to the printer from the computer, the system would become deadly slow, since most printers print information at a maximum rate of only a few hundred characters per second. Instead, your direct access storage device handles spooling. When printer output of a file is requested, the computer instead sends the data to a spool area on the DASD. The printer constantly polls the spool area to see what is there. When information is to be printed, it is read from the spool area of the DASD, not directly from the computer. Hence the computer does not have to slow down for the printer. If the spool area becomes full faster than the printer can empty it, the operating system may not allow you to write into the spool area until there is room.

Let's look briefly at the computer system needed to perform the operations we have discussed above. Every computer must have at least one central processor, where control operations and processing is actually done. Every central processor will have a control unit, whose job is to fetch and decode instructions and to keep track of where the next instruction is located.

Also within the processor will be an *arithmetic logic* unit where calculations are performed and which directs the computer where to store results. Main or *primary memory* is also directly attached to or part of the central processing unit.

Before creating a technical plan for a phase, it is usually worthwhile to create a schedule showing the availability of the phase resources. This covers not only the Team Members, but also the other resources required. Such a plan will include data on when each resource becomes available, when its availability ceases, and when it is not available during the phase. The availability plan also notes holidays, training and allocation to other projects, thus providing a useful check of availability against the technical plan being created.

Approval and acceptance of a phase plan means certain things. The user or customer is committed to a defined level of cost, but in turn expects the project to reach a certain point for that cost by a certain data and with a certain level of quality. If one of these factors should begin to vary beyond an agreed tolerance limit; it is the responsibility of the Project Leader to bring this to the attention of the Project Board. As described in the chapter on control, this is one at a meeting with the Project Board. At this meeting, the Project Leader will present a deviation plan.

The description part of this deviation planning package describes the problem, the reason, the impact, the possible alternatives and the Project Leader's recommendation. The graphic plan will normally cover only the problem area and will extend until either the phase end or the recovery from the deviation, if this is sooner. It is not necessary for the deviation plan to go beyond the phase end. Any recovery work to be done after that will be incorporated in the next phase plan.

The Blueprints

For those who like to approach planning in a methodical fashion, here is a general sequence of actions to follow. Complete the provisional 'duration' and 'end date' lines. This is achieved either by copying from the final estimate, or, if a project completion date is imposed by some external factor, by calculating the stage durations by working back from the end data. Remember that this is elapsed time, not manpower.

Complete the resources section showing how much effort is available if the size of the Phase Team is already known. Examine the task checklists and mark any which are not applicable to the particular project. Identify any special tasks which are not in the checklists. Identify any necessary tasks on the checklists which have already been completed.

Why do we need standards for the control of a project? This chapter considers the need to control various aspects of a project, and covers the control requirements of the various groups involved in a project. It is also deals with the problem of written and verbal communications in a team and project environment. The correct use of control standards enables us to answer the following questions, often asked during a project.

1. What is the quality of workmanship?
2. Are we still producing what the customer wants?
3. Are we on schedule?
4. Are we within budget?
5. Will we fail to realize that schedule or budget problems have occurred until it is too late to do anything about it?
6. How are Project Board members, not normally involved with the project on a day-to-day basis, made aware of the project status?
7. When and how often should the Project Leader meet the Project Board?
8. How do we keep control of customer requests for alterations and additional after the specification and probably the cost have been agreed? How do we prevent such requests from destroying the project schedule and budget?

Chief Aims and Mottos

1. To pass status information upwards from Team Member to Project Board.
2. To enable the Project Leader to spot deviations from budget or schedule as soon as they occur.
3. To keep the team informed.

4. To provide a standard procedure for meetings.
5. To identify the circumstances under which a meeting should be called.
6. To decide who should attend this meeting.

In our solution, we shall consider two ways of interpreting the information and passing it on— the use of meetings and of reports. As far as our project management standards go, the collection of data will be considered from the bottom upwards.

The Project Board numbers represent user and contractor management. They are not involved on a day-to-day basis. If possible, they want to manage by objectives and by exception. As management, they are mainly concerned with the status of the budget. On technical matters, they are only concerned with schedule status and knowing if the customer will get what he wants at the end of the project. They therefore do not want too much technical detail, but brief status information until things begin to go wrong. Then they need early advice of what is going wrong, together with a means of collecting all the relevant details plus technical solution proposals.

The Project Leader needs both technical and financial information regularity. The Team Leader needs up-to-date technical progress and quality information.

Team Members need to be able to measure their own progress against objectives, and know the status of any interfaces within the team. They need to be able to identify with the total product. We can provide a simple recording and reporting structure to suit large and small projects. The phase summary is in graphic form to allow summarized information to be passed in a very brief document. Its main purpose is to pass financial information to the Project Board.

1. The costs of the resources consumed are recorded. A report is sent to the Project Board in graphic form, comparing current phase cumulative costs and completed tasks with the plan.
2. In certain recording systems, one trap into which it is easy to fall at this time is that the team are asked to estimate 'percentage complete' for their current

unfinished tasks. The danger is that this is a subjective estimate, normally optimistic, and therefore misleading. The Project Leader also has the problem of assessing all the team's estimates on different sizes of task and turning these into a single 'percentage complete' for the phase. A much better idea is the one incorporated by BP in their plan. Having produced the phase technical plan, each task in the plan is calculated as a percentage of the total phase plan. This is done by taking the total man-days needed as 100% and calculating each task's effort as a percentage of that. When reporting against the plan, completed tasks are noted and their percentage totalled to give the 'percentage complete'. In reporting this figure, we ignore any tasks which have started but are not yet complete. In order for this approach to be really effective, no task in our plan should be greater than 10% of the total phase effort, or 10 man-days for a small project. Any task larger than this can always be broken down.

3. The '% Work Planned Completed' is calculated by adding up the percentages of the total phase effort of those tasks which have completed so far.

There is one other type of report which is vital if a project is to be kept under control. There must be a document produced for every major change proposed after the feasibility study, and for every major or minor change proposed after the user specification has been signed. The implementation of such changes without proper control and authority has been responsible for many project failures to meet schedule and/or budget.

Having accepted the feasibility estimate, approved the user specification, and committed resources against those documents, only the Project Board has the authority to agree to any changes. Only the customer has the authority to agree to more expenditure, and this must be done at Project Board level. The procedure should be that anyone requesting a modification should document it. The request should be assessed for its impact on the project and its likely cost. All outstanding requests should be reviewed by the Project Board at the next project review meeting.

14

The Reverse Side

A caveat or caution pertains to social arid intellectual development. We should not bring up a generation of computer buffs and hackers to whom their "friendly" computer has become more important than human friends. Social group situations must not be replaced by electronic cocoons, places in which to retreat from reality. In fairness, it also should be noted that computers can be "fun chums" because of the interesting electronic games that are available. The problem is to help young people benefit intellectually and improve their physical coordination without becoming "video junkies" frequenting arcades and feeding billions of quarters into coin slots.

Highly respected scholars have in recent years voiced concerns about the computer as a threat to thinking. Of particular interest is the recent comment made by Professor Joseph Weizenbaum of the Massachusetts Institute of Technology who invented the Eliza computer program and is an authority on artificial intelligence, in an interview for Le Nouvel Observateur he was asked, "do you think, then, that France is making a mistake by trying to put computers in everyone's hands?" Weizenbaum said, "If that is what France is doing, then, yes, it's making a mistake." The temptation to send in computers wherever there is a problem area, be it medicine, education, or whatever, usually creates the impression that grievous deficiencies are being corrected... But often its principles effect is to push problems even further into obscurity to avoid confrontation with the need for fundamentally critical thinking. All the computers in the world won't help you if your unexamined and unconscious assumptions on the nature of reality are simply wrong in their basic conception. All the computers can do is to help you to be stupid in an expensive fashion.

Danger for Brains

The metaphor of a series of wages washing over education is particularly useful in the context of microelectronic technologies. Just as most wages develop in an area for removed from the shoreline on which they break, so much of the original interest in the potentialities of the micro-age began as an array of seemingly unrelated innovations at least partly removed from the school environment. Only since the mid-1970s has the development of relatively inexpensive microcomputers-machines capable of an entertainment function as well as more serious uses-captured the attention of both children and adults.

As of the mid-1980s, as noted earlier, the computer is rapidly becoming the symbol of a new technologically permeated society. Useful in themselves as free-standing decides, whether for instruction, home study, or for administration, much of the potential of the microcomputer is yet to be realized. As microcomputers become even more adequately "networked", they seem certain to become part of a total information-knowledge communication system, involving speech, video, and print.

At the local, regional, national, or international level, diverse technological components are now able to interface with each other. This is the result of the recent convergence of the computer and related microelectronic communications technologies. The synergism that has resulted is now guiding educators into a knowledge-based communications system which is different in character and kind from the more traditional technologies involved in the educational practices of yesteryear. The full implications of the labyrinthine microelectronic technologies associated with extended networks, however, have only begun to be experienced.

The advent of fifth-generation computer systems that can think and may well be able to reason could make possible in the next two decades the development of a total teaching-learning system which is extraordinarily efficient and effective. Although some would view such a system as potentially dehumanizing, this is not necessarily so.

A computerized information-communications system, in itself, is inherently neither good nor bad, but it is powerful. What makes it good or bad is how we learn to use to, how intelligently we apply our skills as thinking people. Micro-technologies will be "good" or "bad" to the degree that we use them with wisdom or folly in education and the wider society. In this sense, electronic micro-biotechnologies seem likely to provide a test for humankind. As Turkle suggests, individuals can use computer systems to establish personal identity, to gain self-awareness, to achieve a feeling of mastery over their present lives, and to direct their alternative futures.

The newly developed body of microelectronic resources epitomized by the computer has an imposing array of brilliant potential solutions for a number of our personal-social problems. It is up to us, as educators, to establish priorities as we address the problems of effective teaching and learning. In this way, we will best be able to utilize our newest resources to prepare learners of all ages for successful living in the new millennium which is close at hand.

There is no doubt that computers and related technologies have had, and will continue to have, for far-reaching effects on the United States and the world economy and employment. There is a broad range of views in the scholarly literature and popular press about the nature and extent of these effects. Despite a rapidly changing present and an increasingly uncertain future, however, vocational educators must provide their students with the opportunity to acquire skills, knowledge, and attitudes needed in order to survive and thrive in what is often called the "information society".

Because of the highly visible and influential roles of computers and related technology in the post industrial economy and society, considerable attention is currently being paid to the concept of computer literacy in preparing students for work. The purpose of this chapter is to assist educators, leaders in industry, and government officials to identify needs and directions for computer-related learning in vocational education. The following questionnaire addressed:

1. How important are computer-related skills and knowledge in preparing students for the workplaces of the information society?
2. What computer-related skills and knowledge are or will be needed in sample occupations?
3. What needs to be done to make vocational education programs more responsive to students' career and vocational needs, give the changing workplace and occupational structures?

Professional Training

Computer-related need in vocational education should be derivable from systematic analyses of tasks performed in the occupations addressed by particular vocational education programs. In the classical approach to instructional systems development, one analyzes the job tasks to be performed and then derives requirements for skill and knowledge requirements are then transformed into instructional objectives. In preparing this chapter, my initial intent was (a) to select a sample of three occupational areas; (b) to gather all available job/task inventories for those areas; (c) to extract all computer- related tasks from these inventories and analyze them for their implications for computer-related skill and knowledge needed for those jobs; and (d) to compare these requirements with existing vocational education curricula in these occupational areas and to identify areas needing revision or improvement.

The methodology was unsuccessful because currently available job/task inventories do not reject computer-related tasks, computer-based methods, or changing job descriptions. It became apparent that the methods, or changing job descriptions. It became apparent that the methods and procedures currently employed for developing and disseminating job/risk inventories are inadequate for handling the rapid pace of technological change in America's workplaces.

A revised approach was to take a broader look at the impact of technology on change in the economy and occupational structures in the United States and to take a long-range look at the implications of these changes on requirements for vocational education objectives and programs. Computer-related needs in the three sample occupation areas were then analyzed in the context of this broader view.

Vocational education is defined in the Education Amendments of 1976 as "organized programs which are directly related to the preparation of individuals for paid or unpaid employment, or for additional preparation for a career requiring other than a baccalaureate or advanced degree". Vocational education provides occupational training to millions of people in many different types of educational institutions across the United States. In 1980-81, the National Centre for Education Statistics estimated that 16.9 million people were enrolled in vocational education programs supported in part by the vocational Education Act of 1963 as amended. This figure does not include students enrolled in the many institutions that are privately controlled. Including those students raises the total to nearly 19 million. However, information on students in programs not supported by the vocational Education Act is sparse and is not included in our discussion. Of the 16.9 million vocational students, about 5.8 million were enrolled in programs designed to train individuals for specific occupations. Occupationally specific programs are offered in grades eleven and twelve as well as in postsecondary and adult education schools.

The vocational education programs supported with federal funds cover education in the following categories identified by the U.S. Department of Education's National Occupational Information Coordinating Committee: agriculture /agribusiness and natural resources, business and office occupations, health occupations, home economics, marketing and distribution, technical occupations, and the trade and industrial occupations.

Industrial arts, which is not included in the list, is not an occupationally specific program but includes courses surveying occupations as well as metal working and woodworking. The two most popular programs are business and office programs and trade and industrial programs, in which a total of more than 60 percent of all vocational education students are enrolled. This pair of programs dominates enrollments at all levels.

Lacking a clear vision of the workplace of tomorrow, educators and their students could well waste billions of dollars and person-years in counterproductive efforts to acquire irrelevant or low-priority skills and knowledge. It is impossible to predict with certainty with the occupational structures will be in twenty or thirty years, much less what the specific skill and knowledge requirements of those jobs will be. Yet the purpose of "computer literacy" especially in vocational education, is to prepare young people for work in the information-rich, highly computerized offices, homes, farms, and factories of the future. This, computer literacy is a high risk educational venture. It is high risk both because of the uncertain pay-off in terms of relevance to tomorrow's jobs and because of the high costs associated with acquisition of computing equipment and provision of teacher training programs needed for adequate computer literacy curricula.

Productive members of society will increasingly be expected to modify, upgrade, and update their knowledge and skills in response to a pace of technological change at least as rapid as occurred during the great industrialization of America a century ago. Given the uncertainty regarding the skill requirements of the economy, it is essential that the education of America's as necessary to these changing requirements.

The vocational education pattern in the past has been to institute computer-related programs of study that are oriented toward technology from the preceding generation of computers. In the early 1970s, computer-related curricula were oriented toward batch processing and keypunching, while the technology was moving toward interactive time-sharing systems. In the mid-1970s, when microcomputers were appearing on the market, educational programs were being, upgraded to reflect the advent of time sharing. In the late 1970s and early 1980s, when the availability of general purpose applications programs were rendering programming skills obsolete for most computer users, many schools began instituting courses to teach all students programming on microcomputers. New that technological advances are rendering many data-entry specialist jobs obsolete, some schools are instituting training in data entry.

Computer-based work stations in business offices are integrating word-processing, data-processing, and communications functions, some schools are instituting training for dedicated word-processing machines and word-processing specialist jobs. How serious a problem is rapid change in technology for teachers and students in vocational education courses of study? The answer depends entirely on the goals and objectives of the courses. If the students are acquiring fundamental concepts and skills in information handling and problem solving, then the characteristics and limitations of the particular machines and methods they are using are more or less incidental. If, on the other hand, students are merely being trained in narrow skills of operation of a particular device or program, then the consequences of using obsolete or nearly obsolete equipment are very serious.

Latest Technologies

Changing technology will be a fact of life in all workplaces for the foreseeable future. Learning to use new machines and new kinds of machines will be a part of every job. Even more significantly, learning new ways of organizing and managing information will be a continuing process for everyone. Consider, for example, the career of a hypothetical secretary over the past five years. She may have begun performing a wise variety of tasks for her employer including typing on a typewriter. Then the organization set up a centralized word-processing centre, and she was transferred there, to specialize in operating a new dedicated word processor. After a year, the company reorganized and she was transferred to another division where a different kind of word processor communicated with an office data-processing machine. Now the company has acquired general purpose personal computers, and she is learning to use not only a word-processing program for the personal computer but an electronic spreadsheet, a database management program, and communications programs. She is setting up procedures for transferring data from the spreadsheet to the word-processing program and is organizing the disk-file library for her group. Viewed in the context of this career path, it would appear to make little difference what particular equipment was used or what specific skills she learned in her vocational education program in school.

There is a broad range of views in the scholarly literature and popular press about the nature and extent of the effects of computer-based automation on he united States economy, on employment, and on job skills. At one extreme it is claimed that the future will require much less skilled workforce. At the other extreme it is said that the future will require a more highly skilled and technologically oriented workforce.

Low Grade Things

The first scenario of technology's impact on future job skills is that, essentially, "machines will do it all". This view implies that many human tasks will be simplified as machines perform the majority of complex operations. Levin and Rumberger's widely quoted thesis is that "the expansion of the lowest skilled jobs in the American economy will vastly outstrip the growth of high technology ones; and the proliferation of high technology industries and their products, is far more likely to reduce the skill requirements of jobs in the U.S. economy than to upgrade them." These authors address two aspects of the changing workforce: the nature of future employment growth and the impact of technology on existing jobs.

With regard to future employment growth, Levin and Rumberger rely heavily on U.S. Department of Labour predictions that the largest increases in new openings in the 1980s will be in low-skill jobs: janitors, nurses' aides, salesclerks, cashiers, and waiters and waitresses. These predictions differ from those that look at the numbers of annual job openings. With regard to the impact of technology on existing jobs, Levin and Rumberger base their analysis on analogy with the industrial revolution.

Mechanization was applied in the workplace in such a manner as to fragment work tasks into simplified operations that required few skills to perform. Basing their reasoning on past experience in industrialization, they conclude that "future technologies will further simplify and routinize work tasks and reduce opportunities for worker individuality and judgment".

Most analysts disagree with Levin and Rumberger's analysis. For example, Leontief and Duchin's analysis results in a nearly opposite conclusion. They developed an input-output model of the United States economy, using four different scenarios of the progressive introduction of computers and various forms of computer-based automation into eighty-nine individual industries. Their model spells out in great detail the probable effects of these technological changes on outputs and inputs of all goods and services and in particular on the demand for labour services in fifty-three different occupations. They find, for example, that "the intensive use of automation over the next twenty years... will involve a significant increase in professionals as a proportion of the labour force and a steep decline in the relative number of clerical workers." A report of the Education Commission of the States agrees with our concern that "by examining the skills needed in tomorrow's labour force we can better prepare workers for the changing conditions they will encounter." The report points out that other factors besides breakthroughs in technology are significantly related to economic growth. these other factors are "advances in new knowledge and increased education levels of the work force." The report states that occupational growth throughout the 1980s is projected to expand most rapidly in the higher-skilled, technical occupations. "Tomorrow's workers will likely need improved skills in the selection and communication of information. Many of today's skills considered to be of a 'higher' level are the potential basic skills of tomorrow."

According to the Commission's report, these skills include evaluation and analysis skills, critical thinking, problem-solving strategies, organization and reference skills, synthesis, application, creativity, decision making given incomplete information, and communication skills though a variety of modes.

Part of the reason for the discrepancies in views of the future may be that as a society we are in a period of transformation or paradigm shifts as characterized by such writers as Masuda, Toffler, and Ferguson. Toffler's view is that in the industrial age the "workers" were trained to perform repetitive tasks requiring varying degrees of skill. The "thinkers" were educated to solve problems, make decisions, and manage workers and information. If on imposes this industrial age paradigm on lowered skill requirements for the "workers". A frequently cited example is Levin's claim that the use of word processors reduces the skill requirements for typists. This kind of thinking is often reported in the public media.

The industrial age paradigm was characterized succinctly in Boyer's discussion of the tracking of students into "academic" and "non-academic" paths: "Students are divided between those who think and those who work, when, in fact, life for all of us is a blend of both." If one applies this "working and thinking" paradigm to the example cited earlier of the claim of reduced skill requirements for typists using word processors, one makes a different interpretation. For example, a "thinker" using a word processor may be performing operations and making decisions that we used to think required higher-order skills, such as planning the organization of document files, designing file templates for repetitive correspondence, writing procedures using variables, programming keyboard macros, developing procedures for integrating data files with documents, selecting appropriate typestyles and document formats, and developing a library of standardized templates. Form this point of view, the person who is typing with a word processor is relieved of lower-level skill requirements such as details of formatting and the checking of spelling and is freed to attend to higher-level information handling concerns.

It is the "worker" versus "thinker" kind of paradigm that leads such analysts as Levin and Rumberger to imagine that computer-based technology will necessarily result in the need for a less skilled workforce. They refer to the ways in which industrialization resulted in specialization and lowered skill requirements on the part of workers and imagine that the same trends will continue with computer-based automation. Their analysis does not take into account the fact that computers can be used to extend the human intellect, thereby allowing humans to be more creative and powerful problem solvers. By participating in the process of creating knowledge, the human adds value to the product or service involved, thereby contributing to the productivity of the overall information-based economy.

Learning and Capability

Traditionally, there computer-related skills and knowledge that have been taught in vocational education have been in the occupational areas of computer operation and data entry clerk. For several years concerns have been voiced about the increasing supply of computer operators and data entry clerks from vocational education programs and the dwindling number of available positions. Furthermore, the people being employed are better educated and are filling more skilled positions. A 1975 survey noted that the number of graduates from the postsecondary vocational and associate level programs might soon exceed the number in the labour market. This report assumed that associated degree institutions were training students primarily for data entry operators and clerical data processing positions. In commenting on institutional resources for computing, Alcorn stated:

"The makeup of the staff of the computer installations is changing toward a higher percentage of analysts and programmers and a lower percentage of operators, toward more full-time and less part-time employees, and toward a slightly better educated staff."

Schools that understood changes in occupations attempted to shift their emphasis to "newer" computer-based jobs and away from heavy emphasis on computer-operator and data entry positions. Though they continued to offer these courses, many programs were expanding their vision.

The traditional vocational education programs in computer operations and data-entry are slowly being replaced by programs in the so-called "Emerging" high-tech occupations such as robotics technician, communications specialist, and computer-assisted design/computer-assisted manufacturing technicians.

By 1990, 80,000 to 100,000 will be in use, according to Walter Wiesel, president of Robot Institute of America, a trade association, and of PRAB Robots, a manufacturing firm. Other figures regarding the robotic revolution are more conservatives. Allan Hunt of the Upjohn institute predicts that 50,000 to 100,000 robots will be is use. But he also warns that over half the jobs created by robotics will require two or more years of college-level training. Wiesel agrees with Hunt's assessment on the amount of training necessary for robotic technicians. It has been assumed by training developers that the design of effective educational and training programs must be founded on detailed and systematic analysis of the task to be performed on the job.

Conducting empirical studies of tasks performed by workers in a particular job category is a costly undertaking, usually beyond the resources of an individual school. Therefore, regional and national centres and consortia have been established, to provide job/task inventories and job-relevant catalogues of performance objectives, criterion-references measures, and performance guides. The High Technology Education Project of the Office for Research in High Technology education at the University of Tennessee attempted to obtain all available job/task inventories for the three selected occupational areas from a wide variety of such centres throughout the United States. Secretarial occupations represent the largest number of annual job openings nationally.

Drafting is being radically affected by computer-aided design and drafting systems. Because computer applications in accounting are older than computer applications in any other field of endeavour, dating back to the 1950s at least, it was expected that accounting occupations would provide insight into how technology is integrated into traditional occupations. For our purposes in this chapter we examined available job/task inventories in order to (a) find out the computer-related skills and knowledge needed by workers in the sampling of occupation areas, (b) discover computer-related skills and knowledge that are common across occupations, and (c) to find out what information is available to vocational curriculum developers and teachers regarding the computer-related skills and knowledge needed by their students. From the stand-point of identifying computer-related tasks, skills, and knowledge, the inventories examined were essentially useless. Even job/task catalogues published as recently as 1983 included few or no computer-related task. Nearly all the secretarial job/task inventories ignored the use of word processes and other kinds of programs on general purpose computers in an office setting. The same is true of the bookkeeping and accounting inventories.

In drafting, few inventories were available; those that were available made no mention of the use of computer-aided design and graphics programs. The one task listing that does identify several computer-related tasks illustrates a major weakness in inventories of the kind reviewed here. In that document computer-related tasks are described almost solely in behavioural terms. The cognitive components of such a task are far more important from any education or training stand-point than the far more important from any educational or training stand-point than the behavioural manipulation of the keys. In reading the task lists, one gets the impression that the one thing workers do not do is think. Rarely in the task lists do they make decisions, analyze information, solve problems, apply principles, and make trade-offs.

Devices for Assessment

Techniques for analyzing tasks for their cognitive components are in their infancy. At the least, however, it would be useful for developing curricula if job/task analyses states the purpose of goals or a task from the viewpoint of the task performer. Such information would be useful in grouping related tasks for instructional analysis and sequencing of instruction. For example, in word processing, statements such is "embeds control characters into text strings" are less useful than statements that reveal the underlying purpose of the operations. To continue with the previous example, the person might be embedding the control characters for such purposes as specifying or modifying document or page formats, documenting procedure, or reorganizing document content. Such purpose are accomplished through different behavioural operations on different machines or software.

A person attempting to become computer-literate needs to develop a cognitive framework that enables his or her to understand basic purposes and functions and transfer these understandings across different machine environments. The present system of creating and updating job/task inventories is of little value as a basis for developing up-to-date curricula or even identifying task, skills, an knowledge needed in workplaces that are in a continual state of change with respect to applications of technology. The inventory procedure takes several years for gathering date, it relies on survey responses from job incumbents in representative firms. The methodology described in the inventory documents does not attempt to take into account the fact that jobs are changing.

To provide an example of the implications of the changing workplace for vocational education, the following section discusses secretarial occupations. Similar considerations apply to other office occupations such as accounting and bookkeeping. In the area of drafting, even more extensive changes are occurring than in the secretarial example, due to the increasing us of computer-aided design, drafting, and engineering systems.

Secretarial jobs will account for the largest number of annual job openings during the 1980s. For perspective, compare the 305,000 projected annual openings for secretaries with the estimated range of 12,000 to 24,0000 jobs for robotics technicians in 1990. Secretarial training programs are one of the most successful vocational education programs, in terms of employment results. These two factors justify paying attention to the continual improvement and modernization of secretarial programs in vocational education. Methods and systems for handling information in offices continue to change due to continuing improvements and reductions in cost for computer and communications based technologies.

Relationships among various organizational groups and subsystems in even small business are being rethought due to changes in the technology available for gathering, storing, organizing, retrieving, and communicating information. For example, five or ten years ago word professing machines were special purpose devices costing tens of thousands of dollars and were considered to require "word processing specialists" to operate. Now, word processing programs are available at a cost of $50 to $400, and they operate on general purpose desktop computers at any desk where there is an electronical outlet. A business person who pays too little for a word processor does not expect to have to capacity is an everyday tool of anyone in an office who needs to produce written documents. One should not expect to have to take a specialist program of studies in word processing to learn to use word processors.

All Purpose Sets

A wide variety of data-management, data-processing, communications, and other functions can easily be performed by non-specialists using the general purpose computer that is the heart of the modern office workstation. This allows for greater integration of various information-handling functions than has been the case in the past. More importantly, it means continual changes in information-handling systems, for the foreseeable future. Implications for vocational education of this trend toward integrated work situations are several.

First, narrow specialist training in dedicated word-processor operations is less valuable in the job market than general information-processing skills. Second, the kinds of applications software a secretary needs to operate are changing. Communications, spreadsheets, databases, and accounting programs are just as important tools for the workstation as are word processors. Third, the integration of the workstation allows for more integration of the functions of information processing. Therefore one can expect less, rather than more, specialization of office jobs. An executive who uses spreadsheets for modelling and decision making, databases for information retrieval, and word processing for preparing reports and correspondence does not want to have a separate secretary or technician to operate each separate program.

The secretary or whatever the person is called must be equally comfortable with typing documents, entering formulas for spreadsheet computations, or requesting sorts from the data management program. Most experts foresee the need for secretarial personnel to have higher-level skills and greater adaptability than in the past. Nearly all of the analyses reviewed for the present study predict that secretarial jobs will continue to require more analytic abilities, greater adaptability, and greater skills in decision making, communications, and interpersonal relations. Understanding of basic concepts of systems analysis, data processing, the telecommunications is seen as necessary in support of this increased adaptability. A fairly extreme version of this point of view was expressed by Stewart:

The day may not be too far off when secretarial jobs will require a master's degree in business administration and be regarded as an entry-level step into management. There will be more creative-type positions, few dog-work-type tasks and there will be far more tasks. Given the inescapable conclusion that business offices will continue to change in the nature of computer-based equipment and in the methods of handling information, what is the most important computer-related skill or knowledge a person preparing to be a secretary could have? Clearly, one cannot point to any given device or program of today and say: "This is the kind of machine of must be trained to operate".

Even the more generic skill of keyboarding is suspect in a world where voice input, optical scan input, and direct computer-to-computer transfer of data could reduce keyboarding demands overnight. The most useful computer-related idea that a secretary could develop is that he or she be able to learn the capabilities, limitations, functions, and operations of any particular computer-based systems when the need arises to do so. The development of this concept, and the related attitude of confidence, can be encouraged by an educational environment that expects students to learn how to learn. For example, students learning to operate an unfamiliar word-processing program would not be taught step-step specific procedures of operation. Rather, they would be introduced to the basic functions of the program and would be provided with a use's manual and/or the online helps and menu built into the program They would be asked to solve problems and accomplish tasks to progressive levels of complexity.

Working independently or in small groups, students would develop confidence and skill in using available information to teach themselves how to solve problems and accomplish new tasks. Reading, writing, oral communications, procedural thinking, keyboarding, familiarity with characteristics of electronic storage media, and a minimal computer-related vocabulary are prerequisite to success in such problem-solving and independent-learning tasks. The kinds of programs secretarial students need to learn how to use include word processors and associated utilities such as spelling an grammar checkers, electronic spreadsheets, data-management programs, graphics programs, and communications programs. Since the way in which such programs actually operate is constantly changing it is important for students to learn not only the specifics of using a particular program. They need to learn the basic information-handling functions that such programs can perform, their capacities, and their limitations.

If one defines computer literacy in functional way, that is, whatever a person needs to be able to do with computer in order to function effectively in a particular role, then one would expect to see the integration of computer-related tools, methods, and concepts into the curriculum in nearly every integration would be reflected in some of the following ways:

1. Job and task inventories for the office and industrial occupations would reflect the computer-related and information-handling task performed and skills and knowledge required in, those occupations.
2. State and local education agencies would be providing guidance on computer-literacy needs in vocational education.
3. Curriculum guides for occupational programs would reflect skills and knowledge needed in relation to technology and information handling.
4. Vocational education conferences would contain sessions and papers on topics related to the integration of

computer-related skills into various vocational education courses.

5. Secondary schools would be sponsoring or conducting in service workshops for vocational education teachers, to increase their computer-related skills.
6. Teacher training institutions would be preparing new vocational education teachers to use computer-based tools methods, and media in their instructional programs.
7. Textbooks and other learning materials used in vocational education would incorporate computer-based methods and materials.
8. Software and educational publishers seeing a market in vocational education for software designed for vocational education curricula, would be offering computer programs to fit into the various curriculum areas.

A survey of the above indicators would be likely to yield useful insights on change processes in vocational education. Although a systematic survey of these indicators in beyond the scope of the present chapter, the following comments on each may be helpful.

According to an October 1984 survey of state education agencies, twenty states has by then passed laws requiring or recommending some form of computer-literacy instruction in their K-12 schools. Many states' guidelines has moved in the direction of integrating computer-related skills and knowledge into the traditional courses. Although few of these state directives and guidelines relate specifically to vocational education, they have strong implications for the computer-related skills that can be expected on the part of students entering vocational education programs.

The California State Department of Education Office of Vocational Education has prepared a draft for a computer literacy guide for business education that addresses three levels of computer literacy—awareness, operations, and competence. The California competence objectives illustrate the idea that students need to learn not just rote procedures, but rather how to apply computer-based tools to the tasks of their jobs. In 1983, Kapp and

Knick-erbocker surveyed state directors of vocational education to determine whether microcomputers were being purchased for use in vocational education in their states, how the computers were being used, and the percentage of teachers using microcomputers. They found that 35 percent of the junior and senior high schools has purchased more than fifty micro-computers, although it is unclear whether all of these were for vocational education. Ninetysix percent of the respondents said that the most frequent use was for word processing. Seventyeight percent of the respondents said that fewer than 50 percent of their teachers were using microcomputers.

Some recent local and regional curriculum guidelines for the areas of occupations, drafting, and accounting occupations were reviewed for this chapter. Although many of the programs reviewed included computer-related competencies or topics, these topics were usually not integrated into the regular curriculum but rather were tacked on as separate courses in computers or information processing. It must be emphasized, however, that the resources for the present chapter precluded systematic evaluation of published curriculum guides.

The topic of computer-related skills has been recently introduced at vocational education conferences. At the First Annual Microcomputers in vocational Education Conference in Madison, Wisconsin in 1982, a collection of papers addressing a very wide range of topics was distributed in a handbook. Some of the papers reflect a revaluation of vocational education courses in view of the availability of computer-based tools. It does not appear, however, that vocational educators have participated in anywhere near the number of local, regional, and national conferences on computer-related issues that have been attended by their counterparts in academic education.

The previously cited study by Kapp and Knickerbocker found that nearly every state or territory had made an effort to provide some information on microcomputers to its vocational educators. The sessions lasted from one-half hour to sixty hours and were held on the local, district, regional, and state levels. No information is available on the number of teachers who have received such training or information. An example of state-supported teacher training is the case of the Vocational Education Services at Indiana University. A series of two-day microcomputer workshops was conducted in the summer and fall of 1984 for vocational educators and administrators. The Vocational Education Services received a fourteen-month grant from the state to become a computer-literacy training centre for teachers in six Indian countries.

One popular textbook in word processing takes a systems approach to office automation by teaching concepts as well as analytic methodology. It addresses the process of change in offices and teaches how to mange all aspects of change. If such a textbook were used in combination with hands-on experience with a variety of office automation equipment, procedures, and tasks, it would have seen that the resulting course of instruction would provide the student with a solid understanding of office information processing.

During past years, education and software publishers have been investing heavily in the development and marketing of software aimed at school markets. Until recently, very few of these products have been specifically for vocational education curricula. It appears that educational publishers have not seen vocational education as a ready market for specially designed software or courseware. This of course will change as the market becomes more apparent.

Multipurpose Machines

Vocational education must be headed towards a functional integration of technology as well as strong basic skills in communication, information handling. and problem solving. If it is not, the curricula will be hopelessly obsolete. The danger to vocational education is that the traditional separation of computer-related occupational curricula will continue to serve as a model for isolation of computer-related skills and knowledge into separate courses. However, the increasing pressures placed on vocational education programs by industry, the popular press, and parents, and the rapid developments in appropriate application software makes such continued isolation unlikely.

The most pervasive problems vis-a-vis the computer revolution and vocational education are the pace of technological and occupational change in the workplace and the inability of traditional vocational education mechanisms and institutions to be proactive with respect to envisioned future requirements. That is, curricula tend to reflect past rather than future workplace requirements.

One important reason for the obsolescence of vocational education curricula is that the schools do not budget for change. Vocational education institutions, both secondary and postsecondary, spend a relatively miniscule proportion of their budgets on program development and improvement. Nearly all of their budget goes for maintenance of existing programs. According to a 1979-80 survey, 74 percent of vocational education institutions at the secondary level spent nothing on new programs, and 90 percent spent less than 5 percent of their budget for new services.

Another problem confronting vocational educators is a lack of current and predictive information regarding the computer-related tasks that will soon be performed by job incumbents in the increasingly automated offices, farms, and factories. Lacking some systematic and accurate basis for reassessing curricula, vocational educators run the risk of investing very large amounts of time and money in developing curricula and operating programs to teach obsolete or low-priority skills and knowledge.

Current approaches to analyzing and cataloging job tasks are almost completely behavioral. To gain more insight into the computer-related skills and knowledge needed in many jobs situations, job/task analysis should focus more on cognitive aspects of the task, such as analysis, decision making, troubleshooting, and problem solving. The need for this increased focus on cognitive processes arises from the increasing amounts and kinds of information handling that must be accomplished in most jobs. To understand this point, it is helpful to consider the characteristics of the information society in contrast to characteristics of the industrial society.

Current literature in vocational education and the popular press reflect considerable interest in and concern about developing new vocational programs for so-called "emerging" high-technology occupations such as robotics technician and telecommunications specialists. However, the changing roles and tasks of the more traditional occupations are far more important in terms of the actual numbers of students and jobholders who will be affected. Curricula in these basic and traditional vocational areas need to be reassessed in relation to need of the information-based workplace. Computer-based tools and methods, for example, should be integrated into the regular curriculum in all subjects, rather than being isolated as a separate subject of study.

Despite differing perspectives and purposes, nearly every recent educational study group and most state education agencies have recommended that computer literacy be included as one of the "basic" in a core educational curriculum and that increased emphasis be placed on higher-level cognitive and social skills in problem solving and information handling. If the trend towards mandated computer literacy at the junior high school level continues, one would expect students entering vocational education programs to have a variety of skills and knowledge related to computers, which should be taken into account in redesigning programs.

15

Technical Aspects of Teaching

Teaching is an essential part of education. Its special function is to impart knowledge, develop understanding and skills. It generally excludes inculcation of values like truth. It is usually associated with the in parting of knowledge of 3 R's - Reading, Writing and Arithmetic- representing various school subjects. Education, on the other hand, has a wider connotation. It implies 7 R's - Reading, Writing, Arithmetic, (All three denoting school subjects), Rights, Responsibilities, Relationships and Recreation (Requirements and ideals of a modern democratic state). In teaching we limit our outlook omitting those more important means of education which are involved in the school as a systematically organised social community, including its tone or general moral environment, its government and discipline, and that potent influence - the personality of the teacher. James Welton observes, "We treat teaching by itself, because it is an aspect of school life which can be singled out in thought, though it cannot be separated in reality, from the whole of which it forms a part and because it covers a fairly consistent body of doctrine. It is true that the value and success of all school teaching depends on those wider and deeper elements of school life-tone, discipline, etc. which are omitting. But it is true that whilst the latter may be excellent the former may be of poor quality.

The Fundamentals

Albert Einstein (A Swiss Physicist 1879-1950): The supreme art of teaching is to awaken joy in creative expression and knowledge.

American Educational Research Association Commission in 'Handbook of Research on Teaching' (1962): Teaching is a form of interpersonal influence aimed at changing the behaviour potential of another person.

Amidon and Hunter (1967): Teaching is an interactive process, primarily involving classroom, which takes place between teacher and pupils and occurs during certain definable activities.

Anatole France (French novelist 1844-1924): The whole art of teaching is only the art of awakening the natural curiosity of young minds for the purpose of satisfying it afterwards.

B.O. Smith (1963): Teaching is a system of actions involving an agent, an end in view, and a situation including two sets of factors those over which the agent has no control (class size, size of classroom, physical characteristics of pupils etc.) and those that he can modify (ways of asking questions almost instructions and way of structuring information or ideas gleaned.)

Burton (1963): Teaching is the stimulation, guidance, direction and encouragement of learning.

Clark (1970): Teaching refers to activities that are designed and performed to produce change in student (pupil) behaviour.

Floyed Well (1958): Children are notoriously 'curious about everything except the things people want them to know. It then remains for us to refrain from forcing any kind of knowledge upon them and they will be curious about everything.

CaWeo Calieleo (Italian astronomer 1564-1652): You cannot teach a man anything, you can only help him to find it himself.

HE. Morrison (1934): Teaching is an intimate contact between a more mature personality and less mature one which is designed to further the education of the latter.

Israel Sheffler (1966): Teaching may be characterised as an activity aimed at the achievement of learning and practised in such a manner as to respect the student's intellectual integrity and capacity.

John Dewey (1859-1952): One might as well say he has sold when no one has bought, as to say he has taught when no one has learned.

John Brubacher (1939): Teaching is an arrangement and manipulation of a situation in which there are gaps and obstructions which an individual will seek to overcome and from which he will learn in the course of doing so.

John Chapman (1960): The gift of teaching is a peculiar talent, and it implies a need and craving in the teacher himself.

Joyce and Well (1972): Teaching is a process by which teacher and students create a shared environment including set of values and beliefs (agreement about what is improvement) which in turn colour their view of reality.

J. Wilton: To know where the pupils are and where they should try to be are the first two essentials of good teaching.

Michael Oakeshort (1966): Teaching is two-fold activity of communicating information and communicating judgement.

N.L. Gage (1962): Teaching is a form of interpersonal influence aimed at changing the behaviour potential of another person.

Ned. A. Flanders (1970): Teaching is an interaction, process. Interaction means participation of both teacher and students and both are benefited by this. The interaction takes place for achieving desired objectives.

Paul Goodman (1980): A good teacher feels his way, looking for response.

Thomas P. Green (1971): Teaching is the task of a teacher which is performed for the development of a child.

W.R. Ryburnt (1946): Teaching includes the training of emotions of the child. It is one of the means of giving right feeling to the children.

William Lyon (1970): In my mind teaching is not merely a life work, a profession, an occupation, a struggle, it is a passion. I love to teach, as a painter loves to paint, as a musician loves to play, as a singer loves to sing, as a strongman rejoices to run a race.

Yoakm and Simpson: Teaching is a means whereby society trains the young in a selected environment as quickly as possible to adjust themselves to the world in which they live.

In the type of teaching as mentioned by Morrison, teaching is reduced to what the teacher does. There is interaction but the flow of instruction is from the teacher. In this type of teaching, the learners may become passive listeners

Brubacher's definition of teaching assigns more place to the learner. This approach tends to be child or learner-centered.

B.O. Smith seems to be more pragmatic in his approach to teaching. He accepts certain limitations of the learner in the teaching learning process.

Smith's definition contains the following three elements:

(a) Teaching is a system of action.

(b) Teaching is a goal-directed action.

(c) Teaching takes place in a situation comprising the controlable and uncontrolable set of factors.

A review of the definitions given above reveals that to play his role competently in teaching, a teacher is expected to understand the significance of the following:

Who is to teach. The teacher is to teach and he must .. understand himself thoroughly - his strengths and weaknesses and strive to present a reasonably good model before his students.

Whom to teach. The child is to be taught. Therefore, a teacher should understand him thoroughly - his abilities, aptitudes, attitudes, manners and temperaments and accordingly cater to the individual differences of students.

Why to teach. The teacher should always keep in view that the aim of education is to develop harmonious personalities, who are culturally refined, emotionally stable, ethically sound, mentally alert, morally upright, physically strong, socially efficient and spiritually enlightened. He should not forget even for a moment that the traditional 3 R's have been replaced by 7 R's, that is, reading, writing, arithmetic (representing various disciplines), rights, responsibilities, relationships and recreation.

Where to teach. The teacher ought not to visualise the school to be merely a place of imparting information but a place where men of tomorrow are trained to take their place as enlightened citizens in the society and contribute to national development.

What to teach. The teacher must have mastery over the subject he teaches.

How to teach. The teacher must use new teaming-learning technology to make his teaching. Effective and inspirational.

When to teach. Appropriate steps need to be taken by the teacher to develop motivation of the student in the entire work.

Instruction is primarily concerned with the development of knowledge and understanding in the pupii about a thing, system or process. Imparting of knowledge and understanding merely represents one of the several objectives which we want to achieve through teaching. Teaching is concerned with all the domains of pupil's behaviour, i. e., cognitive, conative and affective. Instruction is a part of teaching.

The distinction between teaching and instruction may be seen from another angle. The face to face interaction of the teacher and taught found in teaching is not so much essential in the process of instruction . In instruction, a teacher may be replaced by the programmed material, computer, teaching machine, radio and television etc. A teacher cannot be replaced by these aids. Of course, in teaching a teacher makes use of them. Thus, instruction is one of the several modes of teaching.

Teaching is giving Information. There are many things that the students cannot find out for themselves. There are many things that they can never know unless they are told. There are many things the use of which they do not know. These things they have to be told. So one essential part of teaching is communicating knowledge. Knowledge must be given in a systematised manner. Teaching should be-made interesting. It must, however, be stressed that knowledge aspect should not be unduly emphasized.

Teaching is Causing to Learn. It is wrong to think, that knowledge can be passed on from one person to another like money. Knowledge will be received only when the students are prepared to receive it. Real teaching consists in persuading the child, by one method or the other to learn for himself. The teacher is an instrument in helping a child to learn how to do things for himself .

Teaching is a Matter of Helping the Child to Respond to his Environment in an Effective Manner. F.N. Freeman observes, "It is not what is presented to the child which educates him, but rather the reaction that he makes to what is presented. Certain children may fail entirely to respond to a lesson, or may respond in a wrong manner. If a child's response to his geography is to memorize the words, without any understanding of the facts they represent, the lesson is ' educative for him (he has not been taught), although it may be educative for the child next to him who reacts properly."

Teaching is Helping a Child to Adjust himself to his Environment. A child is reacting in some way or the other to his physical and social environment, from his very birth. His reactions are both fruitful and harmful. Teaching should help the child to make successful adjustment. This may be done in two ways. Sometimes we modify the environment and at other times strengthen the child. Teaching should make the child socially efficient, that is, a worthy member of society, making his contribution to the common good. Yoakam and Simpson: write, "Teaching is a means whereby society trains the young in a selected environment as quickly as possible to adjust themselves to the world in which they live. In primitive societies this adjustment means conformity with things as they are. In more advanced civilizations, such as ours, effort is made not only to adjust to things as they are" but also to make an advance in the improvement of conditions of life by training the young in modes of thinking and acting which will help to improve the conditions of living that surround them."

Teaching is Stimulation and Encouragement. Teaching should fire the enthusiasm of the child. It is to encourage the child in the development of his natural desires to work, and to be active.

Teaching is Guidance. Teaching is to guide the pupils to learn the right things in the right manner and at the right time. Teaching is to guide the students to do things in such a way that time, material and energy are not wasted.

Teaching is Training the Emotions of the Child. Ryburn observes, "It is also the encouraging and training of the emotion all life. This is an aspect of teaching which is very commonly neglected', at least in practice. But our teaching will be only one-sided and distorted unless we take into account the 'necessity for helping the child to develop a stable emotional life." Teaching is to develop the emotional life of the child by providing an atmosphere of love, affection and freedom. Teaching is to provide such activities as will sublimate their instinctive urges to action.

Teaching is Both a Conscious and an Unconscious Process. Teaching is both a conscious and an unconsciously process and the most effective part of it is generally the part of which we are unconscious. The personal relationships between the teacher and the taught have a great bearing on the growth of the child

Teaching is a Means of Preparation. Though preparation for future is not the only aspect of teaching, yet it is an important aspect: Teaching is to help the immature child to develop physically, intellectually, emotionally and spiritually to participate effectively in the life of the community.

Teaching is Formal as well as Informal. Formal teaching is deliberately planned, systematically organised and is always purposive. Teachers are just formal agents of teaching. School is not the only agency of teaching. Informal teaching is carried on by the parents, brothers and sisters at home, playmates, student community outside the classroom, etc. The few hours of the school are insufficient for the full development of the child. Formal and informal teaching must coperate, if good results are to be achieved. School should 'supplement' not 'supplant', the training imparted by the home and *vice-versa.*

Teaching as a Skilled Occupation. Every successful teacher is expected to know the general methods of teaching and instruction in creating suitable learning situations. He is also expected to be familiar with the general objectives of education.

Teaching is an Art. Art implies the intelligent action of a human being through which it is possible to modify an ordinary course of events. Teaching is an art which can be improved through research.

Teaching is a Form of Social Service. The teaching profession is regarded to be a sort of social.servjce and the teachers as servants of society in whose hands has been entrusted the task of shaping and developing the behaviour and conduct of the young children for maintaining and improving the social patterns.

Teaching as a Relationship. Teaching is a, relationship which is established between three focal points in education, the teacher, the child and the subject. Teaching is the process by which the teacher brings the child and the subject together. The teacher and the taught are active, the former in teaching and the latter in learning.

Teaching as a Skilled occupation. Every successful teacher is expected to know the general methods of teaching and instruction in creating suitable learning situations. He is also expected to be familiar with the general objectives of education.

Teaching is Both an Art and Science. Silverman (1966) has expressed the nature of teaching in these words. "To be sure teaching-like the practice of medicine-is very much an art which is to say, it calls for exercise of talent and creativity. But like medicine, it is also a science, for it involves a repertoire of techniques, procedures and skills that can be systematically studied, described and improved. A good teacher, like a good doctor, is one who adds creativity and inspiration to the basic repertoire."

Purpose of Teaching

1. Creating learning situations.
2. Motivating the child to learn.
3. Arranging for conditions which assist in the growth of the child's mind and body.
4. Utilizing the initiative and play urges of the children to facilitate learning.
5. Turning the children into creative beings.
6. Inspiring children with the nobility of thoughts, feelings and action.
7. Giving information and explaining it.
8. Diagnosing learning problems.
9. Making curricular material.
10. Evaluating, recording and reporting.

Sri Aurobindo describes the marks of good teaching in these words, "The first principle is that nothing can be taught. The teacher is not an instructor or task master, he is a helper and guide. His business is to suggest and not to impose. He does not actually train the pupils's mind, he only shows him to perfect his instruments of knowledge and helps and encourages him in the process. He does not impart knowledge to him, he shows him how to acquire knowledge for himself. He does not call forth the knowledge that is within, he only shows him where it lies and it can be habituated to rise to surface. The distinction that reserves this principle for the teaching of adolescent and adult minds and denies its application to the child, is a conservative and unintelligent doctrine. Child or man, girl or boy, there is only one sound principle of good teaching. Difference of age only serves to diminish or increase the amount of help and guidance necessary, it does not change its nature."

John Dewey (1859-1952) states, "The more a teacher is aware of the past experiences of students, of their hopes, desires, chief interests, the better will he understand the forces at work that need to be directed and utilized for the formation of reflective habits." Further he writes, "The teacher is a guide and director, he steers the boat but the energy that propels it must come from those who are learning."

Albert Einstein (1879-1955) has observed, "It is the supreme art of the teacher to awaken joy in creative expression and knowledge.

Montaigne, a French philosopher (1533-1592) advises, "A tutor should not be continually thundering instruction into the ears of his pupil, as if he were pouring it through a funnel, but, after having, put the lid, like a young horse, on a trot before him, to observe his paces, and see what he is able to perform, should according to the extent of his capacity, induce him to taste, to distinguish, and to find out things for himself, sometimes opening the way, at other times leaving it for him to open."

Joseph Payne (English educator, 1808-1876) writes, "The teachers part in the process of instruction is that of guide, director or superintendent of the operation by which the pupil teachers himself."

Swami Vivekananda (1863-1902) describes the rôle of the teacher in teaching as, "The true teacher is he who can immediately come down to the level of the student."

Following are the marks of good teaching :

Good teaching recognises individual differences—Good teaching treats each child as unique. Good teaching recognises that catering to individual differences brings strength. It must be remembered that standardized procedures do not fit every pupil.

Good teaching is causing to learn—Good teaching enables the child to learn for himself. It is not stuffing the mind of the child with information. Good teaching is what we can make the child do for himself.

Good teaching provides opportunities for activity—The child is inherently active. Passiveness on the part of the child implies that he is not in good physical and mental health. A good teacher keeps the students active. He is aware of the fact that to keep the students disciplined, he must fill the time with work and he does so accordingly.

Good teaching involves skill in guiding—A good teacher motivates his teaching. He stimulates " through his personality and his activities the personalities and activities of the pupils." He creates such situations as lead to desired types of learners.

Good teaching is kindly and sympathetic—Good teaching must create an environment of acceptance, sympathy and understanding.

Good teaching decreases the distance i.e. to either teacher and the taught—Teachers should come out of their ivory tower and come as close with the students as possible.

Good teaching is not tied to any method—Methods, techniques and devices should be adopted to local situations and considered as servants and not masters.

Good teaching is cooperative—Good teaching is an active and living process. A good teacher seeks the cooperation of the learners.

Good teaching is kindly and sympathetic—A good teacher always creates. A cordial atmosphere in the classroom. He always ensures his pupils's emotional stability and security. He is loving, kind, affectionate and sympathetic to his pupils. He bears in mind this fact "love the child and he will love you, hate him and he will hate you." He avoids scolding and sarcasm.

Good teaching involves careful planning—Good teaching keeps in view that everything cannot be taught to children at every time. A good teacher carefully studies the mental make-up of the pupil he teaches, studies the individual differences of pupils and then prepares his subject-matter. An unplanned lesson often results in a failure and involves a waste of time, energy and money also.

Good teaching is democratic—A good teacher always respects the individuality of his pupils. He keeps democratic ideals, contents, methods and objectives in view.

Good teaching provides desirable and selective information—The good teacher does not try to teach all the available information that he gathers form books and experience. On the other hand he makes a judicious selection and teaches all that is useful to live a good life as responsible member of the society.

Good teaching helps the child to adjust himself to his environment—Man has been struggling against natural forces since ages. He is expected either to adjust himself to these natural forces or to adjust the forces to himself. A good teacher helps the child in both directions.

Good teaching is progressive—A good teacher aims at improving his modes and techniques steadily. He also helps the child to make suitable progress in life.

Good teaching leads to emotional stability—There are very powerful inherited urges which always cry for expansion. A good teacher knows that unguided expression leads to wilderness; and therefore, helps in providing his pupils suitable opportunities which assist in training and sublimating their urges and emotions.

Good teaching is both diagnostic and remedial—A good teacher makes use of the various measuring instruments which have been provided by psychology and discovers the intelligence, aptitudes and interests of children and accordingly plans his work.

Superb Teaching

Challenge of Education-A Policy Perspective (1985). A publication of the Ministry of Education, and a forerunner of The National Policy on Education-NPE 1986, has something worth quoting, on quality of education. It states, "It is difficult to define quality, particularly with reference to educational processes. However, it could be stated that a quality conscious system would produce people who have the attributes of functional and social relevance, mental ability and physical dexterity, efficacy and readability and above all, the confidence and the capability to communicate effectively and exercise initiative, innovative and experiment with new situations. To these personal attributes one could add the dimensions of a value system conducive to harmony, integration and the welfare of the weak and disadvantaged."

Quality teaching also known as effective teaching is the chief instrument of quality education. It is essentially concerned with translating the objectives of education into action and practice. It is concerned with how best to bring about pupil learning by various activities. Quality teaching may be defined as the teacher's ability to stimulate students intellectually and move them emotionally to instill in them love for learning and develop suitable skills and attitudes.

Quality teaching is based on the premise 'All teachers should teach well and all students should learn well'.

An understanding of the following facts would go a long way in quality teaching:

1. Effective teaching is a comprehensive concept. Several variables are involved in teaching.
2. All types of variables play their part in teacher-learning situation.
3. 'What' and 'how' of effective teaching should be carefully comprehended.
4. There are several models of teaching and each should be considered in the overall context of teaching.
5. All models are complimentary to each other.
6. A teacher should adopt an electric approach in the selection of a model.
7. Developing a personal model of teaching in consonance with the requirements of quality teaching should become the cherished goal of every teacher.
8. Skill in creating intellectual excitement has two components· The clarity of an instructor's communications and their positive emotional impact on students.
9. Quality teaching results from a teacher's skill attracting both intellectual excitement and positive rapport with students.

10. The development of good rapport is based on three qualities in the teachers interaction with students: the teacher cares for student progress, the teacher has consideration for students as learners and the teacher respects students as individuals.
11. The three elements involved in teaching competence while contribute to teacher's authority and prestige are: Mastery over the subject, interest in the subject and effective learning situations and experiences.
12. Quality teaching presupposes an understanding mind; a feeling heart and a lofty personality.
13. In quality teaching the environment is of mutual cooperation and of purposefulness. A play-way spirit is the chief characteristic of the work.

Capable Teaching

A 'A' is for alertness on the part of the teacher to the multifarious needs of the learners. Alertness is very helpful in taking appropriate decisions and timely corrective measures.

'A' is also for adaptability in handling several situations.

B 'B' is for businesslike attitude. It is to be ensured that every learner in the class, remains busy in realizing the goals set.

'B' is for balanced behaviour.

C 'C' stands for cooperative teaching-learning. The learners must be made active partners.

'C' is for clarity of purpose. The teacher and the learners must be clear about the goals for the achievement of which they are working.

'C' is for clarity of the subject-matter taught. A teacher must make all possible efforts to make his lesson clear. Difficulties of the learners must be appreciated and clarified.

D 'D' stands for democratic classroom environment.

'D' is for discovery. Children should be guided to find out new facts, ideas and principles. It helps children in becoming independent and resourceful learners.

'D' stands for democratic discipline.

E 'E' stands for expectancies. Each learner should be expected to learn. No learner should be considered without any potential.

'E' stands for enthusiasm. The teacher himself must demonstrate enthusiasm for his work.

'E' stands for appropriate etiquettes.

F 'F' is for feedback. Feedback helps the teacher and the learners to take timely corrective measures for the completion of the task.

'F' stands for faith of the teacher in himself.

G 'G' is for goal-setting. Appropriate goals should be set for the learners. They should also be made clear about the suitability of goals. Efforts may be made to associate the learners with the setting of goals.

H 'H' is for hard work on the part of the students as well as teachers. .

'H'is for humour. Humour on the part of the teacher releases fatigue and tension.

'H' stands for human touch.

I 'I' stands for involvement of all the learners in classroom activities and experiences.

'I' stands for impartial attitude.

'I' stands for inspirational teaching-learning.

J 'J' stands for just attitude.

'J' stands for judicious rewards and punishments.

K 'K' stands for knowing children's abilities, aptitudes and interests.

'K' stands for the knowledge of the sub-matter.

L 'L' stands for linking present, past and future knowledge.

'L' stands for leadership qualities.

M 'M' stands for motivation.

'M' stands for management of the class.

N 'N' stands for needs of the learners and their satisfaction.

O 'O' stands for open-mindedness.

'O' stands for out of class activities.

'O' stands for objectivity in approach.

P 'P' stands for praise. Verbal and non-verbal praise of children can motivate them to hardwork.

'P' stands for personal contact with every learner.

Q 'Q' is for quiz. From time to time, quiz competitions may be arranged in the class.

'Q' stands for quality teaching.

'Q' stands for question-answers.

R 'R' stands for review of the lesson.

'R' stands for relationships.

'R' stands for resourcefulness.

S 'S' stands for success experience. Success motivates the learner to achieve more.

'S' stands for scientific temper.

'S' stands for self-analysis and self-control

T 'T' stands for technology of teaching.

'T' stands for tutoring which involves removing difficulties, individually or in small groups.

U 'U' stands for undivided attention to teaching.

'U' stands for unbiased attitude to the treatment of controversial issues.

V 'V' stands for visual aids.

'V' stands for variety of experiences.

'V' stands for voice-modulated.

'V' stands for variation in the presentation.

W 'W' stands for welcoming attitude.

'W' stands for warmth towards students.

X 'X' stands for X-ray of the teaching process. It implies finding out of the difficulties and potentials of the students.

Y 'Y' stands for yardstick i.e. same standard basis of making a judgement on the performance of the students.

'Y' stands for you, implying that you (student) are the most important element in the teaching-learning process.

'Y' stands for zenith or excellence.

Either J. Swenson in the Teacher's Letter (1952) states that each of the following seven wonders brings a new challenge to the classroom teacher:

First wonder. How much children are ready know before they come to school. They bring with them rich resources of knowledge, skill and understandings-mostly self-learned.

First challenge. How much do I know of these rich resources? How far do I go in searching them out? How do I use what I find?

Second wonder. Children's eagerness to learn. It is natural for children to inquire, to discover. It is unnatural for them to be passive, disinterested.

Second challenge. How do I use this eagerness to learn? In what direction should it be channelled? Am I feeding it or killing it?

Third wonder. The never-ending process of learning. Every hour of the day, no matter where he is with whomever or whatever he works, the child learns.

Third challenge. Is he learning what is best for him, now and later? Am I setting the stage for constructive learnings?

Fourth wonder. The infinite variety of abilities, personalities, needs, and interests of pupils. He who says, "I know children" has not taken time to study the marvels of their growth.

Fourth challenge. Do I know as much as I should about each child's abilities, personalities, needs, interests? How can I learn more? Do I accept differences or rebel against them?

Fifth wonder. The concomity of learning. Simultaneously, children learn subject matters, traits of personality, habits of working, attitudes and appreciations-many of them permanently.

Fifth challenge. Do I push so hard toward a single goal that I push the children away from another of equal importance? Do I leave these "marginal learnings" to chance?

Sixth wonder. The faith, respect, loyalty and tolerance to children. When a teacher treats them well—sometimes even when' he does not—they will respond with respect and understanding.

Sixth challenge. Do I have an equal faith in them and in their motives? Am I as loyal to them and their welfare? Do I treat them with respect and understanding?

Seventh wonder. The ability of children to teach. Each child learns form the other, and even the teacher can learn much from children. .

Seventh challenge. Do I use my opportunities to learn from children? Do I listen, literally and figuratively, to the lessons they can teach?

Ideas in Teaching

Several attempts have been made to analyse activities involved in teaching with a view to understand it scientifically, design teaching materials and methods for realising the specific objectives efficiently, and to evaluate and modify it in the light of the feedback.

Plenlders, Ned. S. (1959) of the University of Minnesota was the first educator to categories all the sets of verbal behaviours (teaching activities) of a teacher in the classroom while interacting with students. He classified these activities into three categories:

1. Teacher Talk. 2. Pupil Talk and 3. Silence/confusion.

1. Teacher talk was further categorised as under:

(1) Indirect influence which includes (a) Accepts feelings, (b) Praises or encourages, (c) Accepts or uses pupil ideas, (d) Asks questions.

(2) Direct influence which includes (a) Lecturing, (b) Giving directions, (c) Criticising or justifying.

2. Pupil talk which induced (a) Pupil talk response, (b) Pupil talk initiation.

3. Silence or confusion.

Komesnr, N.P. (1966) tried to analyse teaching into various specific activities like introducing, demonstrating, contrasting, explaining, proving, justifying, explaining, defining, appraising, amplifying, rating, interpreting, questioning, elaborating, identifying, conjecturing, confirming etc.

Gagel NL. (1968) attempted .to analyse teaching in terms of technical skills. According to him, "Teaching skills are specific instructional techniques and procedures that a teacher may use in the class room. They represent an analysis of the teaching process into relatively discrete components that can be used in different combinations in the continuous flow of the teacher's performance."

Clarles, S.CT. (1970) analysed teaching in terms of some specific activities that are designed and performed to produce change in student's behaviour. Those activities may be of cognitive, affective or conative nature and belonged to different levels.

Brown, B.B. (1968) analyses teaching by considering it as a manysided activity which includes several activities like questioning, giving information and listening etc.

Passi, B.K.. (1976) states that teaching constitutes a number of verbal and non-verbal teaching acts like questioning, accepting pupil response, rewarding, smiling, nodding to pupil response, movements, gestures, etc. These acts, particularly in combination, facilitate the achievement of objectives in terms of pupil growth.

Dhingra, N.K. and Singh Ajit (1982) present the analysis of teaching as, "Teaching can be analysed in terms of teacher behaviour at least at three levels viz, component teaching skills, competent teaching behaviours and atomistics teaching behaviours."

The Two Sides

Teaching Technology : Concept and Meaning

Teaching technology involves the mechanism of instructional process in the classroom situations, levels of teaching, theories of teaching, principal teaching operations and establishing relations between theories and teaching operations.

Teaching technology as a concept can be classified into four well-defined components. These components are: (i) Manpower, (ii) Methods, (iii) Materials, and (iv) Media.

As a method, it implies making use of a few devices such as programmed learning, team teaching, micro-teaching, personalized system of instruction, etc.

As materials, it comprises instructional materials, comprising programmed text-books, manuals, guides, text and other written/

print materials, which expose to the learner the contents of these sources of materials.

As media, it implies audio or visual or both audio-visual media such as radio, tape recorders, films, educational television as teaching aids to supplement effective teaching and to promote better learning.

Whatever be the method, material or media, it requires manpower to operate/ utilise in the teaching learning environment. Thus, the four M's constitute a whole sequence of chains of; inputs/ facilities in teaching technology.

Micro-teaching

Micro-teaching is a significant effort to make teacher education/training programme more effective and meaningful than the traditional programme by making it more scientific. Recent researches in advanced countries in the area of classroom teaching have proved that classroom teaching may be objectively analysed and modified according to the requirements, to develop teaching skills and competencies in the student-teachers and even in in-service teachers. Micro-teaching is one of the important innovations in this direction. It is a controlled practice that makes it possible to concentrate on various aspects of teaching behaviour in the student-teaching training programme. Micro-teaching is a training programme that aims at simplifying the complexities of the teaching process.

Following definitions of micro-teaching throw a lot of light on the meaning and significance of micro-teaching.

Allen, D. W. **(1966).** Micro-teaching is a scaled down teaching encounter in class size and class time.

***Allen, D. W. and Eve, A. W.* (1968).** Micro-teaching is defined as a system of controlled practice that makes it possible to concentrate on specified teaching behaviour and to practise teaching under controlled conditions.

Bush, R. N. **(1968).** Micro-teaching is a teacher education technique which allow teachers to apply clearly defined teaching skills to carefully prepared lessons in a planned series of five to ten minutes encounter with a small group of real students, often with an opportunity to observe the result on video-tape.

Clift, J. C. and Others **(1976).** Micro-teaching is a teacher training programme which reduces the teaching situation to a simpler and more controlled encounter achieved by limiting the practice teaching to a specific skill and reducing time and class size.

Encyclopedia on Education. (Ed. Deighton, L. C :- 1971). Micro-teaching is a real, constructed, scaled down teaching encounter which is used for teacher training, curriculum development and research.

Flanders, Ned. A. **(1960).** Micro-teaching programme is organised to expose the trainees to an organised curriculum of miniature teaching encounters, moving from the less complex to the more complex.

Jangira, N. K. Singh, Ajit **(1982).** Micro-teaching is a scaled down teaching encounter or miniatured classroom teaching.

M.L. Alease, W. R. and Unwin D **(1970).** The term micro-teaching is most often applied to the use of closed circuit television to give immediate feed-back of a trainee teacher's performance in a simplified environment.

Passi, B. K. and Lalita, M. S. **(1976).** Micro-teaching is a training technique which requires student teachers to teach a single concept using specified teaching skill to a small number of pupils in a short duration of time.

Singh, L.C. **(1977).** Micro-teaching is a scaled down teaching encounter in which a teacher teaches a small unit to a group of five pupils for a short period of 5 to 20 minutes. Such a situation offers a helpful setting for an experienced or inexperienced teacher to acquire new teaching skills and to refine old ones.

Chief Objectives of Micro-Teaching

These are as under:

1. To enable the teacher-trainees to learn and assimilate new teaching skills under controlled conditions.
2. To enable the teacher-trainees to gain confidence in teaching by mastering a number of teaching skills on a small group of students.
3. To make use of the academic potential of teacher-trainees for providing much needed feedback.

4. To derive maximum advantage with the available material, money and time.

Real Teaching

'Scaling down' is a key word in micro teaching. In micro-teaching procedure, the trainee is engaged in a scaled down teaching situation. It is scaled down in terms of class size, since the trainee is teaching a small group of four to six pupils. The lesson is scaled down in length of class time and is reduced to five or ten minutes. It is also scaled down in terms of teaching tasks. These tasks may include: the practising and mastering of a specific teaching skill such as lecturing, questioning or leading a discussion; mastering of specific teaching strategies; flexibility; instructional decision-making; alternative uses of specific curricula, instructional materials and classroom management.

The short lesson is recorded on an audio or video-tape recorder and the trainee gets to hear and see himself immediately after the lesson. The pupils who attend the lesson are asked to fill in rating questionnaires evaluating specific aspects of the lesson The trainee's own analysis of the lesson based on the authentic feedback from the tape together with the pupils' reaction and a supervisor's analysis and suggestions, assist the trainee in restructuring the lesson, which he then immediately re-teaches to a new group of pupils. Further assessments by the leaner and the supervisor leads to further improvements when the trainee teaches again, either immediately after or several days later. This micro-teaching sequence is practised usually in a micro-teaching laboratory in a teacher-training institution, or an in-service training programme in regular schools. (Fig.)

Micro-Lesson Plan

Teach	Re-Teach
Micro-Lesson	Another Group
Discuss Feed Back	Replan

Fig. : Micro-teaching cycle.

Three volunteers from the participants the teachers' roles in front of VTR camera and other participants also take part of pupils' improved, three volunteers teach other participants again. The comparison is made between two teaching traits in each teacher on the evaluation sheet. (see Fig.)

Planning for 5 min. teaching

Micro-Teaching (I)
5 min. each, 3 Teachers

Video

Discussion with Video Play-back
3 Teachers

Evaluation Sheet

Replanning
Micro-Teaching (2) 5 min.

Self-Confirmation

Fig. : Micro-teaching flow chart.

Main Propositions of Micro Teaching. Allen and Ryan in their book on the subject give the following main propositions of micro-teaching:

(1) Micro-teaching is real teaching, although a teaching situation is constructed in which the student-teacher and pupils work together in a practice situation. Bonafide teaching does take place.

(2) Micro-teaching lessens the complexities of normal classroom teaching. Class size, scope of content and time are all reduced.

(3) Micro-teaching focuses on training for the accomplishment of specific tasks. These tasks may be the practice of instructional skills, the practise of techniques of teaching, the mastery of certain curricular materials, or the demonstration of teaching methods.

(4) Micro-teaching allows for the increased control of practice. In a micro-teaching setting, the time, number of pupils, methods of feedback and supervision, etc., may be manipulated.

(5) Micro-teaching greatly expands the normal knowledge of results of feedback dimensions in teaching. Immediately after teaching a brief micro-lesson, the trainee is engaged in a critique of his performance. All this feedback can be immediately translated into practice when the trainee re-teaches shortly after the critique conference.

Two related areas can be pointed out where there are clear advantages: (i) training in teaching skill, (ii) research in teacher training.

According to J. C. Clift and others, micro-teaching procedure has three phases; (i) Knowledge acquisition face (ii) Skill acquisition face and (iii) Transfer phase.

N. K. Jangira and Ajit Singh present these phases as under:

Knowledge Acquisition Phase. In this phase, the student-teacher attempts to acquire knowledge about the skill—its rational, its role in classroom and its component behaviours. For this he reads relevant literature. He also observes demonstration lesson—mode of presentation of the skill (modelling). The student-teacher gets theoretical as well as practical knowledge of the skill.

Skill Acquisition Phase. On the basis of the model presented to the student-teacher, he prepares a micro-lesson and practises the skill and carries out the micro-teaching cycle. There are two components of this phase: feedback and micro-teaching setting. Micro-teaching setting includes conditions like size of the micro-class, duration of the micro-lesson, supervisor, types of students etc.

Transfer Phase. Here the student-teacher integrates the different skills. In place of artificial situation, he teaches in the real classroom and tries to integrate all the skills.

Different Levels

The three phases involve certain steps which are given as under:

1. Orientation of the student-teachers to the micro-teaching programme.
2. Discussing teaching skills.
3. Selection of a particular skill.
4. Presenting of a model demonstration lesson on a particular skill.
5. Observation of the model skill by student-teachers and recording their observations on the observation schedule.
6. Critical appreciation of the model lesson by students teachers.
7. Creation of a micro-teaching setting. The Indian Model of Micro-Teaching developed by NCERT gives the following setting:
   (*a*) Number of student-teachers 5-10.
   (*b*) Type of pupils.
   (*c*) Type of supervisor : teacher educators and peers.
   (*d*) Duration of a micro-lesson : 6 minutes.
   (*e*) Duration of a micro-teaching cycle: 36 minutes
8. Practising the skill.
9. Providing feedback.
10. Replanning.
11. Reteaching.
12. Providing re-feed back.
13. Integration of teaching skills.

Assessment Process

Merits of Micro-Teaching. Following are the main advantages of micro-teaching.

1. Superior performance of student teachers on micro-teaching.
2. Training in real teaching.
3. Increased control of practise.
4. Accomplishment of specific skills.
5. Availability of immediate feedback.
6. Helpful in solving some of the problems involved in student teaching.

7. Helpful in the transfer of general teaching competence to classroom teaching.
8. Helpful in building up confidence of the pupil-teacher step by step.
9. Availability of feedback from different sources: (i) Feedback by the supervising educator (ii) Feedback by the peer group (iii) Feedback through audio and video-tape recording.
10. Micro lesson preparing the way for macro lesson.
11. Teaching under simulated conditions.
12. Provision of many opportunities to the teacher trainees to observe the derived patterns of behaviour.
13. Lessening the complexities of the normal classroom teaching by 'scaling down teaching'.
14. Facilitating the combination of a number of teaching devices.

Limitations of Micro-Teaching. Important limitations are:

1. Micro-teaching is skill-oriented at the cost of content-orientation.
2. Broad-based patterns of behaviour are not paid their due attention.
3. Scope of developing micro-teaching skills is limited.
4. Micro-teaching does not take into consideration the overall environment of teaching.

The Acceptance

It should be borne in mind that howsoever excellent the innovation of micro-teaching may be, it should be adopted and practised according to the needs and conditions of the Indian teacher-education system. The number of untrained teachers, number of student teachers admitted to colleges of education, the staff pattern, the curricular demand and the resources available in the colleges are to be taken into account. Absence of technological devices is also a deterrent to the introduction of micro-teaching. But the experts say that micro-teaching can be adopted even without technical sophistication, without a TV network or a tape-recorder. The 'micro' and 'laboratory' elements are the really important ones. The only problem in developing countries, today, is to train teams of teachers, educators and supervisors who will be able to introduce this innovation in their colleges and school systems.

The salient features of Indian Model of Micro-Teaching as developed by NCERT are:

1. The mode of presenting the skill i.e. modelling is done through written material: lectures, demonstration and discussion and not through films, Video, CCTV as in the case of the advanced technology models of micro-teaching followed in USA and U K and other countries.
2. Live observers are used to observe teaching for providing feeback to the student teachers in the Indian mode, while CCTV is used in the developed countries. Peer supervisors are used along with college supervisors.
3. The micro-teaching laboratory can function with minimum of facilities according to the available space, material and equipment. Feedback sessions can be organised even in corridors or in open space.
4. The duration of the micro-teaching cycle is as under:

Teach	6 minutes
Feedback	6 minutes
Replan	12 minutes
Reteach	6 minutes
Re-feed back	6 minutes
Total	36 minutes

Micro-Teaching and Macro-Teaching. Micro-teaching is a technique of imparting training to would-be-teachers in the art of teaching by practising specific teaching skills through scaled down teaching encounter i.e. reducing the complexities of teaching in terms of the size of the class, time and content. By macro-teaching we mean the teaching in regular classes consisting of 40 or more students for 5 minutes. In macro-teaching all the skills of teaching are to be integrated.

16

Tools for Teaching

Developments in teaching and learning materials reflect wider societal and technological advances. The latter half of the twentieth century has witnessed a massive expansion in technological advancements that began cautiously with radio and television and which, via language laboratories and calculators, have now developed into the World Wide Web and the information superhighway. These technological wonders have been adopted by teachers in classrooms and lecture halls with the aim of enhancing the learning experience. Technological teaching and learning aids have assumed greater significance in recent years as one of the major developments that have dominated higher education teaching in the 1990s. We explore the perceptions of computer-assisted learning materials (CAL) from two perspectives: the students who attend the courses; and the tutors who design and teach the courses.

Basic Material

The teaching and learning materials evaluated form part of a suite of computer-aided learning materials known as GeotechniCAL. These have been developed as materials to support the teaching of geotechnical subjects within the syllabus of undergraduate degrees in Civil Engineering, and were funded through the UK Higher Education Funding Councils under the auspices of the Teaching and Learning Technology Programme (TLTP).

The GeotechniCAL project comprises five strands, the primary developers are the Universities of Durham, Glasgow, Portsmouth, South Bank and West of England. Details of each of the strands in the GeotechniCAL project can be found on the World Wide Web at http:// CL24.uwe.ac.uk/geocal/. Other universities (twenty-two in all) have been involved in small amounts of authoring and in the provision of feedback and formal evaluation of the materials.

This article considers the evaluations of two of these strands carried out at Durham University. The first study relates to evaluation of the ConFound package developed at Durham University. Students at Durham University were involved in the formative evaluation of this package. The second study relates to the Site Investigation package developed by South Bank and Portsmouth Universities. Again this was evaluated by Durham students but at a later stage in the development, near the end of the project.

It is important that the evaluation process is not viewed as a one-off exercise at the end of the project but as a continuing process and an integrative element of development, with this in mind, two evaluations were undertaken. Formative evaluations of the Geotechnical materials were carried out at an interim stage to provide feedback to the developers. Summative evaluations were carried out at the end of the project to identify whether the product was seen to be of direct use to users. Both students and tutors participated in the formative and summative evaluations.

Evaluation of Learners

Students are increasingly familiar with mechanisms for course monitoring, evaluations are a means of providing feedback to institutions, course providers and external auditing bodies, and hence students are generally amenable to participating in evaluation processes.

Rather than using whole classes of students as evaluators it can sometimes be more useful to select a small representative group who can provide more detailed feedback. This is particularly true at the stage of formative evaluation when specific feedback to the developers is needed to help them to improve their product. The establishment of a core group of evaluators is particularly important if there are several pieces of software to be compared and evaluated. This core group can also identify whether changes that have been made as a result of previous feedback have been beneficial.

Although it is not always easy to arrange, it was felt important that the student evaluations should be carried out by an independent evaluation coordinator who was unknown to the students. This is one way in which the evaluation of the materials can be separated from other elements such as the course(s), the tutor(s), the assessment of the student's personal knowledge of the subject and of their general progress. That is not to suggest that these are equally important elements of learning that need to be monitored and evaluated, but they are different and to combine them with the evaluation of the CAL materials may cause confusion. The independent evaluation had the additional advantage of allowing students to make critical observations about the learning materials, and to offer insights that they may have felt impeded in offering to known tutors. In this case study, the first author was able to fulfil the role of independent evaluation coordinator.

Temporary Evaluations

For the interim evaluations of the ConFound package at Durham University a core group of eight student evaluators was established. Of the eight students, there were three females and five males. They represented two sub-groups, one group that described themselves as comparatively experienced software users and the other that described themselves as less experienced. Neither group, however, were novices in the use of computers.

The students were identified by numbers (not names) to ensure anonymity. It was considered important to protect identities and to maintain the goodwill of the group so that they could be called upon again, at a later stage, to evaluate this and other pieces of software during the course of the GeotechniCAL project. Not identifying the students by name also stressed that the evaluation exercise was in no way connected with any assessment of their personal knowledge of the subject or of their general progress.

Basic Arguments

The Geotechnical initiative was outlined to the student evaluators. Their role and the reasons that lay behind the various aspects of the evaluation were explained and discussed. This provided the group, and individuals within the group, with the opportunity to ask questions for clarification of particular points and helped to forge group identity.

Knowledge of the Topic

A pre-test of the subject knowledge that the software aims to teach was carried out, using a multiple choice questions test. The Durham test comprised nine multiple choice questions. After completing the test the students were then given a further copy of the test, to complete while using the software. This helped the students and the teachers to assess the subject knowledge content of the software under evaluation.

Utility of Software

The students were given the opportunity to use the software. The learning objective set was to obtain the knowledge required to resist the test. This gave a focus to their use of the software. The students were allowed to spend as long as they wanted using the software, However, to avoid demotivation, the test was designed so that it was feasible to obtain the necessary information in a session lasting approximately one hour. In fact, students chose to spend between 60 and 90 minutes with the software.

Questionnaire for Examination

The students were asked to complete the standard evaluation form developed for use within the GeotechniCAL project.

The evaluation questionnaire was designed to elicit both quantitative and qualitative information. It is based on an earlier questionnaire produced by Dr. Les Davison, coordinator of the GeotechniCAL project. The form used at Durham invites responses on a four point scale to 30 statements grouped under the headings:

- Background (information about the learner);
- Documentation (the documentation supporting the software);
- Content (the level of detail of the subject knowledge of the topic);

- Usability;
- Presentation (of the material);
- General (other general aspects).

The reverse side of the form provides opportunities for qualitative responses under the headings: I particularly liked; I did not like; My suggestions for improvement; and Any other comments.

Interviews to Supplement

A semi-structured interview format was used R group interviews. They typically lasted between 21 and 30 minutes. The interviews were recorded using an audio-tape recorder. The following headings were used to guide the discussion:

- For how long did you use the software ?
- Would you like a teacher/technician present when you use this software ?
- Do you think other members of your course would use this software?
- What did you particularly like about the software?
- Can you make suggestions for improvement?
- Are there features you would like to have included?
- How easy was it to use this software? What precise difficulties did you have?
- Could you understand all of the questions in the questionnaires?
- How helpful was the supporting documentation?
- What other documentation would you have liked?
- Would you prefer to use software, read a book/ do library work or attend a lecture?

These questions were not asked in any particular order.

Information Imparted

It was considered important to provide some feedback to the evaluation group, as quickly as possible. Feedback helps to sustain interest and motivation and ensure continued involvement in the project. At the time of the follow-up interview the students were provided with a set of the correct answers alongside which they could compare their own responses on the subject knowledge multiple choice test. They were also sent a copy of the evaluation report.

The process of summative evaluation followed a different pattern.

After each session using the GeotechniCAL software the student evaluators were interviewed in a group. These follow-up interviews provide a very valuable enhancement to the information gathered from the questionnaires. In discussion some students felt able to provide more specific examples of the points they made in the written feedback. Others took the opportunity to make comments and suggestions that they did not wish to commit to paper. There was also the intellectual stimulation of ideas that a group discussion precipitates. The ideas generated in this way would have been lost if students had been confined to responding to questionnaires and written responses individually.

Evaluations : Summative Way

This section describes an evaluation of the Site Investigation module within the GeotechniCAL suite. The module was evaluated at Durham University with a combined group of final year MEng students following civil engineering options and MSc students following courses in Engineering Geology and Geo-Environmental Engineering. The group consisted of 5 females and 40 males.

Site Investigation is a topic which is taught jointly to the MEng and MSc courses at Durham University.

This would normally have been delivered as a 19 hour lecture course. On this occasion, a three hour supervised CAL session was arranged in place of three hours of lectures. Prior to the session the students had received only one lecture as a basic introduction to the topic. No introduction to the CAL materials was given in the lecture. Instructions to the students at the start of the CAL session were kept to a minimum; they were only instructed which icon to click on. They were then told to work through the tutorial materials until they felt sufficiently confident to attempt the game element of the package. No paper-based documentation was provided, but a lecturer and a demonstrator were on hand throughout the session to respond to student queries. The students were asked to complete the standard evaluation form developed for use within the GeotechniCAL project. Forty-two of the 45 students returned evaluation forms at the end of the CAL session.

Details of the outcomes of the evaluation have been reported by Thompson and Toll. The majority of the students were very positive about the package, preferred it to alternative forms of learning and indicated a clear willingness to spend more time using it. They did identify the need for more guidance and reported that they found the quantity of information difficult to assimilate. However they liked the pictures and video clips; the interactive nature of the software; the humour the 'ease of use and the simulation of a 'real life' situation.

The results of the evaluation were fed back to the student group in a subsequent lecture. Since the evaluation had been so positive, and the majority of students had identified a willingness to spend more time with the package, the option was put to the students that a further three hour CAL session could be arranged in place of three lecture hours. The students were asked to vote for another CAL session with a show of hands. Perhaps surprisingly in view of the comments made in the evaluations, not one student voted in favour of this option. When asked to vote against, 37 of the 45 students raised their hands. Therefore, although they liked the software, found it more interesting than lectures and wanted to spend more time using it, the students clearly did not want it to replace lectures. From the comments on the evaluation forms it was clear they would be prepared to use the software in their own time, or in parallel with the lectures. They felt that conventional lectures provided them with a better means to achieve their main aim of acquiring a set of structured notes for revision purposes.

Evaluations through Teachers

It has already been noted that twenty-two universities were involved in the Geotechnical project, although only five were the primary developers. Tutors from universities other than the developers were involved in the evaluations. In many ways these can be seen as untypical examples of tutors who teach in engineering departments because their involvement in the project indicated a commitment to the use and development of CAL materials. However, they represented an expert view and bad not been closely involved in the development. This group comprised old and new universities, with students from diverse backgrounds on a range of undergraduate and postgraduate courses, including BSc/BEng, MEng and MSc courses.

At the formative evaluation stages of the ConFound package, two tutors were sent copies of the software and a tutor questionnaire. They were asked to complete the questionnaire and/or to provide comments on the software in free format based on their own perceptions of the software. Their comments generally covered half to one A4 page.

At the summative stage, the tutors were asked to provide more detailed feedback on the software after having used it with a group of students. They were asked to comment on their own perceptions and also how successful they felt the software had been when used with students. They were again sent the tutor questionnaire to complete, but were also asked to provide an additional detailed report. The tutor evaluators used the headings on the questionnaire (Documentation, Content, Usability, Presentation, Potential uses) as sub-headings in their reports. These were typically 6 pages in length.

Audio-Visual Aids

Audio-Visual aids, audio-visual material, audio-visual media, communication technology, educational or instructional media and learning resources — all these terms, broadly speaking, mean the same thing. Earlier the term used was audio-visual aids in education. With the advancement in the means of communication and that of technology, educators coined new terms, More specifically media refers to films, filmstrips, recordings, etc. The use of newer terms Educational Technology or Instructional Technology is primarily due to the dynamic expansion of programmed learning, computer assisted instruction and education T.V. This revolution in the field of audio-visual education is the outcome of the development in electronics, notably those involving the radio, tape recorder and computer.

Brief history of the use of Audio-visual aids. A Dutch humanist, theologian and writer Desiderious Erasmus (1466-1536) discouraged memorization as a technique of learning and advocated that children should learn through the aid of pictures or other visuals. John Amos Comenius (1592-1670) prepared a book known as *Orbis Sensulium Pictus.* (The world of Sense Objects) which contained about 150 pictures on aspects of everyday life. The book is considered to be the first illustrated textbook for childhood education. This book gained wide publicity and was used in childhood education centres all over the world. Jean Jacques Rousseau (1712-1778) and other educators stressed the need of pictures and other play materials. Rousseau condemned the use of words by teachers and he stressed 'things'. He pleaded that the teaching process must be directed to the learner's natural curiosity. Pestalozzi (1756-1827) put Rousseau's theory into action in his 'object method'. He based instruction on sense perception.

The term 'Visual education' was used as early as 1926 by Lelson.I.Green.

Eric Ashby (1967) identified four revolutions in education: education from home to school, written words as tool of education, invention of printing and use of books and lastly the fourth revolution in the use of electronic media i.e., radio, television, tape recorder and computer in education.

Burton : Audio-visual aids are those sensory objects or images which initiate or stimulate and reinforce learning.

Carter V. Good : audio-visual aids are those aids which help in completing the triangular process of learning i.e., motivation, classification and stimulation.

Edgar Dale : Audio-visual are those devices by the use of which communication of ideas between persons and groups in various teaching and training situations is helped. These are also termed as multi-sensory materials.

Good's Dictionary of Education : Audio-visual aids are anything by means of which learning process may be encouraged or carried on through the sense of hearing or sense of sight.

Kinder, S. James : Audio-visual aids are any device which can be used to make the learning experience more concrete, more realistic and more dynamic.

Mckown and Roberts: Audio-visual aids are supplementary devices by which the teacher, through the utilization of more than one sensory channels is able to clarify, establish and correlate concepts, interpretations and appreciations.

Audio-visual aids or devices or technological media or learning devices are added devices that help the teacher to clarify, establish, co-relate and co-ordinate accurate concepts, interpretations and appreciations and enable him to make learning more concrete, effective, interesting, inspirational, meaningful and vivid. They help in completing the triangular process of learning viz., motivation-clarification-stimulation. The aim of teaching with technological media is 'clearing the channel between the learner and the things that are worth learning'. The basic assumption underlying Audio-visual Aids is that learning—clear understanding—stems from sense experience. The teacher must 'show' as well as 'tell'. Audio-visual aids provide significant gains in informational learning, retention and recall, thinking and reasoning, activity, interest, imagination, better assimilation and personal growth and development. The aids are the stimuli for learning 'why', 'how', 'when' and 'where'. The 'hard to understand principles' are usually made clear by the intelligent use of skilfully designed instructional aids.

According to Gandhiji, "True education of the intellect can only come through a proper exercise and training of bodily organs—hands, feet, eyes, ears and nose."

Commenting on the use of audio-visual aids, the Kothari Commssion 1964-66 observed that it should indeed bring about an 'educational revolution' in the country. It further stated that the supply of teaching aids to every school was essential for the improvement of the quality of teaching.

The National Policy of Education, 1986 and as modified in 1992 has laid a great stress on the use of teaching aids, especially improvised aids, to make teaching-learning more effective and realistic.

In the words of Edgar Dale, "Because audio-visual materials supply concrete basis for conceptual thinking, they give rise to meaningful concepts enriched by meaningful association, hence they offer the best antidote for the disease of verbalism."

Some of the important values of the proper use of audio-visual aids are given below:

Antidote to the disease of verbal instruction. They help to reduce verbalism. They help in giving clear concepts and thus help to bring accuracy in learning. As observed by Raymound Wyman (1957) "We (teacher) tell students, and we provide them with written material so much of the time. Words are wonderful. They are easily produced, reproduced, stored and transported.

But the overuse or excessive use of words can result in serious problem, chiefly, the problem of verbalism (using or adopting words or phrases without considering what they mean) and forgetting."

Best motivation. They are the best motivators. The students work with more interest and zeal. They are more attentive.

Clear images. Clear images are formed when we see, hear, touch, taste and smell as our experiences are direct, concrete and more or less permanent. Learning through the senses becomes the most natural and consequently the easiest.

Vicarious experience. It is beyond doubt that the first-hand experience is the best type of educative experience. But it is neither practicable nor desirable to provide such experience to pupils. Substituted experiences may be provided under such conditions. There are many inaccessible objects and phenomena. For example, it is not possible for the pupils living in India to see the Eskimoe. Similary, it is not possible for an average man to climb the Mount Everst. There are innumerable such things to which it is not possible to have direct access. So, in all such cases, these aids help us.

Variety. 'Mere chalk and talk' do not help. Audio-visual aids give variety and provide different tools in the hands of the teacher.

Freedom. When audio-visual aids are employed, there is great scope for children to move about, talk, laugh and comment upon. Under such an atmosphere the students work because they want to work and not because the teacher wants them to work.

Opportunities to handle and manipulate. Many visual aids offer opportunities to students to handle and manipulate things.

Retentivity. Audio-visual aids contribute to increased retentivity as they stimulate response of the whole organism to the situation in which learning takes place.

Based on maxims of teaching. The use of audio-visual aids enables the teacher to follow the maxims of teaching like 'concrete to abstract', 'known to unknown' and 'learning by doing.'

Helpful in attracting attention. Attention is the true factor in any process of teaching and learning. Audio-visual aids help the teacher in providing proper environment for capturing as well as sustaining the attention and interest of the students in the classroom work.

Helpful in fixing up new learning. 'What is gained in terms of learning, needs to be fixed up in the minds of students. Audiovisual aids help in achieving this objective by providing several activities, experiences and stimuli to the learners'.

Saving of energy and time. A good deal of energy and time of both the teachers and students can be saved on account of the use of audio-visual aids as most of the concepts and phenomena may be easily clarified, understood and assimilated through their use.

Realism. The use of audio-visual aids provides a touch of reality to the learning situation. By seeing a film show exhibiting the life of the people of the Tundra region, students learn it more effectively in about 2 hours than by spending weeks by reading.

Vividness. Audio-visual aids give vividness to the learning situation. A film on Buddha provides a vivid picture of his life and teachings.

Meeting individual differences. There are wide individual differences among learners. Some are ear-oriented, some can be helped through visual demonstrations, while others learn better by doing. The use of a variety of audio-visual aids helps in meeting the needs of different types of students.

Encouragement to healthy classroom interaction. Audio-visual aids, through their wide variety of stimuli, provision of active participation of the students, and vicarious experiences encourage healthy classroom interaction for the effective realization of teaching-learning objectives.

Spread of education on a mass scale. Audio-visaul. aids like radio and television help in providing opportunities for education to people living in remote areas. They also help in promoting adult education.

Promotion of scientific temper. In place of listening to facts, students observe demonstrations and phenomena and thus cultivate scientific temper.

Development of higher faculties. Verbalism promotes memorisation. Use of audio-visual aids stirs the imagination, thinking process and reasoning power of the students, and calls for creativity, and inventiveness and other higher mental activities on the parts of students and thus helps the development of higher faculties among the students.

Reinforcement to learners. Audio-visual aids prove effective reinforcers by increasing the probability of re-occurance of the response associated with them and thus render valuable help in the teaching-learning process.

Positive transfer of learning and training. Use of audio-visual aids helps in the learning of other concepts, principles and solving the real problems of life by making possible the appropriate positive transfer of learning and training received in the classroom.

Positive environment for creative discipline. A balanced, rational and scientific use of audio-visual aids develops motivation, attracts the attention and interests of the students and provides a variety of creative outlets for the utilisation of their tremendous energy and thus keeps them busy in the classroom work. In this way, the overall classroom environment becomes conducive to creative discipline.

Aids Utility

In addition to reading, vicarious experience can be gained from still pictures, films, filmstrips, resource persons, simulations, mockups, television, and the like. The more concrete and realistic the vicarious experience, the more nearly it approaches the learning effectiveness of the first level. Of course, unless the learner realizes that he is dealing with a substitute, his learning may not be comparable to that of real-life learning.

Interest in the role of the senses in learning was already there in educational circles when instructional media began their ascendancy. It has long been recognized that the various senses condition the reception of messages in the communications act. Research done by Cobun (1968) indicated that:

1 per cent of what is learned is from the sense of TASTE.

1.5 per cent of what is learned is from the sense of TOUCH.

3.5 per cent of what is learned is from the sense of SMELL.

11 per cent of what is learned is from the sense of HEARING.

83 per cent of what is learned is from the sense of SIGHT.

Retention of what is learned is likewise related to sense experience.

Observation and research by Cobun tended to show, holding time as nearly constant as possible, that people generally remember:

10 per cent of what they READ.
20 per cent of what they HEAR.
30 Per cent of what they SEE.
50 per cent of what they HEAR AND SEE.
70 per cent of what they SAY.
90 per cent of what they SAY as they do a thing.

Popular Sayings

I hear, I forget.
I see, I remember.
I do, I understand.

Characteristics

1. They should be meaningful and purposeful.
2. They should be accurate in every respect.
3. They should be simple.
4. They should be cheap.
5. As far as possible, they should be improvised.
6. They should be large enough to be properly seen by the students for whom they are meant.
7. They should be up-to date.
8. They should be easily portable.
9. They should be according to the mental level of the students.
10. They should motivate the learners.

Principle of selection. Teaching aids prove effective only when they suit the teaching objectives and unique characteristics of the special group of learners. Following points may be kept in view in this regard :

(i) They should suit the age-level, grade-level and other characteristics of the learners.
(ii) They should have specific educational value besides being interesting and motivating.
(iii) They should be the true representatives of the real things.
(iv) They should help in the realization of desired learning objectives.

Principle of preparation. This principle requires that following points should be attended to:

(a) As far as possible, locally available material should be used in the preparation of an aid.

(b) The teachers should receive some training in the preparation of aids.

(c) The teachers themselves should prepare some of the aids.

(d) Students may be associated in the preparation of aids.

Preparation of physical control. This principle related to the arrangement of keeping aids safely and also to facilitate their lending to the teachers for use.

Principle of proper presentation. This principle implies the following pioits :

(i) Teachers should carefully visualise the use of teaching aids before their actual presentation.

(ii) They should fully acquaint themselves with the use and manipulation of the aids to be shown in the classroom.

(iii) Adequate care should be taken to handle an aid in such a way as no damage is done to it.

(iv) The aid should be displayed properly so that all the students are able to see it, observe it and derive maximum benefit out of it.

(v) As far as possible, distraction of all kinds to be eliminated so that full attention may be paid to the aid.

Principle of response. This principle demands that the teachers guide the students to respond actively to the audio-visual stimuli so that they derive the maximum benefit in learning.

Principle of evaluation. This principle stipulates that there should be continuous evaluation of both the audio-visual material and accompanying techniques in the light of the realisation of the desired objectives.

While all these aids are becoming more and more popular day by day, there are still some problems to be faced and solved. These are :

Apathy of the teachers. Teachers in general are yet to be convinced that teaching with words alone is very tedious, wasteful and ineffective.

The Classification

Classification Number 1: Projected and Non-Projected Aids

Projected Aids	*Graphic Aids*	*Display Boards*	*3-Dimensional Aids*	*Audio Aids*	*Activity Aids*
1. Films	1. Cartoons	Blackboard	Diagrams	Radio	1. Computer-Assisted Instruction
2. Filmstrips	2. Charts	Bulletin	Models	Recordings	2. Demonstrations
3. Opaque Projector	3. Comics	Flannel Board	Mockups	Television	3. Dramatics
4. Overhead Projector	4. Diagrams	Magnetic Board	Objects		4. Experimentation
5. Slides	5. Flash Cards	Peg Board	Puppets		5. Field Trips
	6. Graphs		Specimens		6. Programmed Instruction
	7. Maps				7. Teaching Machines
	8. Photographs				
	9. Pictures				
	10. Posters				

Classification Number 2: Audio Materials, Visual Materials and Audio-Visual Materials

Audio Materials	*Visual Materials*	*Audio-visual Materials*
(1) Language Laboratories	(1) Bulletin boards	(1) Demonstrations
(2) Radio	(2) Chalk boards	(2) Films
(3) Sound distribution system sets	(3) Charts	(3) Printed materials with recorded sound
(4) Tape and disco recordings	(4) Drawings etc.	(4) Sound filmstrips
	(5) Exhibits	(5) Study trips
	(6) Film strips	(6) Television
	(7) Flash cards	(7) Videotapes
	(8) Flannel boards	
	(9) Flip books	
	(10) Illustrated books	
	(11) Magnetic boards	
	(12) Maps	
	(13) Models	
	(14) Pictures	
	(15) Posters	
	(16) Photographs	
	(17) Self-instructional	
	(18) Silent films	
	(19) Slides	

Indifference of students. The judicious use of aids arouses interest but when used without a definite purpose they lose their significance and importance.

Ineffectiveness of the aids. Due to the absence of proper planning and the lethargy of the teacher and without proper preparation, correct presentation, application and discussion and the essential follow-up work, the aids do not prove their full usefulness. A film like a good lesson has various steps—Preparation, Presentation, Application and Discussion.

Financial hurdles. The Central and State Governments have set up Boards of Audio-Visual Education and have chalked out interesting programmes for the popularization of teaching aids but the lack of finances is not enabling them to do their best.

Absence of electricity. Most of the Projectors, Radio and TV cannot work without the electric current which is not available in a large number of schools.

Lack of facilities for training. Training colleges or specialised agencies should make special provision to train teachers and workers in the use of these aids.

Co-ordination between Centre and States. Good film libraries, museums of audio-visual provision to train teachers and workers in the use of these aids.

Language difficulty. Most educational films are in English. We should have these in Hindi and other important Indian languages.

Not catering to local needs. Little attention is paid in the production of audio-visual aids to the local sociological, psychological and pedagogical factors.

Improper selection of films. Films are not selected according to the classroom needs.

Today, the problem is not whether visual aids should have a place in education. Their place has been recognised long ago. The problem, now, is that of extending the benefits of these aids to all teachers and all children. The future can be bright if there is proper planning on the part of the Government and co-ordination between producers, teachers and students. Useful and effective aids can be produced after getting the reaction of the audience and doing research work in the field. A great deal is being done already but a lot more still remains to be done.

Big Media and Little Media

Big media include computer, VCR and TV. Little media include radio, films strips, graphic, audio cassettes and various visuals.

Three Dimensional Aids

(i) Models
(ii) Mock-ups
(iii) Specimens.

Three dimensional aids are the replicas or substitutes of real objects.

All the learning experiences which can be utilised for classroom teaching are shown by Edgar Dale in a pictorial device—'pinnacle form'—which he called the 'cone of experience'. If we go up the pinnacle from its base, we find that every aid has been arranged in the order of increasing abstractness or decreasing directness. In a simple language, it may be stated that the 'cone' classifies the audiovisual aids according to their effectiveness in communication—aid at the base of the cone as 'most effective'—relative effect gradually decreases.

At the pinnacle of the 'Cone', the direct, purposeful experiences are represented. At the pinnacle of the 'Cone', the verbal symbols are represented.

The experiences included in the cone are as indicated below:

Direct, purposeful experience. The experiences gained through the senses are direct and purposeful. It has been amply observed, "An ounce of experience is better than a tonne of theory, simply because it is only as an experience that any theory has vital and verifiable significance." This, direct experience is gained through the aids mentioned at the base of the cone.

Contrived experience. When the real thing cannot be perceived directly, its simplification becomes necessary. Contrived experience is like a working model which is an editing of reality and differs from the original either in size or in complexity. The real object may be too small or too big, may be confused or concealed. In such a situation imitation is preferred for better and easier understanding.

Dramatic participation. In dramatics, certain real events are presented through the play, the pageant (kind of community drama, usually based on local history), pantomine (actors do not speak, make movements), tablean (pictureline scene in which the characteristics stand still, silently), and the puppets.

Actual Objects. Actual objects and specimens are indispensable in science and other subjects. They are very vivid and impressive. They make a direct appeal to the senses of children. It is not possible for a child to have a clear picture of a river, a factory or a mountain unless he has seen these. The teaching of history and geography can never be effective without visitsing places of importance, valleys, lakes, old forts, monuments, etc. The students get a correct idea of various minerals when they are shown these objects. In framing the multiplication table, counting of beads and sticks prove to be very useful at the earlier stages.

Blackboard. Blackboard and a piece of chalk prove very helpful in illustrating concepts and ideas to the students. These can be used for drawing diagrams and sketches, etc. Blackboard is a simple and unique device which, in spite of new devices and techniques in teaching, is irreplacable as well as indispensable. It is the oldest and the best friend of a teacher. It is the mirror through which students visualise all about the teacher's mind regarding the lesson in hand, his way of explaining, illustrating and teaching as a whole. It is the cheapest teaching device and continues to be the '*sine quo non*' of our educational system. It is the most universally used aid. Writing on clay and sand was the ancient form of blackboard writing. It helps 'crystallizing' the main points, 'summarising' and 'reviewing'.

1. The teacher can illustrate the main points of the lesson on the blackboard.
2. Abstract statements can be clarified in the exposition stage and a summary containing the salient features can be given at the recapitulatory stage.
3. Questions and problems can be listed on the blackboard.
4. Pupils' interest in classwork can be stimulated by blackboard writings and drawings.
5. A teacher can use the blackboard for graphs, graphics, sketches, maps and statistics, etc.
6. A blackboard provides a lot of scope for creative and decorative work.

7. The teacher can erase writings and drawings and start afresh.
8. It helps the teacher to focus the attention of his students on the lesson. It takes heed of varying capacities and rates of grasp of the students.
9. A teacher can review the whole lesson for the benefit of the class with the help of the blackboard.

Types of Blackboards

Fixed blackboard. Fixed in the wall facing the class and normally made of wood or concrete cement.

Blackboard on easel. A portable and adjustable blackboard put on a wooden easel can be taken out of the classroom while taking classes in the open.

Roller blackboard. Made of thick canvas wrapped on a roller mostly used for teaching higher classes.

Graphic board. It has graphic lines and is used for teaching mathematics, science and statistics.

Magna board. A board which enables teachers to make three-dimensional demonstrations with objects on a vertical surface. Small magnets are used to hold suitable objects fixed wherever they are put on this vertical surface.

Chalk Boards of Different Types of Surfaces

1. Paint-coated pressed wood.
2. Dull finished plastic surface.
3. Vitreous-coated steel surface.
4. Ground glass board.

	Colour of the blackboard	*Colour of the chalk*
1.	Green chalk board	White or Yellow chalk
2.	Grey board	Yellow
3.	Red chalk board	Green, Yellow
4.	Orange chalk board	Blue or light Green
5.	Yellow chalk board	Blue
6.	Rose chalk board	Purple, dark Blue
7.	Black chalk board	Any colour

Effective Use of Blackboard

Following points may be kept in view while using the blackboard:

1. Blackboard should be kept clean so-that writing on it could be easily read by the students from all parts of the room.
2. Writing on the blackboard should be legible.
3. Letters and drawings should be large enough to be seen from all parts of the room.
4. Writing should be started from the top left corner.
5. Writing should be in straight rows.
6. Extreme lower corner of the blackboard should not be made use of as writing on it cannot be seen easily.
7. Material on the blackboard should not be covered by standing.
8. Only salient points of the subject-matter should be written on the blackboard.
9. Diagrammatic visual presentation involving many processes should be prepared before the beginning of the lesson.
10. It should be ensured that blackboard is well lighted by natural or artificial means.
11. Everything needed for the blackboard should be got together before the class begins *i,e.,* collection of chalk, rulers, T. Square, Compass, Projector, etc.
12. While writing on the blackboard, the teacher should ensure that the class is attentive.
13. Duster and not hand or handkerchief should be used in cleaning the blackboard.
14. Occasionally students may be asked to write or draw diagram on the blackboard.
15. Teachers should develop the ability to draw freely on the blackboard. The map or chart or diagram that grows before the very eyes of the students is much more useful and valuable than a well finished map, chart or diagram.

16. It should be ensured that the blackboard is periodically serviced.

A chart is a combination of pictorial, graphic, numerical or vertical material which presents a clear visual summary. The most commonly used types of charts include outline charts, tabular charts, flow charts and organisation charts. Other types of charts are technical diagrams and process diagrams. Flip charts and flow charts are also being used. Ready made charts are available for use in teaching in almost all areas in all subjects. But charts prepared by a teacher himself incorporating his own ideas and lines of approach of the specific topic are more useful.

Purposes of Charts

Charts serve the following purposes:

1. For showing relationship by means of facts, figures and statistics.
2. For presenting materials symbolically.
3. For summarising information.
4. For showing continuity in process.
5. For presenting abstract ideas in visual form.
6. For showing development of structure.
7. For creating problems and stimulating thinking.
8. For encouraging utilisation of other media of communication.
9. For motivating the students.

How to use Charts Effectively?

1. Teacher-made charts should be preferred.
2. Students should be involved in the preparation of charts.
3. Charts should be so large that every detail depicted should be visible to every pupil in the class wherever he is sitting.
4. Charts should display information only about one specific area in a subject.
5. A chart should not contain too much written material.
6. A chart should not contain too many details.
7. A chart should give a neat appearance.

8. When a chart is to be used in the classroom, the teacher should make sure that there is provision for hanging the chart at a vantage point.
9. The teacher should have a pointer to point out specific factors in the chart.
10. Straight pins, staples, pegboard lips, gummed hangers, paper-clips, folded making tapes may all be used for fastening charts without damaging them.
11. Charts should be carefully stored and preserved for use in future.

Types of Charts

The following is a list of basic types of charts in terms of arrangements and the kinds of ideas which they may express :

1. The narrative chart, an extended left-to-right arrangement of facts and ideas for expressing: *(a)* The events in a process such as shoe making, oil cracking, or the like, *(b)* The events in the development of a significant issue to its point of resolution or to present status (sometimes a time limit). Example: the events leading to the separation of the Bangladesh from Pakistan, the events leading to the establishment of the idea that an individual should be free and that he should have a voice in his own government and the events leading to increased regulation of business by government, *(c)* Techno-logical improvement over a period of years such as improvement in transportation, communication, manufacturing etc.
2. The tabulation chart, a left-to-right, top-to-bottom arrangement of facts and ideas for expression: *(a)* Numerical data for making comparisons, *(b)* Lists products, mountains, rivers, or the like in selected areas.
3. The cause and effect chart, usually a limited left-to-right arrangement of facts and ideas for expressing: *(a)* Relationship between standard of living and such factors as economic system, availability of natural resources, level of technological advance-ment, *(b)* Relationship between a culture and neighbouring cultures, *(c)* Relationship between rights and responsibilities, *(d)* Relationship

between a complex of conditions and change or conflict, *(e)* Relationship between the elected and the electors, (f) Relationship between community workers and the community which supports them.

4. The chain charts, a circular or semi-ircular arrangement of facts and ideas for expressing: *(a)* Transitions, such as the transition from raw materials to useful products, *(b)* Cycles, such as the water cycle.
5. The evolution chart, a left-to right arrangement of facts and ideas for expressing: *(a)* Changes in specific item from beginning to date, perhaps with projections into the future. Example: origin of the automobile and its subsequent development, early basic homes and changes in basic homes to date, *(b)* Change in standard in food consumption, length of work, weak purchasing power of a rupee, or the like.

Diagrams. Diagrams are very helpful in supplementing vertical illustrations in teaching. Difficult operations may be explained with the help of diagrams. The parts of a flower or leaf can be suitably explained by means of sketches drawn by the teacher in front of the class on the black-board: Simple diagrams can be used to explain different phenomena in geography and science. The diagrams of battle plans and forts can be drawn on the blackboard. The area and volume, etc., in mathematics can be illustrated through diagrams. A teacher is expected to possess the skill of drawing diagrams easily, neatly, rapidly and readily on the blackboard.

Epidiascope. The epidiascope is an instrument which can project images or printed matter or small opaque objects on a screen, or it can project images of a 4" X 4" slide. With the help of any epidiascope, any chart, diagram, map, photograph and picture can be projected on the screen without tearing it off from the book. No slide is needed for this purpose. An epidiascope serves two purposes. It works as epidiascope when it is used to project an opaque object. It works as epidiascope when it is used to project slides (by operating a lever). It works on the principle of horizontal straight line projection with a lamp, plane mirror and projection lens. A strong light from the lamp falls on the opaque object. A plane mirror placed at an angle of 45° over the project, reflects the light so that it passes through the projection lens forming a magnified image on the screen.

Film Strip. A film strip is 35 mm wide and has a series of 12 to 48 picture frames arranged in a sequence so that they develop a theme. A film strip can be prepared by taking a series of photographs using a 35 mm camera and then by taking a positive print of the negative film on another 35 mm film.

Globe. Knowledge of map is unreal without the knowledge of globe-the true map. It is the true representative of earth's physical personality. A globe gives a true idea of the total environment at a glance in a classroom situation. It is through globe that a child can understand the concepts of time, space, wind's planetary relations and proportion. Hence, every school shall have globes. Four types of globes may be kept in every school. (1) Political globes, (2) Physical globes, (3) Washable projection globes, (4) Celestial globes.

Graphs. Graphs are flat pictures which employ dots, lines or pictures to visualise numerical and statistical data to show relationships or statistics.

Several Types of Graphs

Line graph. In a line graph, data is represented with the help of simple lines horizontally or vertically drawn. For increasing the interest and readability of concepts, pictorial illustrations and cartoons are occasionally used on the line graph.

Bar graph. A bar graph consists of bars arranged, horizontally or vertically from a 'zero' base. The colour, length and size of the bars represent different values.

Circle graph. Data may be presented in a circle graph.

Magic Lantern. Magic lantern is the earliest invention in the history of audio-visual aids used for projecting pictures from a transparency (slide) on a wall or screen. When the figure or illustration is very small and it is required to be shown to the entire class, a transparent slide of the small figure is prepared. Then, this slide is placed into the slide carrier part of the magic lantern. This magic lantern device projects it on the screen by enlarging its dimension and making the vision more clear and sharp.

Significance of map study. In several subjects, especially social studies, the learning of many geographical, historical and economic concepts remains unreal, inadequate and incomplete without map media. A resourceful teacher by motivating the pupils will turn the fear of map into the genuine love for them. This, however, presupposes the invariable uses of maps at every possible opportunity by the teacher in the classroom, and the possession of individual atlases by the pupils. Every student should also know certain elementary aspects of map preparation such as copying, enlarging and reducing, symbolizing, colouring, and preparation of key. Most of the students develop an aversion to maps because they do not know skills relating to map preparation.

Meaning of Map. A map is an accurate representation of plain surface in the form of a diagram drawn to scale, the details of boundaries of continents, countries, of etc. Geographical details like location of mountains, rivers, altitude of a place, contours of the earth surface and important' locations can also be represented accurately with reference to a convenient scale with suitable colour scheme.

Identification of Various Aspects of Maps

1. Understanding and interpreting the key of index.
2. Understanding the lines-boundary lines, lines of communication, lines indicating the rivers, contours, meridians and parallels.
3. Understanding the colours, tints, shadows, symbols in a map or globe.
4. The top of every map is not north, but the direction of northern pole is north.
5. Distinction between the various types of maps such as relief, political, distribution maps, etc.
6. Understanding of the position of earth in the universe. Many students suffer from a notion that the earth leans in June towards the Sun northwards and in December southwards and thus the seasons are formed. Earth never dances that way. The student shall understand that the inclination of earth is constant and the learning effect changes due to its rotation around the sun.

Various Types of Maps

Relief Maps (regional and the world). This requires the knowledge of colours, contours, symbols and the other connected ethics of map making.

Historical Maps. Maps in history reveal the changing times and the growth and decline of various kingdoms. Knowledge of lines of boundaries and other symbols is necessary.

Distribution Maps. Generally, the student shall associate with the following types of distribution maps: (1) Vegetation maps, (2) Population maps, (3) Economic maps, (4) Statistical maps, (5) Dot maps, (6) Pictorial maps, (7) Language, race and other human division maps, etc.

Geographical Maps. Contour maps, weather maps, seismological maps, archaeological maps, rainfall maps, geological maps, etc.

Microfilm. The microfilm and microfiche are used widely for storage and retrieval of information. Microfilms contain photographed reading material on 35 mm film, each frame being the reduced photograph of a printed page. Thus, printed matter of a book can be stored in *a* small loop of 35 mm film. When the microfilm is passed through *a* microfilm reader, an enlarged image approximately of the size of the printed page is formed on a ground glass (rear-view) screen and the observer can read the matter. By moving the film through the microfilm reader, images of different pages can be obtained and read.

Models. Models are substitutes for real things. A model is a three-dimensional representation of a real thing. Models are concrete objects to explain clearly the structure or functions of real things. A model is a replica of the original. Models enable students to have a correct concept of the object. Being three dimensional, models evoke great interest and simplify matters. Models enable us to reduce or enlarge objects to an observable size. It may not be possible or even practicable to make students see the whole of a large industrial unit or even a large machine unit, but a model will give the correct perspective. Preparation of models could, form a topic for project work. It is essential to create interest in creative activity in students. Models are working as well as static. A working model will secure immediate attention and serve as motivation to learn. Model can be prepared with several kinds of materials like cardboard, plastic, plaster of paris, wood, clay, and thermocol etc. (See also under three Dimensial Aids)

The Secondary Education Commission, on the role of school museums observed, "Museums playa great part in the education of school children as they bring home to them much more vividly than any prosaic lectures, the discoveries of the past and the various developments that have taken place in many fields of science and technology." Again the Commission observes, "We believe it is necessary from the educational point of view to establish such museums in important centres at least wherein both ancient and modern collections will be exhibited and in some cases even demonstrations given of the actual process of development of various scientific discoveries. Nothing can impress students in the formative age so much as the actual visualising of these experiments in a graphic manner,"

Museums are made up of materials used in classroom teaching which, in many cases, are collected, classified and exhibited by students, with or without the help of a teacher. The museum activities may be an extracurricular function of the class or the school or they may be incorporated into a scientific-experimental method of teaching. The objectives of this type of nuseum are:

(a) to form within the school or the classroom an embryonic community dedicated to the usual occupations reflected in the school life of adults;

(b) to permit visual instruction and experimentation with actual museum specimens;

(c) to stimulate enthusiasm for study and research among both teachers and students;

(d) to stimulate interest, co-operation and participation in the cultural activities and scientific research conducted by the larger museums;

(e) to instruct students in proper scientific methods of laboratory, research and museum conservation and exhibition techniques;

(f) to form, in the absence of larger museums in the community, a nucleus from which the classroom museum can grow beyond the limits of the school to serve ultimately the community and the region as a whole.

Exhibit programmes, interpretation, visual communication. What then are some of the ways in which museums as cultural and educational centres of the community can communicate successfully with their transitory visitors of heterogeneous composition? Based on various audience-testing experiments the following media can be used to heighten the effectiveness of visual communication.

Dramatic labels. Usually they are far too short in the museums or far too long. They actually frighten away rather than entice the average museum visitor. Experiments suggest that large letters placed at the focal point of the case or exhibit area will successfully headline the exhibit and catch the visitor's attention. Like a newspaper headline, the main label tends to direct the eye to smaller, less conspicuous letters that outline the most important points of the exhibit.

Dramatic lighting. Light is a means of visual communication as well as an attention getter. Coloured lights that change, fade or highlight an exhibit can be used with great dramatic effect. Light can also be used to tell a story and to convey a sense of passing time. Light is particularly important in art museums.

Dramatic utilization. Again experiments suggest that museum visitors should be given a chance to touch exhibits as well as to see them. Of course, much depends on the nature and expendability of the object involved but certain types of material-objects of wood, stone and metal and special "touch me" samples of animal skins and fabrics-can be used with great success to satisfy the visitor's urge to which while permitting a minimum of danger.

Dramatic sound effects. Sound, like light, can be used to heighten the dramatic effect of visual communication. For example, an Amazon rain forest exhibition can be made vastly more effective by adding the sound of tropical rain, the croaking of frogs, the chattering of monkeys, and the beat of drums. An exhibit of mediaeval art can be made more meaningful if it is accompanied by music of the same period:

Effective use of space. Special concepts are also important in planning visitor traffic patterns within the exhibit areas.

Illustrated Demonstration

Pictures are very much liked by children and especially of lower classes, pictures provide an environment of 'reality'. A lesson in history can be made interesting and stimulating by showing the pictures of kings and queens, costumes and dresses, forts and weapons, monuments and tombs, etc. Similarly in a geography lesson, we can show the pictures of animals, deserts, lakes, mountains and rivers, etc., and also the various aspects of lives of people of other lands with great effect.

Following points need to be kept in view while showing pictures to the students:

1. Child's point of view should be the main criterion in the selection of pictures.
2. Pictures should be relevant to the topic.
3. As far as possible, pictures may be coloured.
4. Pictures should be accurate and of a suitable size.
5. It is desirable if the teacher himself prepares the pictures and takes help from the students.
6. Pictures should be shown in such a way that all students in the class can easily watch.
7. Too many pictures should not be displayed in one lesson.
8. After showing the picture, it should be removed from the view of the students.
9. Sufficient time should be given to see the picture.
10. Students who are good at drawing should be encouraged to draw pictures.

Through Movies

Micro-Projector. The combination of a microscope and a slide projector is an instrument called micro-projector. The microscope is used to see very minute parts of objects by magnifying the same hundreds of times. The minute part usually of a plant or an animal is put on a glass slide and a magnified image formed by a combination of leuses in a microscope which can be seen by an individual through the naked eye. The micro-projector attachment consists of a projection lens; a plane mirror fixed at 45 degrees to the vertical plane and a vertical ground glass screen. It is very useful in teaching science.

Overhead projector (OHP). Over head projector is a device that can project a chart, a diagram, a map, a table or for that matter, anything written on transparent plates, upon a screen or the white wall before students in a class. This makes teaching illuminative, illustrative and impressive. It also saves a great deal of the teacher's time used in drawing or writing. These transparencies can also be preserved by the teacher for future display while taking up the same topic. It is very simple to prepare such transparencies. All that a teacher has to do is to draw or write, as the case may be, upon transparent plates with any dark ink with a fibre tipped pen. Any material meant for display before the class while teaching can also be typed on such transparencies using a good carbon paper. In case transparencies are to be washed out for use, washable water colour can also be used for writing on the transparencies.

Slide Projector. With a slide projector, photographic slides can be projected on the screen or the wall before the class. Photographs of relevant matter meant for teaching in the class can be developed on celluloid slides and displayed with the help of such a projector. The teacher's lesson can also be recorded on an audio cassette and played with a tape recorder suitably synchronising with the slides by manipulating a remote control switch. Such an arrangement is called a tape-slide sequence. In case there are several slides to be shown in quick succession, the tape-slide sequence can bring as interesting an effect on the viewers as do the movie films. An ordinary slide projector has a frame containing two slits into which slides are put for focusing. They are manually and continuously replaced by other slides one after another. An improved type of a slide projector consists of a circular disc with more slits where even a hundred or more slides can be inserted in a sequential order which can be projected on the screen with the help of a remote control switch to be suitably manipulated by the teacher as he delivers the lesson.

Puppets. Puppetry is one of the old and popular arts in India. The use of puppets has been very popular in China, Egypt, Greece and Japan. Puppets can serve as an effective aid to learning. They can be made to illustrate lessons in civics, geography, history and hygiene. Puppets throw a lot of light in an interesting way on the life of historical personages if they are accompanied by effective narration. There should be plenty of dancing and music in the display of puppetry. While presenting puppet programmes, the age and tastes of the pupils should be duly considered. A short puppet play is always preferable to a long play. Puppets are of three types: (i) Hand puppets which fit in the hand like a glove and are operated from below by fingers. (ii) Rod puppets which are operated from below the stage by a combination of rods and springs, (iii) Marionettes or string puppets which are figures with moving limbs. These are operated from the above by means of strings.

Reprography Instruments

Reprographic is a branch of technology dealing with methods of duplication or reproduction. Duplication involves making a number of identical copies of the original. Reproduction enables preparation of one or more identical copies of the original, same size or of different size in monochrome or colour. Equipment and processes, included are: duplicators, reflex printing and photography.

Record players are a means of audio playback. They are older types of hardware using records of discs for the needed playback. Four sizes of records 7", 10", 12" and 16" are in common use. There are also high speed record player with standard stylus. The record players now in use are equipped with speed changer mechanisms permitting the playing of the slower long-playing 45, 33⅓ and 16⅔ r.p.m. records played by microgrove stylus. The use of recorded pieces in education has great value in language learning, appreciation of poetry and literature and presentation of brief dramatised episodes from history, from development of musical knowledge and discrimination. Long-playing records with 20 minutes of recorded information per side provide several diverse selections inscribed on each side and are very suitable for classroom instructional purposes. The needed selection for a particular learning situation can be easily identified by the specific microgrove ring it occupies on the record. 'Talking books' for the blind also consists of recordings of essential literature for the visually handicapped. The older, manually wound spring powered gramophone's place now has been taken up by electrically powered multi-speed record players and changers with built-in amplifying unit or linked to separate amplifying units and speakers. Likewise, the older mechanical recording has given place to electrical imprinting involving greater clarity and fidelity.

Tape-recorder. A tape-recorder in its own can be very effective for classroom instruction. Pre-recorded tapes consisting of lessons by eminent teachers on any subject can be played in the class. Such instructions become impressive not only because of the novelty but also because of their being well-thought out and planned. The tape-recorder has proved to be a boon in teaching foreign languages like English. Pre-recorded tapes on English lessons can be played in the classroom to teach not only the contents of the lesson but also proper accent, pronunciation and intonation which an average English teacher very much lacks.

Video tapes played through TV. Pre-recorded video tapes can be played through TV in the classroom. Video films on educational topics shown through TV in the classroom have the same effect on the students as the ordinary cinematic educational films do. Video films have the added advantage over ordinary films in that the arrangement is compact and requires little space and time for manipulation. It is the most convenient of all audio-visual teaching-learning materials.

The potential advantage of video cassette lies in the fact that control of the equipment and the learning process is placed in the hands of the learner through control over the mechanics of the machine, i.e. stopping, starting, timing, reviewing and previewing and consequently the capacity to order the sequence of events, controls the rate of learning, and facilitates practice sequences.

The potential exists for providing the basis for learning a wide range of motor, intellectual and cognitive and interpersonal skills, as well as affective aspects. These are important aspects which printed materials cannot deal with adequately.

This facility could be particularly useful where distance education programmes are involved with updating skills and techniques of workers in the field. .For example, new horticulture techniques can be transmitted to field workers to improve farming techniques. Mid-career retraining can also be catered for.

In some countries as a way of regionalizing a centrally produced programme, video cassette programmes are being built round the study centre concept, a location where several video machines are available to which students bring their study notes. The students run the programmes as individuals. Sometimes study centres provide for group sessions during which video cassettes are played. Unless some supplementary teaching is provided, this technique can become another version of broadcast technology.

In other countries some institutions assume that students can gain access to such equipment and make programmes which will be used on an individual basis as either supplementary learning material or integral to the teaching programme.

The problems associated with video cassettes are of two kinds: (i) cost; and (ii) production of programmes.

(i) Equipment costs cannot always be kept down by using lower quality equipment. Cheaper equipment formats do not enable technical material such as animal or plant tissue to be represented adequately or tapes to be reproduced in quantity without loss of fidelity.

(ii) Video production for educational purposes calls for new techniques different from the entertainment modes. Producers, directors, scriptwriters need to be knowledgeable about teaching and learning. Many of the old techniques of film and television will no longer be of use. For example, the very basic concept that programmes must have a beginning, a middle, and an end will no longer apply as a cassette could just as easily consist of a series of short video events which sets a problem, teaches a technique, or brings together a range of visual material to make concepts or principles clear.

Devices of Three Dimensions

Three dimensional aids serve as good substitutes for the real objects. There is no doubt that an encounter with real objects serves as an unmatchable source of learning. But on account of several reasons it may not be possible to bring the real objects in the classroom. The real objects may be too large to move or store in the classroom. It may be too small to be seen for a group of students. It can be too complicated in real form to be understood. Its movements may be too slow to be studied completely. It can be too expensive to be purchased by an educational institution. Being handicapped in such situations, a teacher has to search for some good substitute for the real objects.

Models diagrams, mock-ups and specimens are the important three dimensional aids.

Models. Models are the replicas or copies of the real objects. Models are usually of three types: solid, cross-sectional and working. Models are concrete objects, some considerably larger than the real object. Sectional models explain clearly the structure or functions of the original. In some cases working models of the original are used where the specific function of the original is duplicated and could be explained easily.

Following are the important functions of models:

1. Models simplify reality.
2. Models concretise abstract concepts.
3. Models enable us to reduce or enlarge objects to an observable size.
4. A model provides the correct concept of an industrial unit or a bridge or a dam like, the Bhakra Dam etc.
5. A working model explains the various processes of objects and machines.
6. Preparation of models could form a topic for project work. This is very helpful to create interest in creative activity in pupils.

Cardboard, plastic, plaster of paris, wood thermocol' and metal, etc., can be used in the preparation of a model.

Mock-ups. A mock-up refers to a specialised model or working replica of the object being depicted. In a mock-up, a certain element of the original reality is emphasised or highlighted to make it more meaningful for the purpose of instruction. While a model is a recognizable limitation of an object (though larger or smaller than the original one), a mock-up may or may not be similar in appearance. Mock-ups of aeroplanes, automobile engines, bridges, ships and tunnels, etc., may be demonstrated for explaining their structure and actual working. Mock-ups are often used in technical institutions for training purposes.

Dioramas. A diorama is a three dimensional scene in depth incorporating a group of modelled objects and figures in a natural setting. The diorama scene is set up on a small stage with a group of modelled objects kept on the foreground which is blended into a painted realistic background. Dioramas are very effective in the teaching of biological and social sciences.

17

Preparing Curriculum

The major impact of the proliferation of computers in just about all walks of life, has been on the content of education and training, rather than on the methods. As more and more people use computers in their work, it has become necessary to include instruction about computers and computing in more and more courses. Seigel and Davis refer to three 'waves' of the technology and the related know-how. The first wave was related to the new technology itself-the design and programming of computers and computer applications. This involved a relatively small proportion of the population.

New Streams

The second wave came with the advent of the cheap microcomputer and its use by a much greater section of the population. This led to a 'hobbyist' approach to computing, everyone 'having a go' at programming and the growth of a movement in education towards 'computer literacy' for everyone. Finally, the 'third wave' is characterized by the permeation of all sectors of social and professional activity by computer systems. This wave brings with it the need for a variety of new skills and attitudes, which will enable us to use their tools and systems efficiently, without necessarily being expect in the skills of programming, or having any specialist knowledge of computer science. In this 'third wave' people will use computes as today they use cars or television sets or telephones. They have to acquire the specialist knowledge and skills to control the equipment and get the best possible performance out of it, but they do not expect to have to fix it when it malfunctions, or devise new applications for it. They just acquire the equipment that is designed for the task they wish to perform learn to use it efficiently and if it breaks down, or their requirements expand beyond the equipment's present capabilities, they call in a specialist. This image of three consecutive 'waves' is useful in the educational computing context, as it illustrates the different, and changing, requirements for education and training about computers.

We might also add that the two are to some extent inseparable. A good example is the effect on teaching methods that the mere existence of word processing, spreadsheets and database management software is already having. In most universities it is quite rare for students to type out their work on conventional typewriters. Soon, work processors will be as common in the secondary schools. As students become more skilled in the use of this tool, the way they think about written assignments is changing. Once written, a page or a paragraph is a block of information that has an entity of its own. It may be shifted about and pasted in at will. Experimental composition and rewriting become painless.

It is our view of the 'field' of discussion in respect of computers and education. Our field is divided into two main sectors, which we may call 'informatics as content of education' and 'informatics as an instrument of education'. This distinction separates the problems of designing curricula for computer specialists or for general computer literacy, from the problems of utilizing computers in the educational process. Interesting and important as the first of these two sectors is, we shall not be able to devote time and space to it in this book. Our aims her are concerned with the use of computers as an instrument of education. We have divided this sector of the field into three sub-sectors, dealing respectively with the use of computers as an administrative tool, as a tool to assist the teacher and as a tool to assist the teacher and as a tool to assist the learner; we prefer to call it a learner's tool, for the learner may use the computer to help him learn or to take over routine tasks and thus reduce the drudgery of the learning process.

Alongside the specific examples of applications of computers in education, we have placed some brackets to indicate how we are using the three principal technical terms CAL, CAI and CML. Our usage does not necessarily agree with that of all other authors. Indeed, every author seems to have his own definitions and classifications for the same technical terms. One marked difference is in the use of the terms 'instruction' and 'Learning' on either side of the Atlantic. In the USA particularly, the term 'Instruction' tends to be used in a more global sense, for any type of teacher/ learner interchange, whereas in Britain the term CAI has of late become restricted to 'programmed instruction' types of exercises the preferred generic term being 'computer-assisted learning'.

The elements of CAL suggest that perhaps the British view that learning may be assisted in many diverse ways but only some of them have the characteristics of true instruction-seems to be gaining ground. However, detailed differences exist between the usage of CAL/ CML/CAI in the works of British authors, even though they do agree that CAI is a subset of CAL. Some consider CMI as a variety of CAL. After all, the continuous formative evaluation of a student's progress and the feedback of the results, either to improve course materials, select different options or merely to inform the student of his progress/errors/weaknesses is one very effective way of assisting the learning process. Others exclude CML/CMI as a separate category, not a part of CAL in the strict sense. For Godfrey and Sterling, the development of a CML element is part and parcel of the development of any CAL materials. Nicholas Rsushby, on the other hand, in his book An Introduction to Educational Computing, seems to separate these two modes, dealing with them in quite distinct chapters. He also differs from us slightly n other aspects of technology, using a four-paradigm classification of CAL:

1. The *instructional* paradigm.
2. The *revelatory* paradigm.
3. The *conjectural* paradigm.
4. The *emancipatory* paradigm and also its use for 'serendipity' learning, or the 'browsing' through databases without clearly defined specific objectives.

Various authors have presented somewhat different schemata for organizing the different ways in which computers are being used in education and training. A simple but very useful classification was used by Taylor in his book 'The computer in the school': TUTOR, TOOL, TUTEE, Taylor's TUTOR category includes most of the applications listed in our 'tool for TEACHING' sub-section. His TOOL category is equivalent to our 'tool for the LEARNER to SIMPLY of DELEGATE tasks.

His TUTEE category includes most of the applications we would include in 'tools for the LEARNER to THINK WITH', especially the programming of computers in order to gain a deeper understanding of a given problem solving strategy or knowledge domain. In the remainder of this book, we shall occasionally use the 'tutor, tool, tutee' classification schemata. Note, however, that Taylor's classification does not include the upper sub-section of our schema; the use of the computer to manage the instructional process. This is because Taylor's schema is set up from the viewpoint of the learner-for example, the 'tutee' category contains applications in which the learner 'teachers the computer and in this sense the computer becomes the learner's 'tutee'. Our schema is set up from multiple viewpoints-learner's, instructor's and managers.

To close, we might mention Kearsley's classification. When discussing computer-based training, he divides the field into CMI, CAI and CAL as follows:

- CMI-Computer-Managed Instruction, which includes all the routine data processing tasks that an instructor might wish to have performed to assess students, revise materials.
- CAL-Computer-Assisted Instruction, which includes drill-and-practice, tutorial and Socratic but not testing; and
- CAL-Computer-Assisted Learning, which is taken to include simulations and games, database search/ Inquiry methods and programming of computers. Note that this classification uses similar terminology with quite different meanings from our own. Kearsley's use of 'CAL', is quite different whereas, CAI is seen as a sub-

set of a much broader category termed CAL. He uses these two terms as mutually exclusive sub-categories of computer-based training, or, presumably, education.

The other difference concerns the breadth of the concept of 'instruction'. Kearsley's categories imply that simulations and games and database-search exercises are not examples of 'instructional' materials. We defined the term 'instruction' somewhat more broadly. Whereas some existing examples of these type of computer applications would not qualify to be considered instructional systems or system components, there are many that do qualify to be thus classified. Let us come back to earth, however, from these rather philosophical comments, to stress that the reader might come across a variety of classification system in the literature, but the example applications being classified are in all cases the same.

Using the Net

Computer-managed instruction can best be defined as the use of computer programmes for the on-line management of the instructional process. This may include the planning, organizing, controlling and evaluation functions as they occur during the instructional process.

CMI is not a recent concept. Indeed, the use of the computer to store, analyse and interpret data about a process is a very typical type of application. No wonder that CMI was one of the first applications of computing to the instructional process. Note that CMI can be an integral feature of a computer-assigned or administered instructional system, or it can be a 'stand-alone' application of computer-based management of more or less conventional classroom instruction. As such, it may use an existing computer, installed for other data processing purposes, to assist the classroom teachers in the management of their courses.

Almost all serious CAI systems do have a built-in CMI component. However, in many microcomputer-based systems or recent years this is quite rudimentary, restricted perhaps to the scoring of a student's success on the questions in a given lesson and summarizing this in a final report. As soon as the student switches the computer off, these data may be lost. Other micro-based systems are a little more sophisticated, in that they store these student records on the diskette, allowing more sophisticated analyses of results by the instructor/ author.

Computer-based CAI systems, designed for use by large numbers of students at distributed terminals, are much stronger on CMI. A good example is the PLATO Learning Management system built into Control Data's PLATO computer-based-instruction system. We shall discuss the PLATO system in more detail later, when we analyse tutorial CAI. For the time being serves to show the wealth of data storage, organization and analysis options open to the instructor using the PLATO system.

Apart from such obvious facilities as the recording and monitoring of student progress, the system offers very extensive formative evaluation possibilities geared to both the diagnosis and correction of weakness in the instructional materials design, as well as individual weaknesses and difficulties of each student. Other facilities include: control over 'who has access to what', allowing one to vary the extent of learner control over the learning process, as well as access to progress statistics; an electronic mail facility allowing individual communication between instructor and student or between students.

A large-scale example of the second type of application was Project Plan, which was developed in the late 1960s in the USA. This project used computer-marked objective tests, to accompany all the primary and some of the secondary school curriculum in American schools. The schools subscribing to the system were equipped with special 'post office' terminals, one to a classroom. After covering a particular unit, of, say, three or four objectives, the learners, either individually or as groups, would take a pre-printed objective test, in multiple-choice format. They would respond on special cards, marking the choices by scoring the appropriate letters alongside the question's number, already preprinted on the cards. They would also mark their individual code numbers. Then they would 'post' the cards into a slot of the terminal, to update their individual file, kept in a computer at a distance.

The individual student received feedback of results and suggestions for further study. The teacher could compare the individual student's progress with that of his group and of other students and groups in other schools, right across the country. The computer was programmed to follow a highly complex control algorithm, that could use this extremely large bank of data to generate individual student profiles, individual guidance, suggestions of the best methods and materials of study for particular students or particular course objectives, predictions of success in particular types of career and so on. The system involved several thousand American school children and used an even larger database on long-term success in life, related to school performance, which had been collected in an earlier project-PROJECT TALENT-that had involved five million children.

Project PLAN used a large mainframe computer dedicated to the instructional management functions. During the life of the project, which was sponsored by the Westinghouse Corporation, schools on both sides of the USA were effectively in communication, linked through the one computer at Westinghouse in California. There were even some American schools as far away as Saudi Arabia, receiving on-line management services from the one computer. This may be one of the principal reasons why the project lasted only a few years. At that time-late 1960s and early 1970s-the costs of running such a service were very high, and the long distance data communication links were not all that reliable. Neither of these limitations are true today and, although project PLAN is no longer with us, many similar large-scale CMI systems are currently operating in various countries. Perhaps one of the biggest is the system operated by the US Navy. However, the British Open University operates a somewhat more limited sort of CMI capability. Other open learning systems are following suit, the Open University of China for example, with over one million students, would have difficulty in achieving effective instructional management without extensive computer assistance.

However, stand-alone CMI system do not have to be so big, not do they need a dedicated computer system. Some of the earliest systematic research and development on computers in education used a little bit of spare time in an existing multipurpose computer to manage classroom-based or print-based programmed instructional systems. At the University of Aston in Birmingham, U.K. Croxton and Martin added a simple computer-based management system to an existing engineering structures course, using printed modules, and in so doing more than doubled the frequency of distinction passes on final national examinations.

The traditional 'system-control' model of CMI is seen to assume three general characteristics for the course that is being managed. These are:

1. *Individualization.* The instruction is assumed to be individualized to a greater or lesser extent, in terms of learning rate, methods, media, even content and objectives in some cases.
2. *Behavioural objectives.* The instruction is assumed to be designed on the basis of a task analysis that established a set of specific behavioural objectives.
3. *Educational technology principles.* The instructions assumed to be designed /developed in accordance with general educational technology, principles, including some model for the selection of methods and media, some model for the measurement and control of mastery of the pre-specified objectives, and so on.

In recent years, with the development of database management technology, there is a new trend that may prove very important. This is the trend towards the structuring of bodies of knowledge in the form of so called 'knowledge bases'. Such knowledge bases are essential components of the new 'AI' generation of problem-solving software but they may also be used as resources by learners to identify the knowledge required for a purpose of the learner's own choosing.

The management system of such a knowledge base is not centred on specific behavioural objectives, but must identify and present the knowledge content relevant to some personal objective that the learner brings to the exercise, which may not be fully predictable in advance. Such knowledge-base management systems may be important elements in CMI systems of the future. An example of such a system is embedded in a digital electronics course. I helped to develop for the rapid and flexible retraining/ updating of electronics technicians. This is basically a laboratory/

workshop-based course, organized in a series of two-week modules. The instructor spends most of his or her time on the practical laboratory /workshop exercises.

The underlying electronics, mathematics and logic theory is available in a large number of reference sheets which are organized in the form of a knowledge base. This is intended to include all the knowledge that an electronics technician working with digital logic circuits may require, whatever the specific industry/ application/ state of sophistication of the technology, etc. Anyone entering the course should be able to locate, quickly and completely, all the information relevant to current activity in the laboratory, be presented with specific relevant example, at an appropriate level of difficulty, and receive appropriate self-testing questions and exercises. This completely random-access system of information presentation is managed by a simple database applications package.

A Particular Device

Computer-based testing may be part of a CAI system, or may be a stand-alone facility. Some computer-based testing facilities are no more than an item bank, which can be used to generate two or more tests of equivalent content and difficulty, to be used at different moments in conventional classroom teaching/ testing. Such systems are no more than a specialist application of databases; each test item is classified according to several parameters. The instructor may request the print-out of a test of X items, of Y difficulty level, with Z content-type on a given set of objectives.

The item bank contains a sufficient number of test items in each of these categories to enable random selection of items to generate several quite different test-papers which are, however, equivalent. Such an application is stand-alone, does not require the student to interact with the computer and does not score the test or analyse the results. As it stands, such an application would not be considered by anyone as an example of computer-assisted-instruction. It is 'computer-assisted-test construction'.

When, however, the student takes the test on-line at a computer terminal, when the test is automatically scored and the results analysed, and when that analysis results in some final guidance message to the student then we have a level of assistance in testing that takes on part of the instructional function. For example, in the case of the 20-module remedial maths course mentioned earlier, early versions of the CMI system were based on a 20-part diagnostic paper-based test, that all students took on entry. This was scored by a monitor who then entered the test results into the computer for analysis, prescription of an individual study plan and control of student progress. In later versions, however, the students would take the diagnostic test on-line. This offered one immediate benefit. In the earlier system, a weak student would spend a lot of time getting all the items of the massive diagnostic test wrong. When taken on-line, the computer keeps track of student performance as he or she takes the test and, as soon as error rates on a given section of the test exceed acceptable limits, the testing stops, a partial prescription is given and the student goes off to pick up the module in the resource centre.

After studying, the student returns to the computer terminal, automatically picks up the test at the point where he or she had difficulties, gets post-tested on the skills just studied hopefully succeeds this time and proceeds further into the diagnostic system until another weakness is identified and the appropriate study module is prescribed. In this set-up, the diagnostic pre-testing and post-testing are completely administered and managed by the computer. These are, of course, essential components of the instructional system, so we can look on this computer-assisted testing procedure as a form of partial CAI. It would only require the study material to be converted into computer-based information screens, to transform the whole system into a CAI tutorial.

Some of the earliest research and development related to drill and practice exercises on computers was performed by Patrick Suppes and his collaborators at Stanford University in the 1960s. The major findings of these studies supported the thesis that, at least in the area of mathematical skills, well designed drill and practice routines could develop higher levels of competence, in less time than was normally the case when other means of organizing the practice sessions were tried.

Since those early days, the number of different draft applications has increased and, of course, the costs of computers and software development have fallen, turning Suppes' effective, but exceedingly expensive, techniques into everyday reality. The type of sophisticated, matrix-based, model of complexity and difficulty in a given set of problems, may be quite easily accommodated in even quite a modest computer.

As a guide, the memory needed to run the type of complex drill and practice routines designed by Suppes is much less than that required to run a reasonably sophisticated version of VISICALC, SUPERCALC or one of the other spreadsheet programmes now available for most home computers in the 32K RAM or upwards range of memory. The basic organization of a set of practice maths problems in a given skill domain. The practice items are classified according to complexity and difficulty.

Drill and practice is unduly criticized by some people, as being a 'lesser form' of CAI. We would not agree. There are, of course, whole areas of the curriculum and whole classes of objectives, for which this mode of practice is not appropriate. However, there are also whole areas where some form of drilling is necessary in order to develop basic skills or to reinforce essential knowledge. No one learns a foreign vocabulary without the need to practice and repeat the words. This may occur in the natural context of using the language. But if one is in a hurry, some artificial drilling exercise is needed.

If the computer can offer entertaining and efficient drill exercises at an economic cost, there is nothing 'second class' about it. If a clerk has to develop a high level of skill in the performance of a routine task, such as the error-free calculation of pay-as-you-earn tax deductions from employees wage packets and a computer based drill proves to be the most effective and efficient means of developing this skill, why should we frown on this form of application? We are rather of the opinion that drill ad practice, though not very spectacular, is destined to be one of the main uses of CAI, as long as people have to learn routine and repetitive tasks of any nature.

A number of versatile packages, rather like the test packages described earlier, are now available, that allow the teacher to change the content of the exercise while maintaining the general format of the exercise. The difference between these drill exercises and the test packages mentioned earlier, is in the form of feedback supplied to the student and in the conscious effort to develop the mastery of specific objectives. Once again, many of these exercises are disguised as games and are often, indeed, based on well known games, adapted to the computer based format. Some of these, marketed by Wida Software, are specifically designed to develop associations, as in the learning of a new vocabulary. One version is an adaptation of the card game of SNAP. Two words or phrases appear on the screen at any one time, one in each language.

Without a Proper Choice

The words change in a random fashion, first one then the other. At times the two words which are visible are equivalent-in that case, the player must register that he/she observed the association, by depressing a key. If the key is not depressed within a certain time limit, the computer gains a point. If the player responds within the time limit, he/she gains a point. There are nine different speeds of play that can be pre-set at the beginning of the exercise. The game can be used for any association-learning, where rapid identification response is an asset; e.g. in understanding a foreign spoken conversation, in learning map codes ad conventions, in identifying traffic signs and in many other association and discrimination learning situations.

Another exercise, named odd man out presents four words or short phrases on the screen, three of which belong to one class and one belongs to another. The player must identify the odd man out, by keying in the appropriate code number. If correct, the player obtains confirmative feedback, together with an explanation of the classifying concept used. If incorrect, the player receives corrective feedback and, once again, an explanation of the basis for the classification. In this way, a whole range of concepts can be drilled to perfection.

One application would be in the recognition and classification of parts of speech. The game would be 'loaded' with four adjectives four verbs, four adverbs, four prepositions and son on. The computer then selects, randomly, three examples from one group and one from another. Other applications for which we have used this format of drill include the training of supermarket checkout staff in the classification of products sold according to stock-control categories, the training of postmen to classify streets according to postal delivery rounds, the drilling of 'town and river' type of factual information in geography and the classification of animals and plants in biology. It is a drill format that is suitable for the development of most concepts, especially groups of interrelated and easily confused concepts.

Yet another drill game, supplied by Wida Software, is based on the simulation, on the computer screen, of a 'one-armed bandit' fruit machine. Three cylinders can be rotated, by pressing appropriate keys. Imaginary 'coins' have to be fed to the computer to make it play. At certain, randomly occurring moments in the game, the player gains the right to hold or to 'nudge' one or more of the cylinders, just as in the real-life gambling machines. However. instead of attempting to line up three lemons, or other winning combinations of fruit, the player must line up three works that, together, 'make sense'. Once again, the content of the drill may be changed at will. The game was originally designed to drill correct sentence formation in foreign language teaching. However, with a bit of ingenuity, other applications may be invented. One history application involved the matching of who did what and when.

However, simulators, based on computers, have many applications in the drill and practice mode. A classic and very illuminating example is Gordon Pask's SAKI, developed in the early 1960s, but only recently generally available, due to the fall of computer prices. The SAKI machine was initially devised to train the skills of punching a numerical keypad of ten digits. A later, more sophisticated version was developed to train and drill typing skills. The trainee is presented with a keyboard that has no markings on the keys and two screens. One screen presents information to be typed and the other shows a picture of the keyboard layout on which the keys light up to indicate the position of the key to be pressed at a given moment. The trainee approaches the simulator after some initial instruction on correct technique, typing rhythm and related essential knowledge.

Randomly selected letters appear on screen 1 and the position of each appropriate key is 'cued' by the lights that appear on the simulated keyboard on screen 2. As practice progresses the general speed of presentation of data to be typed increases, and the intensity of the lights not he simulated keyboard decreases. However, all this happens in function of the error pattern and response rate of the trainee. He/she gets longer to respond to the letters which give difficulty, gets more intense cues and over longer period of time for these letters and, furthermore, these letters begin to occur at a frequency proportional to their level of difficulty. All this occurs in response to a particular trainee's individual pattern of errors. He/she gets more practice more time to respond and more help, adjusted on a continuous, 'on-line' basis by the control algorithm built into the trainer. This highly adaptive learning environment is extremely efficient, leading typical learners to achieve first-rate typing speeds in only a few hours of drill and practice. Similar adaptive, computer-based, training devices now are fairly common for developing psychomotor and perceptual skills, such as radar tracking, missile firing and aircraft gunnery.

Many arcade and home video games also develop, perhaps not all that intentionally, certain basic coordination or manipulation skills. It is more difficult to classify such devices as the full scale flight simulators, or Moore's 'talking typewriter' used for the automated teaching of writing and reading skills. Basically, they too are simulated environments that provide the opportunity for intensive practice of some basic skills. However, a lot of initial learning may also take place during the experience. An illustrative example of this category, which contrasts with the SAKI system, is the EASY LEARN keyboard training station, initially developed for the British Post Office and now marketed by Hi-Port Systems in the United Kingdom. This is a full-function keyboard trainer, that can be used as a stand-alone individual trainer, or linked in groups to an instructor terminal for use as a form of learning laboratory.

Only one screen is used and this can be used to present a variety of displays, including stimulus material to be copy-typed by the trainee and explanatory presentations, to teach the basic rules of efficient keyboard technique. It is some of the variety of presentations that the trainee receives at different stages of the programme. The system may be used in the 'conditional' mode in which trainees only progress to new material after a correct response and correction of any errors, or in the 'unconditional' mode which allows progress irrespective of errors.

A Different Mode

The programmed tutorial mode of CAI is indeed akin to 'computer-based programmed instruction'. All the most commonly used techniques of the early days of programmed instruction are now being revived and applied in the design of CAI programmed tutorial sequences. Both linear and branching structures are used, through many people argue that the use of a computer to present a linear instructional sequence is rather like using a steam-hammer to crack a nut. This may, in general, be true, though there are some instances in which computer generated effects or the computer control of ancillary media or equipment, may justify the application.

In relation of branching, the computer opens up a range of possibilities that would have been difficult to arrange in the scrambled text, or primitive teaching machine, days of the 1060s. Theoretically, the computer can be programmed to branch to any number of alternatives, not to a limit of four or five at most, restricted by the number of plausible choices that the instructional designer can invent for one given multiple choice question, and also by the difficult of organizing the pages in a scrambled text when there are very many different routes through the book.

In theory, a large library of computer-based instructional materials could be cross-referenced and indexed in a way that permitted students to back-track to a new context but has unfortunately been forgotten through lack of use. Branching decisions, to faster or slower streams of instructional presentation, can be taken on the basis of a cumulative analysis of several responses over time and not just on the last, possibly atypical, response made. A variety of other non-computer-based materials may be incorporated into the system, their use being prescribed by the diagnoses of individual student progress and needs, that are constantly being prepared and updated by the computer. These alternative materials may be visual, as in videodise and intefactive videocassette systems already on the market. They may be print-based reading assignments, annotated bibliographies for free study, laboratory or workshop-based experiments and practical exercises, or specific group-learning activities. They may be all of these, knitted into a complex, multi-media, computer-controlled, truly individualized instructional system.

Unfortunately, in practice, few real CAI systems exploit these possibilities to the full. Too many are totally computer-based when they could be more effective and more economical if they were partly based on other media. Too many are a mixture of linear and branching sequences, not very different from programmes that actually existed in print and paper form some 20 years ago. Too many are not even good examples of ostensibly CAI systems that did not really differe much from a standard textbook-presented electronically. They did not even follow the three basic principles of instructional programming:

- Active participation, by learners, in the learning process.
- Immediate knowledge of results and corrective feedback.
- Avoidance of excessive errors on the part of the learners.

  Still less did they show creativity and perspicacity in the analysis of typical students' errors and difficulties, and the design of appropriate instructional solutions.

For want of a better starting point, the basic principles and techniques of programmed instruction, which have stood the test of time should be systematically and creativity applied in the design of programmed tutorial CAI. However, if one merely applies the basic techniques of programmed instruction, it is often difficult to justify the use of a computer to present the material. The figure presents the original version of a step in a CAI sequence on set theory. This step introduces the concept of 'UNION'. It is reasonably well designed in that it supplements the formal definition by an example. Then the exercise that follows tests comprehension of the concept, by application to a specific case. It would have been better, though, to ask students to generate a response rather than merely selecting one from a set of suggestion. This is the difference between construction and recognition of an appropriate response.

However, the author seems to have been so conditioned by the multiple-choice single-letter response format that was required by early teaching machines and most scrambled text branching programmed, that he/she has overlooked that in a computer-based application we can ask the student to construct a response ad then write a routine to analyse and classify and response in relation to its source of error, thus matching it to an appropriate feedback comment. The modification in the method of asking for a response, introduced, is the least that could be done in order to make use of the capabilities that computers offer over and above those present in textual presentation. The feedback comments in the two versions illustrate another point.

In the original version, the feedback is very categorical and the corrective strategy is to suggest rereading the present screen of information and try to answer again. This is a further legacy of print-based self instruction. Any more complex branching would lead to excessive page turning and any benefit from enrichment of the branching might be out-weighed by lost time looking for correct page and the possibility of losing one's place together. When presented by computer, however, any amount of to and fro branching can be handled quickly and smoothly.

As the error illustrated may be a mere slip on the part of the student, or may have deeper causes, why not plan for alternative forms of corrective feedback. We can allow for the student who immediately sees his error when presented with the feedback message and for the student who found the bare formal definition insufficiently clear and would like more and more practical examples to improve his understanding of the new concept. We can allow for the very unsure student, who would like to back track to the earlier concept that he has confused with the new one. We have left these options under student control, but we could bring these alternatives under programme control, by asking subsidiary questions which would help to diagnose the seriousness and source of the individual student's misconception.

Another possible enhancement that would be easy to introduce would be the substitution of a different practice example of equivalent difficulty for each subsequent wrong answer so that students do not have the chance to get zero in one the correct answer by a process of trial and error. One could, of course, use many other computer-based tricks, like animating the Venn diagrams and showing the union of two sets forming a new set with all the elements included in one circle. Whether this would enhance learning, or would just be a gimmicky application of the 'bells and whistles', is a moot point. Finally, of course, we could abandon the basic original tutorial design and opt for a discovery-learning conversational strategy, or a simulation perhaps, if we can justify it.

Different Ways to Work

There are many different approaches that may be classified in this category of CAI. Some are referred to as 'Socratic' dialogue and are based on a mixed-initiative strategy, where both computer and student may either ask or respond to questions. Such tutorials are based on 'artificial intelligence' models of the teaching learning process and require very complicated and time consuming programming in little used and difficult to learn programming languages, such as Lisp or Prolog. It is not surprising, therefore that, at the time of writing most of these systems are research laboratory playthings, rather than widely used and practically cost-effective instructional systems. They include such early systems as SCHOLAR and CASTE and more recent ones such as SOPHIE. They differ very much from each other in terms of the specific models for interaction and learning or teaching, upon which they operate.

But they have the common element of adaptiveness to the individual learner by some means of 'learning about the learner'. This is where they attempt to model the expert human tutor more closely than other forms of CAI and, therefore, they have gained the popular name of 'intelligent tutoring systems' or more coloquially 'Intelligent Computer Assisted Instruction'. However, not all conversational, in-dept dialogue, CAI methodologies are based on the concept of the computer learning about the learner and thus improving and further individualizing the instructional strategy being used.

It is possible to build some very complex interactive dialogues purely on the basis of deep questioning techniques and multi-faceted analyses of the responses given by the student. After all, this is what happens in many university courses as the general rule, especially when student/staff ratios are high. The professor teaching a large group seldom gets to know all the students.

However, by setting suitably deep and multi-faceted 'essay' or 'seminar' type assignments the professor can get a very accurate picture of the individual student's present conceptual schema on a given topic. In his or her' reply to the essay or the seminar presentation, the professor can be very perceptive and helpful to the individual although the only data available to the professor is the content of a complex written or spoken argument on the topic, prepared by the specific student in question, together with accumulated experience of how students in general react to the topic, what difficulties or misconceptions they have, etc.

One very successful approach to the simulation of such professor-student interchanges on specific complex problems on a computer is the technique of Structural Communication, developed by Hodgson and his associates in the United Kingdom at the end of the 1960s. This method is based on the analysis of a multi-faceted multiple choice response which the student constructs by selection of a combination of response components from a 20 to 40 item 'response matrix. The construction of such in-depth interactive tutorial dialogues is quite complex from the viewpoint of subject-matter expertise and knowledge structure analysis, but relatively simple in terms of the computer hardware and software required.

Whereas the conversational, or dialogue, modes of CAI are perhaps among the least practised on a large scale, SIMULATION is probably the most used and fastest growing mode. This is probably due to a series of factors.

- Computer-based simulations are sometimes the only way of developing certain types of learning experiences.
- They use the particular advantage of the computer as an ultra-rapid calculating and data processing machine, to the best advantage.
- The computer may often play a part in a more elaborate, not entirely computer-based simulation-game.

- Unlike the conversation mode, simulations are often quite simple to plan form the instructional viewpoint. Thus, the instructional designer may delegate a major part of the production task to specialist computer staff.
- The use of simulations is usually an adjunct to normal teaching procedures; it does not disrupt traditional organizational practices, upset conventional teachers by threatening the jobs of anyone, or tie up the computer on a nearly permanent basic for instruction.
- Many computer-based simulations are in the science area, where staff are most receptive to the new technology.
- There are, however, ample valid applications for this mode in almost any educational or training context.

One area in which dozens, perhaps hundreds of successful simulations have been developed, is medical education. Trainee doctors learn how patients with diabetes react to the intake of sugar in various quantities. Other simulations teach abut the reactions of the body to different drugs or medicines. Yet others deal with environmental factors that promote epidemics, the control of a common disease by the vaccination of different proportions of the population. In all such simulations, the student may vary some of the critical variables and observe how other variables are affected.

Another popular area for process simulations is in the sciences. Ellington, Addinall and Percival list dozens of examples, including a simulation of process of discharge of a capacitor, the flow of fluids through nozzles, gaseous diffusion, gravitation, interference and diffraction patterns of light waves, motion of satellites in orbits, and many others.

There is one other application to be mentioned here the flight simulator. Simple navigational simulators one down the road, for operation on most makes of home are a form of decision-making exercise. They teach more or less accurately, the factors that must be taken into account when flying and navigating a plane. In playing with these simulators, one learns when to drop the undercarriage, in relation to air speed, when and how much to trim the flaps, how to allow for a cross wind when approaching an airfield, and so on.

Such a software package, sold as a game for recreational purposes, does therefore give practice in the decision-making aspects of flying. At it presents the player with up to three visual displays the instrument plane, the view in front of the cockpit and a map of the area on which the plane is situated; it is a simulation of the navigational and instrument-flying tasks in the pilot's job. When this same decision-making package is incorporated in a model of a real plane, that also supplies the correct physical feel, guidance and feedback for the manual skills of control, we have introduced the element of apparatus operation.

The final classification in our schema of CAI only just qualities to be included as a category of institution': it is really a mode of information retrieval from some form of organized bank of information, or database. However, if the database is organized to supply all the information necessary to achieve certain groups of educational objectives and if the learner is given a set of specific objectives to be achieved, then we have a form of instructional system indeed, a very flexible self-instructional system.

There is, on the other hand, the unstructured, 'browsing' use of a computerized database, analogous to browsing in a public library, which is not aimed towards specific learning objectives and is therefore not 'instruction in the sense that we are using the term. This is what Nicholas Rsushby termed 'serendipity learning'. The planning of a bank of information for unstructured, serendipity learning, is not unlike the planning of the purchasing policy of a public library. We do not know exactly who will turn up to use the resources, or what they will be looking for.

One potential growth area for the application of the computer in education is, no doubt, the creation of computer-based libraries, computer-based information tanks on specific subjects, etc. One such application already in use in UK is Prestel. Other videotext systems, available to the public in general and devoted to educational and cultural purposes, as opposed to advertising and new casting, will no doubt appear in increasing numbers, throughout the world. Pundits already draw mental images of immense national or even international networks linking dozens of specialist libraries into one huge system which, to use the words of Roy Jenkins, 'can allow the contents of all the world's great libraries to flow through every living room in the land'.

The organization of information to become a functioning reality, will need a lot of work on the organization of the information of these 'great libraries' in such a manner that the not-too-skilled potential user can find his way about, locate what he wants, or what he might want if he only knew that it existed. The task of organizing such immense databases is not all that well understood. Many people are now interested in the topic and much research is under way. In relation to educational, scientific and other specialist use of such systems, the need is felt for a technology of subject-matter-analysis and organization that can produce a database on a given subject that is as helpful to the learner/ researcher as a human expert on the subject would be, if available for a personal interview. This has led to the concept of Expert Systems-computer-based information banks which emulate a human expert in a given subject area.

Electronic Library

A database on a specialist subject is, however, little more than a well organized and cross-referenced library. It is an important and useful tool in the hands of an expert. However, it does not take over the role of the expert. The important aspect of a true expert system is that it takes on at least part of the problem-organization and problem-solving roles on the human expert. It is capable not only furnishing the information solicited, but should be able to interrogate the user for relevant input information, prompt the user in the steps to be followed in solving a problem, or even take over the problem-solving process as a whole.

The special-purpose scientific software that solves a set of pre-determined equations has been with us for a long time any computer programme is a 'problem solver' in this sense. But the solution of complex problems that require one to weigh various factors in relation to each other and make a decision on incomplete data, that is, *heuristic* problem solving, has only recently been successfully computerized. The 'expert system' is one form of a computerized heuristic problem solver.

Taylor's classification of the computer in education as 'Tutor, Tool and Tutee' emphasizes that one major way in which computes are used by learners is to learn how to programme them. The computer is Tutee, in the sense that it is the learner who takes on the role of 'tutor' or rather, programmer. There are two justifications for such as an approach, one related to the development of specific programming skills, the other related to the development of general problem-solving skills and 'powerful ideas'.

The argument that learning to programme the computer is best achieved through practice in programming the computer is unassailable. However, who needs computer programming skills? Well, those who earn their livelihood by programming computers. But the idea, born with the appearance of cheap microcomputers, that all computer users would engage in some programming, is last dying.

The 'vocational training' argument for teaching computing to every one is not strong, and we can see how recently the concept of 'computer literacy' and been changing-whereas in the early 1980s just about all such programmes in included instruction in one or more computer languages, the late 1980s tendency is towards much less emphasis on programming languages and much more on the efficient use of special purpose applications software. This trend is spurred on by expediency by the need to concentrate on what is immediately useful. But there are many educators and computer scientists who argue that a knowledge of computing has general value as a discipline in logical thinking, problem formulation and solution, etc. They argue that experience in programming is time well spent in any student's general education, whatever their future vocational needs might turn out to be, not all educators agree.

Some remember that for centuries the inclusion of Latin as an obligatory subject in the general school curriculum was defended largely, on the grounds that 'Latin is a logical language and therefore, through learning Latin, students would learn to think logically'.

There was no shred of evidence to suggest that this was in fact so, but the pressure group for Latin was so strong that many generations of argument were needed in order to introduce a change in the curriculum. Are we witnessing a similar 'pressure group' situation developing in respect of computer studies in the general curriculum? Or is there some real evidence that learning to programme has some more general educational effects? The answer from the 'pressure group' is that of course it depends on what language you learn and on how it is taught. The majority of computer scientists criticize the inclusion of BASIC as an introductory computing experience, arguing that the structure of this language is not conductive to the learning of good programming strategies.

The educators, on the other hand, argue that the programming experience should be planned to include concepts of more general utility. The juxtaposition of these two opinions largely explains the popularity of LOGO, since its appearance in microcomputer versions in the early 1980s. Before we look at the evidence, let us examine just what LOGO is and how it is being used in schools.

LOGO was developed at Massachusetts Institute of Technology by a team of educators and computer scientists interested in logic programming and Piagetian concepts of child development. This, at first sight, rather strange combination of interests came about when Seymour Papert, a student of Praget and interested in implementing his ideas in education, joined the faculty of MIT, at that time on the leading research centres on artificial intelligence. The current 'AI' programming language LISP, is powerful but not too easy to learn tool. The MIT team was working on the development of a simpler version.. Papert saw, in this development, the opportunity to introduce young children to logic programming at a very early age and through this, to create a computer-based learning environment in which children could discover for themselves most of the concepts and relationships of mathematics. Papert's ideas stimulated a lot of excitement in the AT fraternity and led to a number of projects in the mid ` 1070s. Notable among these was the Brookline LOGO project. Projects like these were exploratory 'let's see what can be done' studies, rather than strict research.

The Edinburgh project was perhaps the more rigorous; in that standard mathematics tests were administered to students participating in the project. However, these projects served more to illustrate the potential for creative use of computers with young children, rather than any spectacular learning improvement towards the accepted school mathematics objectives. The experience gained in these projects, was synthesized in Papert's classic book Mindstroms which appeared at the same time that microcomputer versions of LOGO were released on the market. Thus the LOGO movement was launched.

One aspect that Papert built into LOGO was the 'Turtle', triangular cursor that can be moved and rotated by the user, to create a geometrical drawing. How a child can build a simple shape by writing a short programme and the use that shape as a component to build much more complex figures. The capacity of LOGO to allow the user to define his own commands and thus extend the power of the language, is one of its main attractions and strengths. The programmer uses the idea of 'recursion' to simplify the structure of the programme.

Recursion means 'repeat what you already know, well illustrated in the 'SPOINSQUARE' programme. The complex figure is drawn by using the previously defined command and repeating several times with small changes in size and rotation. By experimenting with such programming, Papert argues, children gain insights into how complex ideas are structured from simpler ones. This insight, gained in the context of 'turtle geometry', is claimed to transfer to other domains of learning as well. We shall examine later on some of the research on whether the claims made for using LOGO really do stand up. There is no doubt that the introduction of LOGO in schools has contributed much to the de-mystification of computers and has created some very entertaining educational activities.

With some notable exceptions, well designed comparative research has shown, at best, a slight improvement in learning for the mediated version of the lessons compared. More often, analysis has shown 'no significant difference'. We have seen that a more sophisticated approach to the analysis of the data from many similar studies has been tried by Kulik and his collaborators. Not surprisingly, Kulik has performed a series of such 'meta analysis' studies on the very large number of comparative studies on CAL-one analysis of comparison studies in higher education and one in elementary education. All there of these 'meta-analyses' involving the combination of hundreds of separate comparative research studies, showed significant, if not spectacularly large, advantages for the computer-based materials, over the teacher administered lessons.

Possible limitations of comparative research and Clark's position on effect of media on instruction. These meta analyses have come under fire from several writers. Some have argued that many comparative studies may induce the teachers involved to take extra pains over their lesson-planning and delivery as they find themselves 'on trial' and thus the CAL benefits normally attainable would be reduced or masked. Others argue that the opposite effect may be present-the extra effort, time and instructional design skill that has gone into the development of the computer-based materials, results in superior lesson designs and exaggerate the effect of the computer. Clark indeed re-analysed the results of the' Kulik studies, discarding the poorly designed studies and separating those in which the same teacher was responsible for the development of the CAL material and for the conventional class teaching, from those where different teachers taught the control classes. He found that when the same teacher was both author of the CAL materials and instructor of the classroom-based control group, the advantage for the computer-based instruction was much reduced.

He argues that, probably, this is because in those studies there is more similarity in the basic instructional design of the two alternatives being compared and, if this similarity were to be controlled rigorously in all studies, there would probably be no significant advantage of the computer administered lessons over the teacher-delivered instruction. He concludes by arguing that, as was the case with his findings in the case of video and other mediated instruction, computers make no more contribution to learning than the truck which delivers groceries to the market contributes to improved nutrition in a community. Purchasing a truck will not improve nutrition just as purchasing a computer will not improve student achievement. Nutrition gains come from getting the correct groceries to the people who need them. Similarly, achievement gains result from matching the correct teaching method to the student who needs it.'

The Outcomes

This apparent criticism of CAL is really no more than a criticism of the comparative studies that form such a large percentage of the research. When all possible variables have been controlled and balanced, 'it is not at all surprising to find no difference between any two presentation media.' However, this implies that the content of learning selected for a comparative study must be such that it is equally capable of being presented by the various media being compared. It also implies that the teaching methods implemented in a study must be capable of being implemented equally well in all the media being compared. And there is ample evidence to suggest that the really effective way of using computers in teaching is to implement by the unaided classroom teacher. One use of CAL which is so defended is the computer-based simulation/ games, in that it presents real life-like experience to all students within realistic timeframes, in a way that was hitherto impossible.

Another argument is that many instructional designs that could, in theory, be implemented by the unaided teacher do not generally get to be implemented because they are too time consuming or difficult to use on a day-to-day basis, But the high speed of data, processing offered by the computer makes these designs practically viable. To find the real benefits of the use of computers as instruments of instruction, we should look for real problems that have been solved, or real improvements that have been gained by the use of CAL. These 'case studies' may turn out to be more informative than formal research studies. They are capable of showing the effect of a number of the medium's characteristics over a significant period of time. They may also suggest benefits which are not measured by the standard testing procedures of formal research.

To start with computer-managed instruction, one should note the many reported success stories that document the benefit actually achieved when previously existing non-CAI courses were enhanced with an element of computer-based management. The case of the Engineering Structure course at the University of Aston in the UK, mentioned earlier, is a notable example in this category. By adding a computer-managed diagnosis system to an existing, self-study module-based, university level course, the authors succeeded in raising the success rates of their students on nationally administered examinations to such an extent that all their students' results fell in the top 10 per cent of the national score distribution. This result was so outstanding, in relation to that particular university's previous record and in terms of the students' outstanding results in structures but not necessarily in any of the other engineering examinations, that the examining body initially refused to believe that some form of 'cheating' was not involved. Only after the students took a second 'cheat proofed' structures exam and achieved similar outstanding results, did the new teaching method get the credit that was due to it.

The main reason for the spectacular improvement was in fact nothing more than the increased level of diagnostic control that could be exerted when the computer was used to process the results of the week-by-week study assignments. With 300 or more students registered on a lecture-and-modules based course, there was no way for faculty to keep track of individual progress until it was too late to do anything about individual learning problems. With rapid computer-based diagnosis of learning progress, it was possible to use all existing teaching resources to give the maximum of individual coaching (not-much, with the staff-student ratio available, but the little possible made all the difference).

The use of computer-assisted testing also has its share of success stories. One, already described earlier, was the added smoothness and practically that on-line diagnostic testing introduced into a remedial mathematics 'learning-by-appointment' system that had been running previously on the basis of paper tests.

Other benefits of the on-line 'adaptive' testing approach are documented by Weiss, who shows that to achieve similar levels of precision in diagnosis, computer-based adaptive tests use 30-50 per cent fewer test questions than a similar paper-and-pencil test. This saves testing time, cuts down on student effort and reduces the frustration of the weaker student faced with many over-difficult questions to tackle and knowing that he/she will almost certainly answer incorrectly.

A further form of benefit that has often been gained in practice is increased facility in the construction of appropriate levels of tests and, therefore, increased use of systematic diagnostic testing procedures. This benefit comes about through the mere existence of a test item bank on a given subject matter, organized according to objective, difficulty level, etc. Such an item bank may be constructed by small contributions from many teachers and is then available to all teachers as a service. Lippey describes how such computer-assisted testing may be used and gives examples of the benefits achieved.

Uses and misuses of drill and practice and case studies of keyboard skills drill and practice. The drill and practice mode of CAI has often been attacked as an uncreative and anti-educational use of the computer. But really, this criticism should be levelled not at the medium but at the method-WHEN USED INAPPROPRIATELY. To be sure, kids are often drilled into memorizing useless information or into executing useful procedures without real understanding of what they are learning. But these are also quite valid for drills in both education and training.

The learning of foreign language vocabularies is one example where repeated use is essential and some form of drill exercises, whether computer base or not, are appropriate. High-speed reflex skills, like typing and computer keyboard operation, are another outstanding example of a type of learning which is heavily dependent on drill and practice and where computer-based drills have shown themselves to be vastly superior to any previous training method. We mentioned in previous sections of this chapter, the early SAKI keyboard trainer and the later easy learn system developed for the British post office. These systems have shown themselves to be most effective, achieving results that were unknown under conventional classroom instruction. 'Twice the typing speed in half the learning time, or your money back,' are slogans that can safely be used in marketing these systems, as practical experience has shown that such results are nearly always achieved by motivated learners.

Coming now to TUTORIAL CAI, we should remember that all the previously mentioned modes are often, and indeed should almost always be, present in tutorial. Individual student progress is monitored and managed by the changing of the path through the materials in response to individual needs. This necessarily involves computer-based testing which is adaptive in nature. When drills are appropriate, they may be built in and may also be made more palatable by the use of game-like contexts for practice.

Bright Aspects

The extra characteristic of the tutorial is the presentation of new information to be learnt. This may be more or less effective than it would have been by means of other media. Until recently, for example, there were serious limitations on the degree of resolution of the graphic materials that could be presented on most school use micro-computers. This aspect has improved significantly as more powerful graphics packages have become available. Also the current trend towards the linking of CAI tutorials with video material from laser discs has effectively overcome the problem of visual resolution for most purposes. But this does not make the computer screen the ideal presentation medium for all the types of information that the learner may require. The very size of the screen is sometimes a severe limitation, leading one to break down a complex network or a map, into separate screens, or to use an inconvenient 'windowing' technique in order to allow the learner to see the 'big picture'. However; for most typical instructional content, the modern computer system, enhanced with interactive video, is a pretty adequate presentation media. The benefits, if any, should be looked for in the speed and precision of storing, accessing, presenting, revising and individualizing of the information

Discrepancy between the not-so-spectacular findings of formal comparative research studies and the reported successes of individual case studies, Kulik's meta-analyses typically showed advantages to CAL over classroom instruction of the order of 15 percentage points. This is not to be 'sneezed at', if it represents a gain that can truly be expected over a long-term period, in real life instructional conditions. Clark seems to argue that the bulk of this difference is due to superior instructional design of the lesson structures given by computer and that there is no reason why similarly efficient lesson structures could not have been given in classroom instruction.

The tendency in real life classroom instruction is to have varied success with different teachers and even with different classes, taught by the same teacher. It is difficult to always maintain the same standard of teaching that was achieved during a relatively short comparative study when 'everyone was watching'. It is not surprising, therefore, that many case studies of large-scale CAI use report instructional improvements well in excess of those 15 percentage points found by Kulik.

Of course, not all tutorial CAI is the large-scale substitution of classroom instruction by machine instruction. Much the more common situation, especially in schools, is the integration of short CAI- tutorials on specific topics, into an overall course design, planned, implemented and partly delivered by the classroom teacher. In such a case, it is very difficult to separate out any benefits of CAI over alternative instructional designs. What can be measured is the overall effect of the teacher-computer media combination, as opposed to the teacher alone. There seems to be much less formal research along these lines. But informally, it is this sort of situation that impresses the enthusiast teacher most.

The bulk of the more popular literature on the use of computers in the classroom abounds with examples of the creative integration of the computer as one of the media at the teacher's disposal. There is insufficient space in this book to explore the richness of possibilities for the integration of computer-based courseware into the conventional classroom teaching situation. Many books especially devoted to the classroom use of the computer have been written and interested reader should study some of the practical suggestions reported.

The trend towards the development of conversational CAI was in part spurred by the limitations of the 'programmed instruction' models as a basis for the effective use of the computer as a medium of instruction. Already in the late 1960s there were several alternative models proposed. We have already mentioned the conversational approach built into the CASTE system and the 'structural communication' approach. Both of these methods were successfully tested in paper-based tutorial versions, but the computer technology of the time was inadequate to support their use as models for the development of large-scale CAI applications. Now that the technology has caught up, we find these techniques are little used because of the great skill and effort needed to design effective materials that exploit the systems' capabilities of interaction. There are a few examples of successful implementations of conversational tutorials, but hardly any large-scale regular use.

A similar situation exists with respect to the 'intelligent' tutorial systems that we read so much about. There is a history of research and development that spans over 30 years. Experimental systems have been operational for at last 20 years but no real impact on everyday instruction, whether in the school classroom or in job trainee situations, has as yet been felt. As Frank Roberts, of Control Data, remarked at the 1986 conference of the Association for the Development of Computer-assisted Instructional Systems, 'to my knowledge, some 15 or so intelligent tutorial systems have so far been developed beyond the conceptual design stage... of these, only five or six have been used at all extensively in real life instructional situations... and none have been systematically evaluated. As far as research on ICAI is concerned, we are still in the laboratory stage.'

The situation is very different with respect to the 'simulation' mode of CAI. This has been the fastest growing art in recent years and has the largest number of enthusiastic adherents among teachers and trainers alike. By its nature, a computer-based simulation is usually a component in a lesson. The computer is used to dynamically illustrate the cause-effect relationships that hold true in some real-life phenomenon.

An example is the famous simulation of Mendel's laws in action in a computer-based fruit-fly mating experiment. In an hour or so on the computer, it is possible to simulate many generations of fruit-fly offspring for many different mating patterns. This allows students to deduce the Mendelian laws for themselves-to discover and painstaking observations. Similar discovery experience can now be conveniently arranged in just about every area of science education, as well as economics, management, etc. The educational success of such simulations is however, much dependent on how well they are introduced and followed up by the teacher.

As with all experimental or discovery learning, it is important to reflect on the specific cases and identify the general principles at play. This is best achieved by careful initial orientation of the students and, even more importantly, deep final analysis and evaluation of what was learned. Most simulation packages do not perform these functions. The way the teacher plans and executes the briefing and debriefing is the key factor in the overall instructional effectiveness of computer-based simulations, used in the classroom for conceptual learning.

A Sort of Departure

The use of computer-based simulation to teach machine-operation is somewhat different. In this case, the instructional objectives are to learn a specific procedure. A well designed simulator may present more varied practice, more concentrated; experience of rarely occurring situations and enhanced feedback and guidance, all in a safer and possibly less environment than 'real life'. The reports on the use of computer-based simulations tend top be generally positive. Business games, using the computer as an interactive data bank, have been used and praised for nearly 30 years now. Computer-based simulations for procedural learning have a similarly long history, especially as embedded training for computer-related procedures but also in all branches of military training.

In the cognitive learning field, the research is less conclusive. This is partly due to the points made earlier, with respect to the simulations often forming only part of the teacher's overall lesson plan. This makes it difficult to sort out whether improved learning was due to something inherent in the simulation exercise or to the skill with which the teacher exploited the experience in subsequent activities. There is a certain body of research that suggests that simulations used on their own are sometimes less effective than they appear to be. Light reports studies which show rather poor learning of factual information from business simulations that were, on the face of it, excellent and absorbing exercises. Not were concepts or principles sufficiently well generalized. There seemed to be some learning of a general 'feel' for management decision making, which was difficult to measure by normal testing methods. Oakey reported studies with situational simulation-games in which students worked in groups to solve complex problems.

The objectives of the simulation games studies included general problem-solving skills and working effectively as a group, as well as content-related objectives. He found that very little real learning had occurred, especially as related to the general problem-solving and inter-personal skills.

We are now stepping beyond what may be strictly called 'computer-assisted instruction'. A database located in a computer is an information resource. As such it may be no different in content from some other resources, say a filing cabinet or a section of a library. It is different, however, in terms of the case and speed with which specific items of information may be located. Improving the efficiency of access to information has obvious effects on the efficiency of learning. This 'tool' use of the computer thus brings automatic benefits to the instructional process, whether that process itself changes or not.

18

Mass Media in Action

Medium of New Technology

Among the most significant forces for change in recent years is the technological sophistication we now possess, for this sophistication not only affects our lives in profound ways but also seems to hold tantalizing promise for increasing our efficiency in education (Kinder, 1973). The last 80 years have seen the development of steam-driven, high-speed rotary presses, advanced optics, films, wire and tape sound recordings, simple and complex duplicating and copy machines, radio, television, computers, and communication lasers.

This technological escalation has bestowed upon education proliferation of equipment and materials which can assist in the reorganization and redefinition of educational experiences. In the past, most teaching depended almost entirely on verbal communication between teacher and student, or written communication to the student from printed materials. Although, these communication channels continue to play important roles in the learning process, today's students are learning facts, skills and attitudes from pictures, television, recorded words, programmed lessons, and other media. Once technology enters the school building, dramatic renovations usually begin. With the technological magic touch, a simple school-house turns into a systematized learning centre.

Today, many countries around the world use some form of technological media in education. In a few countries, the use is fairly widespread. Most technological devices and programmes, however, are structured around the needs of the teacher and are employed as teaching aids in the classroom. In other.words, most educators are using technology to answer the question : how can technology help the teacher? In a few areas, however, focus is on the needs of the student. There. educators ask the question : how can technology help the learner?

In the instances where the student is the centre of attention, technology is catalyst for educational change. Its absence would made a significant difference to the educational process, because technology is an integral part of a well-thoughtout system, not merely a teacher's aid:

Locatis and Athinson (1984) define media as the means (usually audio-visual or electronic) for transmitting or delivering messages. Media includes such things as prints, graphics, photography, audio-communication, television, simulating games and computer.

Schramm, Wilber (1973) in his book *Big Media – Little Media, Aid Studies in Educational Technology,* categories computer, VCR, TV as 'Big Media' and 'radio, filmstrips, graphic, audio cassettes and various visuals' as 'Little Media'.

Meaning and Significance. Nelson Henry has very rightly observed in *Media and Symbols,* "Educational institutions, left to themselves may not be successful in achieving the educational objectives of the developing societies without the support of the new media." New media, implying mass media, as channels of education gain relevance from their capacity to disseminate information to a great number of people (masses) and make the present educational programmes more effective and meaningful.

According to Dr. Marshall McLuhan whose books *The Gutenberg* and *Understanding Mass Media* throw a lot of light on the subject of mass media, it is the medium which is the message. This means that the medium by which a piece of information or knowledge is communicated to us exerts a profound influence on us. The effectiveness of a piece of information depends upon the medium through which it is imparted. Dr McLuhan thinks that electronic media affect the sensibilities greatly because they tend to massage the sense. Thus, the medium is not only the message but also the massage because it massages the sensory organs and stimulates them to respond actively. Therefore, it is important that the mass media be utilised in the classroom teaching so that the students may obtain sensory stimulation as a part of the process of instruction.

As observed by Wilbur Schramm in his book *'Big Media-Little Media'*, mass media can be made use of in education "as support models in two basic but overlapping ways."

(1) They can beamed part of environment into which learning activities are designed as seen in distance teaching institutions.

(2) They can be brought into the environment as indirect partners or as tools in the hands of the teachers, by supplementing additional or supportive information that is educationally important and useful.

Mass media are means of impersonal communication via some medium, imported through mediated situation. Mass media are means or instruments of communication that reach large number of people or pupils with a common message. The matter may be printed like newspapers or it may take the form of radio, television and cinema. Carlton W.H. Erickson observes, "In recent years technology has swept through society from research laboratories into manufacturing communications, the space age, and finally now, into education."

In early times, the teacher was the only medium of communication for children. He taught his students orally. During the course of time the invention of the printing press, led to the printing of books. Then came newspapers. Now for quite some time new mass media like radio and T.V. are increasingly used in education. They reach large members and also help in improving the quality of education.

Schools and colleges for long have been the sole medium for imparting information and aiding in the acquisition of knowledge. But with the technological development and fast expanding knowledge, new avenues of education have come up. These media disseminate information which the schools can no longer ignore but needs to be integrated into the teaching-learning process.

The National Policy on Education 1986 and modified policy, 1992 has observed, "The media has profound influence on the minds of children. The mass media make the constraints of time and distance manageable. Modern educational technology must reach out to the most distant areas and the most deprived section of beneficiaries simultaneously with the areas of comparative affluence and ready availability."

Mass media serve some important functions. They are helpful in reaching large number of people. They are helpful in the spread of compulsory education and adult literacy. Recently their use is being made increasingly in distance education. They are useful in making instruction more effective and meaningful.

The use of radio, supplemented by correspondence programme has proved to be very successful in Kenya. Radio forums as a means of adult and continuing education have proved to be extremely successful in Canada, India, Nigeria. Sweden, Tanzania and many other countries.

It is sometimes felt that the mass media tend to diminish the importance of the teacher. It is also claimed in certain circles that they are likely to replace the classroom teachers. A close look at the use of these media of education indicates that they are supplementary media. A lot of work by way of pre-telecast, during telecast and post-telecast remains to be done by the teachers. Many gaps are to be filled up by them. In spite of the explosion of technological media in the developed countries, they still occupy the place of importance. Fears about the replacement of teachers are unfounded.

Radio Technology

There is hardly any doubt regarding the potential of the radio as an instructional aid. Frederic Wittis has rightly remarked "I like to think of education by radio as a timely, vital and dramatic thing; a system of learning or acquiring more information, a means of widening one's horizon or enriching one's life and breaking down prejudices through inspiration and not perspiration; an education by desire and not by discipline; a pattern of swiftly changing pictures, events with keen interpretations, not statistics and formula's; a moving panorama of the world in which we live—right now, while we are living in it—not a dreary drill of textbooks and tests. In short, I feel that one of broadcasting's most helpful contributions to education and one of its real responsibilities to itself and its listeners is the popularising of education itself."

R.G. Reynolds writes: "Radio is the most significant medium for education in its broadest sense that has been introduced since the turn of the century. As a supplement to classroom teaching its possibilities are almost unlimited. Its teaching possibilities are not confined to the five or six hours of the school day. It is available from early morning till long after midnight. By utilising the rich educational and cultural offerings of the radio, children and adults in communities, however remote, have access to the best of the worlds's stores of knowledge and art. Some day its use as an educational instrument will be as common place as textbooks and blackboards."

Merits

1. Bringing the school into contact with the world around.
2. Helping in the spread of elementary education.
3. Helping in the promotion of adult education.
4. Assisting in the spread of non-formal education.
5. Enrichment of school programme.
6. Furnishing up-to-date material.
7. Developing critical thinking.
8. Developing leisure time interest and appreciation.
9. Providing opportunities for student participation.
10. Providing an alternative approach to the education of out of school children.
11. Imparting vocational skills.
12. Popularising science with a view to developing scientific outlook.
13. Promoting emotional and national integration.
14. Providing information about population education, energy conservation, preservation of wild life etc.
15. Serving as a training component for teachers.

Limitations

1. Radio broadcast is a one-way communication. Students cannot put questions to the broadcaster.
2. The educational value of radio broadcasting depends merely on the use of sense of hearing.
3. The students have little opportunities to participate in the instructional activity. They are passive listeners for most of the time.
4. In several cases, broadcasting time does not suit all educational institutions.
5. The number of receiving sets is not adequate in the case of several educational institutions.
6. It becomes very difficult to integrate school programmes which radio broadcasts.
7. A continuing listening on the part of the students may make them inattentive and uninterested in the task of gaining learning experiences.
8. Usually there is paucity of adequate pre-information, manual or guides regarding radio broadcast with the result that the students and teachers both face difficulties in making necessary preparation for the utilisation of these programmes.

Suggestions for Effective broadcasting

1. The school broadcasts should not be merely course lessons but should have a wider horizon of application in day-to-day life.
2. The school broadcasts should be planned according to the needs of the syllabus, students and concerned teachers.
3. Teachers should occasionally meet, discuss and plan the type of assistance required on mass media instructional facilities.
4. The radio programmes should be intended to give supplementary information to the various topics in the syllabus.
5. Good planning and administration is highly needed so as to make the programmes effective and worthwhile.

6. Broadcasting time should be suitable to schools.
7. Adequate feedback should be provided.
8. There should be proper follow-up on school broadcasting programmes.
9. Adequate listening facilities should be provided in schools.
10. Broadcasts should be made in easy and simple language.
11. Broadcasts should be made in a pleasing style.

In short all the six main stages of a radio broadcast namely, production, preparation, listening to the programme, feedback, consolidation of acquired knowledge and evaluation should be carefully attended to.

History of school broadcasting. Ever since the start of school broadcasting by British Broadcasting Corporation (B.B.C.) in 1920, it has made rapid strides in making sound contribution to formal education, In the U.S.A., in 1923, there were programmes in accounting from New York: programmes in arithmetic and literature from Oakland in 1924, 20 States in U.S.A. had provision for educational broadcasting. Around the same time about 98% of the schools in U.K. were equipped with radio and there were regular daily programmes. Bombay Station put out items of special interest to school children. Madras had regular school broadcasts for half an hour on all weekdays. Similar programmes were introduced by Calcutta Station in 1932. The programmes for schools produced by Akashwani Stations are for the following categories of people.

(a) Children of primary classes; (b) children of secondary and higher secondary classes; (c) Preparing lessons for secondary and higher secondary classes near examination times; (d) Teachers; (e) General enrichment programme for children.

These broadcasts can either be 'live' or 'transcribed' depending on the physical presence of the person broadcasting or his recorded speech. Broadcasting organisations throughout the world, including AIR, include in their output various school broadcasts. Such programmes are normally arranged in consultation with the heads of various institutions. This liaison between the radio and educational authorities helps in bringing out effective and useful programmes for the pupils. The planning of such talks is undertaken with great care and by persons of repute. The programmes are prepared termwise and copies are supplied to schools sufficiently in advance to enable the teachers to discuss the subject with the pupils.

T.V. for Learning

ETV in the World. TV has become child's third parent and a first teacher. The history of television shows that it is a very powerful, informative socializing and mobilizing force. Most of the countries of the world have gone for television to solve their difficulties and problems relating to education. Direct television instruction started four decades back in progressive countries like UK and USA The regular programmes were sent on air in November 1936 by BBC. Remote areas were provided with television sets. By 1958 more than 98% of the population was covered by television transmission. By 1961 Moscow and U.K. shared the programmes with each other. By 1962 Americam engineers, succeeded in bouncing television waves across the Atlantic on a Satellite-Telestar. In 1967 the first regular service of coloured televisions in Europe began on BBC-2.

For the first time, television for instructional purposes was used in the USA. A large number of experiments in instructional television were conducted there. In 1958, a project entitled continental classroom started instructional television for the whole of USA. It telecasted a programme "Physical of the Atomic Age" for science teachers. About 40,000 teachers received instruction through this programme. Later on, several programmes such as modern chemistry, contemporary mathematics and new biology were also telecast by this project. In 1961, a project called "Mid-west Airborne Instructional Television" started instructional television. About 13,000 schools received the programmes benefiting about five million students, at a cost of 7.5 million dollars or at an expenditure of 1.5 dollar per student. At present there are hundreds of instructional television programmes being telecast in USA and other countries.

Significance of educational television. Television is the most potential instrument in educating masses and thereby narrowing down the gap of progress between the developing and developed countries of the world. For a country like India which has vast and inaccessible areas, different climatic conditions, large and ever growing population, TV can be an important central media in providing functional, formal and non-formal education to the masses. It can also help in bringing about social and cultural changes bearing on art, music, drama and literature. It is through television that stimulating and thought-provoking views of renowned statesmen, scientists, educationists, artists and teachers can be shared by all. Television helps in enforcing the public understanding of social, political and scientific advancement of a country. Following are the important merits of television.

Chief Merits

1. It permits the use of the best available teacher to teach a subject for a large number of student viewers. It preserves the expert teaching skills of such teachers on video tape or film for later use.
2. It provides a common experience to all students when they all see the same basic ideas or techniques on television.
3. It provides the teacher an opportunity to observe the instructional methods and ideas of their experts and to increase his own knowledge of teaching methods and stimulate new ideas.
4. It provides technical advantages not readily available in normal classrooms for illustration or demonstration.
   (a) It makes possible close-up magnification of small objects, components, intricate mechanisms, diagrams, etc; giving student a "front-row seat."
   (b) It allows instantaneous change of perspection by switching from a wide camera angle to a close-up or by "zooming" in.
   (c) It permits relationships between two illustrations or time lapse between two stages of a process by dissolving one picture into another.
   (d) It provides for comparison of two or more illustrations by superimposure or 'split screen' effects.
5. It directs the attention of the student to the exact detail of object which he should see by eliminating distracting surroundings.

6. It makes quick and lasting visual and rural impressions which can often reduce the time necessary to teach an idea or technique.
7. It makes it possible to bring large, scarce, new or refined equipment "into the classroom" electronically.
8. It incorporates useful film sequences, slides, graphic art and makes available teaching aids within a television presentation, tailored to meet the needs of a particular course or subject.
9. It saves time, effort and cost of setting up classroom projection equipment.
10. It brings instructional films into classrooms as needed with no special classroom preparation, no darkening of rooms or use of special ventilation in the room.
11. It provides more "immediacy" than instructional films.
12. It brings live demonstration, video-tape or film presentations to the classroom at the instant or immediately after they occur.
13. It permits inclusion of up-to-date information, modification, new equipment or techniques into the classroom instruction.
14. It allows the teacher time to observe individual students or to assist them during the television presentation, or to determine what needs further application after the presentation.

Limitations

1. The medium is limited to one-way communication from teacher to students. Students cannot put any question.
2. The total cost of teaching by television is more than normal classroom instruction, unless television is used to reach large number of students at one time or sequentially over a period of time.
3. Television has special and unique techniques and requires occasional re-arrangement of subject sequence.
4. Individual differences of the students are not attended to in a TV lesson.

5. TV lessons may not suit the school timings.
6. TV lessons are not flexible.
7. Instruction through TV is not child or learner centred.

Kinds of Educational

1. Total TV teaching.
2. TV as a complementary basic resource.
3. TV as a supplementary environment.

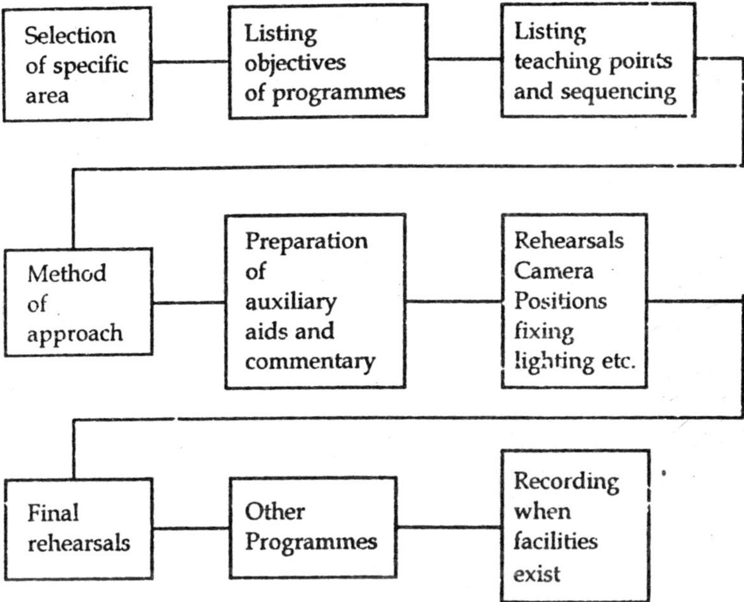

Fig. : Basic procedures in programming ETV.

Kinds of Educational TV

Open circuit television. It is the usual type of telecast by commercial or non-commercial stations.

Closed circuit television (CCTV). It is the selective telecast which can be used only by specially equipped receivers. Its range is limited to the length of the cable. CCTV can be used to great advantage in educational institutions. Its capabilities are as under:

1. It increases the range of instruction to one or more locations beyond the classroom.

2. It enables institutions to present televised instruction in accordance with their specific needs and schedules.
3. It provides opportunities for the exchange of professors and courses between one institution and another linked to a circuit.
4. In teacher training institutions CCTV with video-tape-recorders can be used to record performance of the teacher trainee during micro-teaching lessons. Video-tape provides the necessary feedback.
5. CCTV is used in many medical colleges in developed countries. The entire operation can be covered by using a single television camera or a battery of cameras located at vantage points.

School TV programmes have five main stages and it is necessary that the teacher should be associated with each stage.

1. Planning and Preparation
2. Presentation
3. Production
4. Utilisation
5. Evaluation

Teacher in the planning and preparation of TV programmes. No TV programme for schools can be planned and prepared unless the classroom teacher is effectively associated with this work. To plan and prepare a good TV lesson, a thorough knowledge of the requirements of the students of different age levels, the suitability of the materials, the sequence and the contents are very vital and this can be met fully only by the classroom teacher. Experience tells that the classroom teacher can contribute effectively in this area if he has a good grounding and knows very well the mechanics of a good TV lesson.

Teacher in the production of TV programme. Production is a technical thing but the knowledge about the mechanics of production must be known to the classroom teacher if he is to appreciate a good lesson, i.e., to locate its strong and weak points and suggest improvements.

Teacher in the presentation of TV programme. Again, in the presentation of a TV lesson it is only the classroom teacher who can deliver the goods—no doubt a teacher with initiative, imagination and subject competency. The presentation involves only a selected number of teachers but the scope of selection involves all the teachers of a subject. A good selection can be possible only from a TV trained group. It is noted that without necessary training in this field even a very good and competent teacher in a school fumbles and stumbles in the studio.

Utilisation of TV programme and the teacher. Pre/post telecast utilisation is the area where the teacher is the master of the situation. It may be emphasised that no TV lesson is complete without the introduction and follow-up exercise in the classroom by the subject teacher. An average lesson with proper and well thought introduction and follow-up can become a very effective lesson whereas a good lesson in the absence of one or both can go flat. The teacher has to inspire the students, prepare them and arouse their curiosity before the telecast of the lesson and afterward has to clarify the doubts, if any, provide the missing links and re-inforcement in the follow-up. He has also to integrate the TV lesson with his classroom teaching. He has also to take care of many other factors and provide congenial conditions to enable his students to really benefit from a TV lesson.

Teacher in the evaluation of TV programme. Evaluation is another important area. If tackled properly, it contributes considerably to the quality and usefulness of TV lessons. No evaluation is possible or worthwhile without the involvement of the classroom teacher. Moreover, simply involvement of the classroom teacher does not help much unless he is fully conversant and properly trained to evaluate and assess the TV lesson from all angles and has acquired competency to do the job well. Without proper training the teachers even fail to fill up the check-sheets properly—an exercise to be completed by the classroom teacher after every lesson.

Resources at Disposal

Once the television becomes an integral part of classroom teaching, the physical facilities available in the schools are as important as the quality of the programme, from the utilisation point of view. No matter how rich and valid the TV programmes are, they cannot reach the audience unless optimum physical facilities are available to the viewers. The availability of physical facilities appears to be quite simple yet it requires a constant vigil to keep them all in operational readiness.

Broadly speaking we can classify the physical facilities into three categories :

(a) Space and seating arrangements.

(b) TV sets, Antenna and other accessories.

(c) Literature.

(a) In each TV viewing school, suitable space area must be earmarked for television viewing depending upon the number of viewers. Ideally speaking each class that has to view a TV lesson, should have TV set, fitted in the classroom itself but it is not possible. Therefore provision of a room, which can be converted into a TV room should be made, Hall is another alternative for large number of viewers. Other points to be taken care of are:

(i) Placement of TV set and its adjustment

(ii) Seating arrangement

(iii) Lighting

(iv) Ventilation

(v) Space for demonstration, per-telecast and post-telecast activities.

(b) It is needless to say that the TV sets should always be in operational condition so that these can be switched on at a very short notice. The various factors that put operating off are:

(i) Defective power points and plugs

(ii) Defective Antenna

(iii) Misadjustment of TV controls

(iv) Major defect in the TV

(v) Voltage fluctuations

(vi) Operational procedures like locked cupboards etc.

(c) The school television programmes by and large are syllabus based programmes and therefore the students must know the connecting links between their classroom teaching and the television programmes. These should reach the classroom teacher in the beginning of the session or term as the case may be.

The Celluloid

Broadly speaking, a film is a multiple media of communication. It presents facts in a realistic way, dramatizes human relations, arouses emotions and transmits attitudes. It may be used for the communication of ideas, attitudes and experiences to the masses of people. It is very effective in adult education. An educational film has been described as the greatest teacher because it teaches not only through the brain but through the whole body. It has a very powerful influence on the minds of children and is shaping their personality. The main aim of educational film is to elevate and educate them according to the patterns and principles set by the society. A good educational film should help the students to develop a sense of citizenship. A film on national integration can be prepared to help inculcate ideas of oneness and unity. 'Live and let Live' can be that theme. A variety of topics—historical, biographical and of current interest can be covered.

Some of the main advantages of motion pictures are given below:

Increased reading interests of the students. Various investigations conducted in USA. show that film producers arouse increased reading interest in children. They are stimulated to get more information about the fact they have observed in a film show.

Real learning situations. The film puts before us the learning situations which look to be quite real and actual. The child sees something happening and his experience is direct. Therefore, he is deeply impressed.

Selected learning situation. A child learns from his actual life experience more than he learns from the lessons which he gets passively in the school. But life experience comes as a routine.

Sometimes it has no educative value. Sometimes it may have adverse influence. But in an educational film, all the learning situations are selected ones. They have a great educational value.

Quickness of movement. The events in a film show run very swiftly but without losing continuity and essence of development. Therefore, the effects are also received swiftly in a concentrated form.

Vividness. The learning situation is quite vivid. Everything is happening in such a way as if it is more than living and actual. All the activities are quite vivid.

Motivation. The film motivates teaching. The child takes a great interest. A long study of many weeks may not be able to bring home the acts of the French Revolution to a child but he will at once understand and learn everything about the movement if he is shown a film of the events.

Recreation. A film show is recreational also. It is a play for the child and not work. Thus he learns through playway. He feels light and happy after the show.

Development of study habits. Educational films develop study habits as children like to know more about the facts they have leant in the show.

Illustration of all the learning situations. We cannot give an adequate idea of an ocean to a child who has never seen a lake even. A child cannot understand what a mountain is like if he has never even come acros a hill in his life. But it is not possible for us to take every child to the ocean and mountains, to the deserts and valley, to the Tundras and the Tropics. The film serves us here wonderfully. It brings the ocean, the mountains, the deserts, the valleys the Tundras and Tropics, all in their form and with all their grandeur into the school hall.

Charles, F. Hoban and E.B. Ormer summarise the educational advantages of films as: means of imparting information, development of skills, development of attitudes, enlarging interests and development of the will to solve problems.

1. Educational films sometimes include an element of fiction in historical events.
2. Recapitulation in not possible on the spot. Sometimes the teacher likes and the pupils too wish to dwell longer on a particular shot in the show. But the film does not wait. It goes no.
3. Really good educational films are not available in our country.
4. The whole process is very costly. All the schools cannot afford to have good halls, projectors and other equipment for the purpose.
5. It may have some bad effect on eyesight.

6. Generally teachers are not trained to handle the projector and organize the show.
7. It needs electricity. Many village schools have no electricity.

Suggestion for making the optimum use of Educational Films

The most important point to be taken into consideration is that the film must be relevant and purposeful.

When a film show is going to be arranged, the teacher should see that it is really needed in connection with the studies which are going on. He must discuss the background of the learning situations to be presented in the film show, previous to presentation. It should serve the purpose of recapitulation. The whole process may be arranged in the following steps :

1. Preliminary talk about the film.
2. Presentation of the film.
3. Discussion and follow-up on the film.
4. Recapitulation and recording of salient features.

The Children's Film Society India (CFSI) was established in 1955 as an autonomous body with the objectives of promoting and encouraging the Children Film Movement in the country. It also aims at providing children and the young people, films with clean and healthy entertainment. The organisation is engaged in production, acquisition, distribution and exhibition of the films suitable for the children and young people. The main office of the Society is at Mumbai and Zonal offices are at New Delhi, Chennai and Kolkata.

Since its inception, the society has produced and purchased about 100 feature films and 104 short films.

A pilot project to reach the rural children in Maharashtra by means of Mobile Film Unit has been in operation for a number of years.

Four children film clubs are functioning, viz., one at Kolhapur (Maharashtra), two at Porbandar (Gujarat) and one at Mumbai.

The society organises film festivals and participates in important international films festivals abroad. In India, the first international film festival was arranged in Bombay in 1979.

In the year 1981, the Indian festival was accorded 'A' Category status by the International Centre of Films for Children and Young People (ICFCYP), Paris.

The society has set up a National Centre of Films for Children affiliated to the International Centre of Films set up at Brussels under the sponsorship of UNESCO. Some of the important films a teacher can make use are : (1) *Scout Comp,* (2) *Guru Bhakti,* (3) *Ganga Ki Lahren,* (4) *Bachon se Batten,* (5) *Gulab Ka Phool,* (6) *Ekata,* (7) *26 January.*

Newspapers and Magazines

The press is an informal but very influential agency of education. The press includes newspapers and magazines. They provide a variety of information. They cover almost all areas of knowledge. They keep us well-informed. They are very useful in the teaching of various subjects. Instruction through newspapers introduces variety and an element of 'play-way'.

The newspapers are very useful for the study of languages. Pupils learn many new words and many new expressions. They learn how to express themselves and how to follow the expression of others. As regards social studies they learn how the society is developing day by day. They learn a lot about the society. There is much geographical and scientific information also in daily papers and magazines.

For international understanding the study of newspapers is essential. Children come to know how the world is progressing, how we are woven internationally, how the events occurring in one country affect all the other countries of the world and how we shall have to suffer if the Third World War breaks out.

In the teaching of arithmetic, the newspapers can furnish examples concerning banks, interest on savings accounts, deposits is also very helpful in the teaching of economics and commerce. Likewise a lot of information on various subjects is available form newspapers which can be used in daily teaching.

19

The Revolution

The Computer is the revolutionary invention of the modern times. The field of micro-electronics emerged rapidly after 1946 when ENIAC, the first digital computer became operable. In the thirty years that followed, the number of works who disseminated knowledge grew rapidly, and by 1977 the information economy employed approximately 50 per cent of the population including computer operators, teachers, media personnel, and the like. If we assume that ENIAC marked the birth of an information age in 1946, it seems reasonable to contend that the information society reached its lusty youth by 1956-1957. In 1956, as John Naisbitt points out, a "megashift" from the industrial or "smokestack" society took place. In that year, for the first time, blue-collar workers were outnumbered by people in white-collar jobs. Then in 1957, a global communications revolution began when "the Russians launched Sputnik, the missing technological catalyst in a growing information society".

The first computers were essentially mechanical contraptions. Development began with the introduction of the abacus in ancient China and flowered in medieval times with the invention of mechanical clocks. The seventeenth-century philosopher-mathematician, Gottfried von Leibnitz, viewed calculation as an activity unworthy of people as intelligent as himself. As a result, he developed a mechanical counting device to save time. His invention, with its stepped wheels, became the mechanical heart of many of the- calculating machines used until the early 1970s. Mechanical calculator technology reached its creative peaks in the midnineteenth century.

After the mid 1940s the second stream of computer development created an increasingly sophisticated and expensive alternative to mechanical calculators, one epitomized by ENIAC. And, so rapid did the accelerating rate of change become after World WAR II, that ENIAC was virtually obsolete by the time it was completed. In 1947, Bell Laboratories developed the transistor, using in the process tiny pieces of semiconductor material such as silicon and germanium. This development made it possible to combine many circuits in a tiny fraction of the space required by vacuum tubes and at greatly reduced cost.

Important Phase

Another significant even occurred in 1959 when integrated circuits were devised. These involved single chips, each of which contained several complete electronic circuits. By 1970, when the microchip made its debut, thousands of integrated circuits could be placed on a silicon chip 6.35 mm. square, roughly the size of a child's fingernail. As of the 1980s, over 100,000 transistors can be integrated on a single microchip, each of these bits of silicon containing the same computing power as the original thirty-ton ENIAC. Examples of recent hyper miniaturization ventures include the following: (1) In 1983, Professors Kenneth Hanck and Keith De Armond of North Carolina State University were undertaking to replace microchips with individual molecules capable of storing information in one-millionth of the space silicon chips require; (2) in 1984, Digital Research announced a single computer disc capable of preserving the entire contents of Encyclopedia Britannica; (3) in 1984, work was underway at Cornell University to etch salt crystals with words ten nanometers high which, if successful, would permit putting the contents of Encyclopedia Britannica on a bit of hardware approximately the size of a postage stamp.

At the same time, small magnetic bubbles were being incorporated in the microchip to create VLSI circuitry. These bubbles increase tenfold the present huge memory capacity of the chip. Furthermore, unlike conventional chips, when power-flow is interrupted, information continues to be stored in the chip-memory, ready for retrieval as needed. Dramatic changes are also taking place in conventional chip technology. Currently chips are made by preparing slices or wafers of silicon four inches in diameter. Up to 400 chips are then chemically etched on to the wafer, the memory and processor of cutting up chips and then putting them together is wastage of time and money and places limitations on a computer system because of the physical distance electric signals must travel between chips on the board.

A way has now been found to use the whole wafer with memory and processor and thus avoid all the separate steps. This will result in computer systems that are twenty times faster, less power hungry, more compact, and less expensive. In addition, the wafer will have a fail-safe mechanism that will enable it to reconfigure itself automatically so as to eliminate failed chips. Such a development lays the groundwork for the third stage of development.

Positive Aspects

A promising development in microelectronic technologies, one applicable to the computer field, is just getting underway. Conceivably, the shift will be as dramatic as the shift from mechanical to electronic systems. The new technology uses laser beams in lieu of electric current to permit the creation of optical computers. Their novel characteristic is the use of transphasors, which will function as the equivalents of transistors. In a transistor, a small electric current is used to switch an electric voltage between a high and low value.

The high voltage is equivalent to 1 in the binary system and the low to 0. The transphasor performs the same function as the transistor but uses a laser beam which enables it to operate several hundred times faster than the already fantastic nanosecond speed of the transistor and with greater versatility. It is becoming apparent as we go more closer to the 1990s, that the new "Third Stream" generation of optical computers should have many advantages over earlier models. Optical computers will be much faster, and programming will not longer be confined to binary arithmetic since transphasors can represent more than high and low values. Even more important, the new breed of computers promises to be able to carry out a number of different operations simultaneously.

Human knowledge, at its 1983 rate of accumulation, has been doubling every two years. It seems fortunate, therefore, that future pocket-sized transphasor computers can be (1) inexpensively produced, (2) capable of performing multiple operations simultaneously and (3) freed from the constraints of binary programming, thus promising to help us cope with accelerating change and proliferating information.

Modern Computers

Sine the development of the first two modern computers in 1946, there has been a phenomenal growth in their number and in their acceptance as efficient and indispensable tools. In 1956, there were about 600 computers. They grew in number to around 30,000 in 1966 and 400,000 in 1976. Today, there are over six million of them, and it is estimated that by 1990 more than half the households in America will have invested in computer systems. As might be expected, opinions vary as to the speed and extent of the proliferation of computers.

Regardless of conflicting views as to the precise rate of their penetration, computers are rapidly becoming in integral part of our lives. They are to be found in the factory, farm, and office; the sore, bank, and hospital; the school, university, and home. Society has constructed for itself the "electric surround" foreseen by Marshall McLuhan in the early 1960s. Further progress, however, depends upon the development of a computer systems and already become a barrier to many applications. Most areas of professional activity involve expertise of one kind or another in decision making.

The development of computers and associated programs that will effectively simulate professional decision making is only now beginning. A research on "artificial intelligence" begins to make an impact, there should be major forward leaps in fields ranging from education to medicine towards a fifth-generation computer. In the diverse phases of computer development each generation marks a distinct stage in technological advance. As noted earlier, the first generation of computers utilized vacuum tubes; the second, transistors; the third, microchips; and today's fourth generation, extremely powerful superchips. These rapid developments through four generations represent remarkable progress in the refinement of microelectrode technologies. Current attempts to develop a fifth-generation computer system for the 1990s-one capable of operating intelligently in a manner somewhat like that of the human brain-may demand a radical rethinking of basic educational principles as well as the development of entirely new coping skills on the part of both students and adults as they move into a more complex "electronic surround".

Present-day computers do what they are programmed to do. neither more nor less. They have become remarkably efficient tools for learners, teachers, and school administrator. The development of "intelligent" fifth-generation computer systems offers not only the likelihood of enhanced efficiency, but, even more important, increased effectiveness. There is also the prospect of potential increases in the task of coping with the social turbulence created by the microchip. A potential for hyper-turbulence lies in the development of a computer system which is capable of operating intelligently in a manner rather like that of the human brain, capable of "thinking" for itself. If this comes to full fruition, silicon will in effect take over from carbon the current building block of human evolution.

Before beginning to probe some of the implications of micro-technologies for education, we will consider briefly a few aspects of the hyper-turbulence generated by technological developments over the past forty or fifty years. Because of the focus of the present volume, we shall give particular attention to the social hyper-turbulence that has occurred since the microchip breakthrough a dozen years ago-a breakthrough which enabled a transportable home computer to be sold at a price within the scope of many family budgets.

Hyper-turbulence in a social environment is a term which describes "the condition that results when available resources and institutions prove inadequate to deal with the speed and diversity of change". While rapid, unsettling changes are not a unique concomitant of an information society, a comprehensive inventory of proliferating signs of hyper-turbulence is unnecessary sine the media report those signs so extensively on a global basis that further elaboration is needless.

Suffice it to say that the extent of the turbulence is mirrored, for example, in wars and terrorist attacks; a national debt in the United States in excess of 37.2 percent of the gross national product; a technologically oriented, $7 billion a year business in pornography; and an increasing use of hightech devices in homes. The sources of potential and already extant turbulence are virtually endless, but the small sample above will suffice as we turn attention to some of the ways in which the United States has become a micro-permeated society to a degree beyond Orwellian imagination. The permeation, quite understandably, nurtures turbulence. For example:

1. The United States government embarked, as of 1983, on a program of computer expenditures that will total at least $28 billion by 1988. Recipients of an estimated one million computers include air traffic controllers, customs and passport personnel, and Social Security workers. Electronic mail networks link the white House to federal agencies. The Treasury Department receives global economic data via statelite. The Veterans Administration, Department of Agriculture, Department of Commerce, Library of Congress, National Library of Medicine, Internal Revenue Service, and FBI are more and more computer-based. The Food and Drug Administration has programmed a computer to react like a mouse.
2. Electronic invasion of privacy has become more and, more common. Credit card "protection" bureaus now distribute comprehensive lists of credit cards to prospective customers via computers the bureaus patently have access to personal affairs, suggesting one more item on the roster of high-tech threats to our private lives.
3. The media, particularly television, permeate daily life. "Selected" news for the public consumption, diverse types of mind-numbling entertainment, and hidden or visible persuasion in many forms were deliberately or inadvertently made a part of our lives as Americans

spent 1.5 billion hours per day viewing television in 1984.

4. The workplace has begun to be permeated by microelectronics. Some employees have been "telecommuting" and choosing their hours of work.

The roots of the sources of hyper-turbulence and "present shock" are nourished by changes in the nature of change generated by high tech. It is highly important for educators to be aware of what has been wrought or facilitated by microelectronics. Changes in the nature of change. For uncounted millennia, change has been more than glacially slow. Carl Sagan deftly points out that if all of time, sine time began, were squeezed into one year, then the single-cell life in the warm seas of past eons would not appear until September.

The tread of the dinosaur would not shake the earth until the Christmas season, and early humans would not begin their long struggle for survival until 10 P.M. on new Year's eve. Furthermore, it would be 10:30 P.M. before our neolithic ancestors learned to chip tools from stones. The era for which history has preserved remembrance, occurs in the last few seconds prior to midnight in our "evolutionary year".

There have been crucial system-breaks in the pst, such as occurred at the end of Western Roman power in 476 A.D. But when Roman hegemony no longer existed from the Mediterranean Sea to Hadrinan's Wall, lifestyles did not change dramatically. Spears and arrows continued to be used in battle. Fields were tilled by oxen, and horses remained beasts of burden. There was little "techno-change" until the out, the world entered an ear off "technoshock". There was a dramatic change in the nature of change because of the creation and application of new technologies. In approximately fifty years, Platt tells us, there has been more acceleration in the rate of social evolution than in the previous six centuries. As an outcome, life on earth is at "the greatest turning point in four billion years". He goes on to say:

The convergence of today's technological forces, has produced a roaring waterfall of change. It leads onward to a great sea of new evolutionary possibilities on the earth and reaching into space. But right now we are in the torrent and our only hope is to work together with energy and intelligence if we are to come through successfully into that boundless ocean of hyper-turbulence and holism. One of the lessons humans must learn, particularly educators working in administration and curriculum development-that it is a period of hyper-turbulence, whatever educational changes are contemplated must be viewed holistically and systematically. We are now well into an epoch in which humans can never do one thing, an epoch in which any single action is certain to have consequences greater than the one (s) intended.

Change in Technology

As was pointed out recently, the technological changes that occur (as in the various stages of computer development) have (a) intended (b) largely unexpected, and (c) unintended consequences. Microelectronic technologies, therefore, which have implications for education require that a holistic or "total picture" assessment be made of a proposed educational policy, program, or innovation. The primary intent as television entered homes was to purvey education and entertainment. Representative of an unexpected outcome was the vast number of elementary school children who would sit up beyond midnight to watch late, late movies. An unintended impact was the decline of academic test scores which began in 1964 roughly twelve years after a cadre of 1952 kindergartens in the "TV generation" began taking the Scholastic Aptitude Test.

Between the mid- 1940s and the mid-1970s most technological advances occurred in the area of computer' hardware. Raw computer power was used to sell computers. What mattered was how many instructions a computer could handle, how much data it could store, and how fast it could process information.

Dramatic reductions in the size and cost of computers, however, have made them increasingly attractive to the domestic, educational, and business markets. As a result, computers have now become largely on off-the-shelf commodity. They are no longer the specialized marvels of yesteryear. Indeed, they sometimes share such similar characteristics that in their marketing manufacturers often are forced to exaggerate the importance of the differences which presumably distinguish them. Recently, the other "twin", software, has become more significant, especially to educators.

The quality and diversity of software is of great significance in classroom instruction, curriculum development, and distance learning. It has meaning for aspects of administrative leadership, too, as noted elsewhere in this volume. This is why we have chosen the status of software art to conclude the first part of this chapter and also to serve as a bridge to our inquiry into general implications of micro-technologies for education.

Growth of Software

Since 1980, many educators' interests have shifted from hardware to software. A decade or more ago, computers tended to be concentrated inside centralized data-processing areas where they were used primarily for clerical, accounting, and statistical purposes. Today, they are much more visible in living rooms, offices, classrooms, and work stations of all kinds. They handle a rapidly increasing range of tasks or functions including world processing, computer graphics, computer-assisted or computer-managed instruction, statistical analysis, financial data, inventory control, video games, and much more. Computer owners initially tended to buy the computer first, then choose the software to go with it.

Today, particularly in pursuing educational goals, it is advisable to examine the software one plans to use, then to select a computer than can run it efficiently. In addition, compatibility of software and hardware is also a problem, even with those systems purported to be compatible. "Compatibility" is governed not only by the capacities of hardware, but also by the way that the software is protected by the manufacturer. Therefore, the "friendliness" or compatibility of the system has also become an important consideration.

It is a consumer-oriented property which is beginning to be a priority as software companies compete more vigorously with one another. Friendliness has particular implications for education, because it creates a decreasing need for users to learn programming. Word-processing programs, spreadsheets, and database managers are emerging as the main programming "languages" of the 1980s.

As software became a more important concern of parents and teachers, computer programming ceased to be of secondary concern in our "Silicon Valleys". Many of the small companies of the 1970 have now become sizeable corporations. Hardware companies, even giants such as Apple And IBM, are finding that they do not have sufficient resources to write all the programs needed for the overgrowing list of new uses for computers. Until recently, most software companies tended to specialize, but distinctions are becoming increasingly blurred.

As the competition between software houses has grown and offerings have become more comprehensive, customers also have become more demanding. As a result, prices of programs have been reduced, customer feedback has been heeded, manuals have become more readable, and training programs have been made more widely available. One improvement of particular importance in our schools is the recent development of flat television screens weighing less than two pounds and only three-quarters of an inch thick. Thus, true portability has become possible. Of all recent developments, however, none is more important than the evolution of integrated software for home and classroom. Integrated software replaces "stand-alone" programs.

One integrated program of particular merit for secondary and postsecondary education can do complex statistical projections on a spreadsheet, create graphics and charts from the database to illustrate the projections, enable the user to write a report merging the information, and, if need be, to transmit it by telephone to one of the several electronic universities that opened in 1984-85. Moreover, since integrated programs use the same commands and instructions, it is not now necessary to learn the intricacies of three, four, five, or more computer programs. Programs do not need to be changed, nor does information have to be re-entered. In the 1980s the task of using a single computer system for both teaching and administrative purposes has thus been simplified.

The high-tech communications at Los Angeles were appreciably more extensive and impressive. The Games transported electronically to our homes were spread over 4,000 square miles, persons from fifty-one nations who spoke eighty-three languages were in the Olympic Community, and 17,000 terminals were brought in and placed at over sixty sites in order to insure comprehensive coverage. Why do we begin this section of the chapter on the implications of micro-technologies by recounting the remarkable Olympic coverage in 1984?

During the present decade the silicon ship, as it infuses us with information, has begun to approach and sometimes to transcend certain aspects of the input traditionally provided by schooling in the Unites States. As one outcome it is now increasingly necessary to consider as a single interwoven topic (a) the milieu created by the microchip and satellite and (b) the increasingly electronic surround provided for young learners by more and more schools and homes in America. Documenting the extent and suddenness of the electronic explosion is report from Dataquest, a California-based research group, which reported that in 1980 twenty-four firms sold fewer than 750 thousand personal computers. By 1982, more than a hundred companies marketed approximately three million units.

Of the many electronic developments with a direct or indirect bearing on the teaching-learning process, educational networking apparently involves the largest cluster of challenges, advantages, and problems. Before examining the network concept in some depth, however, the fascinating complexity of a few of the inventions or events infiltrating complexity of a few of the inventions or events infiltrating human lives merits passing mention. They suggest the shape of things to come.

1. A nationwide portable cellular telephone service has become available as of 1984-85.
2. OMNI magazine recently published a short story written by a computer without human help.
3. At the Toko Auto Show a car which could respond to twenty-six pre-registered voice commands was introduced.
4. In various sports, coaching by "biomechanical computer analysis" was developed.
5. A calculator wrist watch came on the market. It "reads" and records the numbers pressed on its glass covered dial by a finger and then calculates as instructed. It also serves as a stopwatch and tells the hour.

At the same time, the world is becoming both a bigger and a smaller place. As we become submerged by information, the challenge is to extract knowledge from the flood of paper and electronic signals that bombard us. Information is transitory; knowledge is durable and self-propagating. The world is made of information, simple forms of which are matter and energy, but the biggest achievements of humankind are knowledge-based.

The concept of the network as a means of keeping informed and as a means of coping with pyramidal bureaucracies or hierarchies is an ancient one. The "Committees of Correspondence" in colonial times, "Old Boy hierarchies", and the "grapevine" are examples of traditional communications structures devised to keep ourselves informed. In the realm of telecommunication information networks, there is a growing range and variety of electronic linkages, which are commonly known as databases.

Development at Fast Pace

Microcomputer telecommunications seem fated to be the fastest growing segment of microchip-based industries. This because the proliferation of databases not only helps an individual to be informed but also to communicate, to engage in lifelong learning, and even to telecommute to work or to "tele-shop" rather than wait in line to be served at a store. So rapidly has the home and office database grown in popularity that by 1985 there probably will be well over 350,000 subscribers to the various network services available from the "Big Three", and perhaps hundreds of other vendors. Just as ABC, CBS, and NBC continue to dominate television-although pressed in some areas by cable competitors-so three comparable "Big Three" purveyors of databases are Jominant

The nature of available information services equipment. The gear needed for home, school, or corporation participation in microelectronic networks varies in price from a few hundred dollars to well over $10,000 depending on individual or institutional needs and aspirations. If one already owns a personal computer and has a touch-tone phone, the additional requirements are (a) a modem that transforms computer data into acoustical signals, or vice-versa; (b) a software communication package; and (c) a communications interfacing component that physically coordinates sending and receiving information to an from other parts of the network via the modem and telephone circuit. If these items of equipment are available, the client can obtain series such as those mentioned in subsequent paragraphs by (a) dialing the local or WATS number for a given service and (b) providing the identification number and password. One is then "tuned in" or "on line" given data source.

One need not be a programmer or understand a computer language to engage in networking.

Various networks, such as those listed above, provide a growing list of services. For example, COMP-U-STORE of Stamford, Connecticut, purveys over 60,000 products; Tradenet permits persons "to network" barter deals; and a Canadian firm will lease a database dealing with demographies and marketing prospects in a given geographical area. Information on Demand (IOD) Specializes in Exotic questions and will even translate technical Japanese or Chinese characters into other written languages.

The extent to which networking is contributing to education is substantial. Compuserve has arranged an advisory service in which faculty members from between 200 and 3000 secondary schools provide on-line advice regarding such matters as preparing for SAT's or selecting a compatible university. The constantly updated research-retrieval information available through DIALOG and the opportunity for students to request reference materials on wide variety of topics from librarians are of obvious value.

Two rival computer networks in Britain now make it possible to link all of that country's 6,500 secondary schools. Schools will be able to "network" with other schools and to interact with business and industry. It is envisaged, for instance, that employers will relay career information and job applications directly to terminals in the schools. Students will complete the application forms on the terminals in the schools and "return" them instantly via computer mail services.

Electronic on -screen reference books, updated from day to day, also are available. As of mid-1984, on two networks there were around 90,000 subscribers resting the idea of a network encyclopedia and, at present, are also exploring other electronic alternatives. Some limited and controlled experiments had been undertaken by 1983-84 in schools in the United States in an effort to improve basic reading skills by means of computers.

Teleconference networking and electronic mail also are beginning to be used in education. Teleconferencing is similar to electronic mail in that it transmits data, audio and video, from one location to another, but interactively. In time communication within or between school systems seems likely. There is ample precedent in the business community. By mid-1984 a company making electronic instruments, Hewlett-Packard, was exchanging some 100,000 electronic messages daily with 15,000 employees in fifty locations around the globe.

Educators within larger cities, or when separated by thousands of miles, can exchange information. For instance, in a "wired" school a teacher, principal, or nurse can type a note to a school physician on a computer and describe the symptoms of a child suddenly taken ill. Return advice can be expected in a matter of a minute or two. "Voicemail" systems, where spoken messages are recorded via telephone-computer units, also are in their early stages.

If we are to accept views expressed in much of the literature we have reviewed in preparing this chapter, it is likely that in the next two decades microelectronics and network databases will virtually become educators' partners in the classroom, office, and laboratory. If this is the case, we will need to answer with prudence, reasoned by Chorover: How will microcomputers and associated microelectronic technologies affect the form and content of education? What effect will their introduction have on the personal and professional lives of students, teachers, and administrators? How will it effect relationships, as well as the quality of the interactions, between the individuals and groups of people involved in the educational process? We now consider each of these queries. Changing form an curriculum content. Here, educators confront the basic challenge of the impact of microelectronics on the curriculum and instruction. It seems likely, as computers become even more sophisticated, and as they retrieve information even more efficiently, that there will be not a decreasing but an increasing need for reading, speaking, and writing skills. There also seems certain to be a need for expanded knowledge with respect to the content and application of the subject matter of the natural and social sciences.

The computer and networks purvey information; they do not dispense the ability to understand or interpret this input. As a result of increased input, the meaning of meaning needs to be emphasized. This includes helping young learners to recognize flawed communication, trival or "junk" communication, manipulated news, and the ways in which those forms of communication, including books and journals, that bring wisdom can best be exploited. In short, redesign of the curriculum must eventuate in the widespread literacy-based know-how that is essential in a society with a high "survival quotient". Furthermore, even the presumed "great leap" that the artificial intelligence of fifth-generation computers may initiate will demand more, rather than less, knowledge and wisdom of humans.

The importance of judgment, perception and intuition in both teaching and learning is likely to increase as computerized knowledge systems assume more of the burdens of memorization, retrieval, and analysis. Changing personal professional roles: Students, teachers, administrators not only will the personal and educational roles and young learners undergo mutations in coming decades; mature and senior learners and professional educators can anticipate new experiences for the new epoch.

Various experiences and exposures are suggested for administrators and teachers. The following sampling of possible innovations in our schools merits particular attention not just in view of the revolutionary developments we have already described but because of their implications for many members of the community—

1. A basic knowledge of the increasing complexity and versatility of the computer and of the overall microelectronic milieu should be acquired. Special heed must be given to the growing range and variety of network input for both faculty and students at home as well as at school. As Neil postman has pointed out, by 1980 students who were graduated from high schools in

the United States had spent some 15 or 16 thousand hours watching television, versus the 12 thousand hours they spent in elementary and secondary classrooms. The computer in the home, including videogames, is increasing the discrepancy. Clearly, ways of monitoring and utilizing the total electronic surround must become a greater part of the preparation of teachers and adult lifelong learning skills, and the use of access to networks need to follow new paths. Technological unemployment created by increased robotization lends an increasing urgency for retrofitting or retraining the jobless.

2. First-hand acquaintance with the range and variety of software available for elementary and secondary pupils and adults is needed. Also, the adaptability of hardware to proliferating information on networks must constantly be reviewed by teachers and, as appropriate, shared with learners.
3. Course work in administration at both the undergraduate and graduate levels should include a study of (a) the basic nature of the skills of computer operation plus some "hands on" contacts; (b) an introduction to curriculum planning that anticipates and is derived from developments that are shaping the future; and (c) improved and increased input from arts and science college courses dealing with megatrends that are shaping society. Continuing "literacy upgrading", including basic skills testing, is essential in all course work.
4. Because of the rapidity of change in microelectronics, continuing "competency updates" through short-term workshops and conferences should be sponsored at the university level for school employees and parents.
5. Content of course syllabi and of policy books in such areas as school plant, law, finance, public relations, and basic administration should be checked periodically by the school administration and faculty to help insure that the implications of current microelectronic developments are included and emerging developments anticipated.

6. When feasible, sabbaticals for administrators and teachers, or at least short-term residencies, should be arranged so that participants have access to electronically equipped "vanguard" schools or university computer centers.
7. Finally, teaches and administrators should be helped to understand that their teaching and leadership potential can be threatened and perhaps sharply diminished if they allow themselves to become dependent on (a) "micro-wise" assistants of (b) too dependent on a computer system as a substitute for their own personal critical thinking.

Angle of Humanity

In the emerging electronic educational realms, one short statement has acquired greatly enhanced significance. Carefully planned teamwork and cooperation have never been more vital than they will be in the future. Successful teamwork already is coming into being among parents and other community residents, students, teachers, administrators, school boards, and trustees because of the tremendously versatile silicon chip.

The opportunity for human beings to work together and to live well with their micro-biotechnological creations has never been greater, and never has it-been fraught with greater potential peril in a time of ecological and nuclear dangers. As we acquire the higher skills of successful interaction, our success as team-workers will be greater as we recognize that there are multiple facets of the learners' intelligence in the widest sense of the term. We have tended to stress and to test verbal and mathematical skills. Far less has been done to polish the artistic, musical, and kinesthetic forms of intelligence. By and large interpersonal or social intelligence skill in working with others-and interpersonal or self-knowledge insights have often been taken for granted. They now need careful cultivation. A part of successful human relations in the educational world of tomorrow will involve shaping a wide range of talents to strengthen the faculty and to obtain the best of the varied social and intellectual skills that each member possesses.

Although the prospects for the positive application of microelectronics in education are bright, a few caveats and cautions need to be kept in mind. The EMP, first society and its schools need to preserve some effective back-up strategies because one single nuclear blast would be likely to give off an electromagnetic pulse (EMP) that could lobotomize computers along with other circuitry. The EMP phenomenon, which travels with the speed of light, is an intense burst of magnetic energy that burns out electrical systems. A nuclear bomb exploded 250 miles above a mid-western state presumably would envelop the United States with EMP which has peak fields of 50,000 volts per meter-probably enough to make most of our power and communications systems useless-including those operated by the military. Since EMP was identified as a threat in 1962, billions of dollars have been spent by the military in a unsuccessful effort to safeguard our electronic gear. The maintenance of freedom from overdependence on sophisticated microelectronic communication systems seems crucial.

Additional Reading

Bhaskara Rao, Digumarti (1994). *Scientific Aptitude*, New Delhi: Ashish Publishing House. ISBN 81-7024-658-X.

Bhaskara Rao, Digumarti (1995). *Animal Kingdom*. New Delhi: Discovery Publishing House. ISBN 81-7141-274-2.

Bhaskara Rao, Digumarti (1995). *Batracology*. New Delhi: Discovery Publishing House. ISBN 81-7141-279-3.

Bhaskara Rao, Digumarti (1997), *Scientific Attitude*. New Delhi: Discovery Publishing House. ISBN 81-7141-308-0.

Bhaskara Rao, Digumarti (1996). *Scientific Attitude vis-à-vis Scientific Aptitude*. New Delhi: Discovery Publishing House. ISBN 81-7141-308-0.

Bhaskara Rao, Digumarti, Editor (1996). *Encyclopaedia of Education for All*, 5 Volumes. New Delhi: APH Publishing Corporation. ISBN 81-7024-759-4 (set).

Vol. I *Education for All: The World Conference*. ISBN 81-7024-760-8.

Vol. II *Education for All: The EPA-9 Summit*. ISBN 81-7024-761-6.

Vol. III *Education for All: Quality Education for All*. ISBN 81-7024-762-6.

Vol. IV *Education for All: Planning and Monitoring*. ISBN 81-7024-763-4.

Vol. V *Education for All: The Indian Scenario*. ISBN 81-7024-764-0.

Bhaskara Rao, Digumarti, Editor (1996). *Global Perceptions on Peace Education*, 3 Volumes. New Delhi: Discovery Publishing House. ISBN 81-7141-319-6.

Bhaskara Rao, Digumarti, Editor (1996). *National Policy on Education*. 2 Volumes. New Delhi: Anmol Publications Pvt. Ltd. ISBN 81-7488-323-1.

Bhaskara Rao, Digumarti, Editor (1997). *Care the Child*, 2 Volumes. New Delhi: Discovery Publishing House. ISBN 81-7141-394-3.

Bhaskara Rao, Digumarti, Editor (1997). *Education for the 21st Century*. New Delhi: Discovery Publishing House. ISBN 81-7141-389-7.

Bhaskara Rao, Digumarti, Editor (1997). *Reflections on Scientific Attitude*. New Delhi: Discovery Publishing House, ISBN 81-7141-319-6.

Bhaskara Rao, Digumarti, Editor (1997). *Success Story of a Primary Education Project*. New Delhi: APH Publishing Corporation. ISBN 81-7024-850-7.

Bhaskara Rao, Digumarti, Editor (1997). *World Food Summit*. New Delhi: Discovery Publishing House. ISBN 81-7141-386-2.

Bhaskara Rao, Digumarti, Editor (1998). *Adolescence Education*. New Delhi: Discovery Publishing House. ISBN 81-7141-432-X.

Bhaskara Rao, Digumarti, Editor (1998). *Community and School Nutrition Education*. New Delhi: Discovery Publishing House. ISBN 81-7141-435-4.

Bhaskara Rao, Digumarti, Editor (1998). *District Primary Education Programme*. New Delhi: Discovery Publishing House. ISBN 81-7141-396-X.

Bhaskara Rao, Digumarti, Editor (1998). *Earth Summit*, 2 Volumes. New Delhi: Discovery Publishing House. ISBN 81-7141-435-4.

Bhaskara Rao, Digumarti, Editor (1998). *National Policy on Education: Towards an Enlightened and Humane Society*. New Delhi: Discovery Publishing House. ISBN 81-7141-426-5.

Bhaskara Rao, Digumarti, Editor (1998). *Reforming School Education*. New Delhi: Discovery Publishing House. ISBN 81-7141-403-6.

Bhaskara Rao, Digumarti, Editor (1998). *Teacher Education in India*. New Delhi: Discovery Publishing House. ISBN 81-7141-406-0.

Bhaskara Rao, Digumarti, Editor (1998). *World Summit for Social Development*. New Delhi: Discovery Publishing House. ISBN 81-7141-420-6.

Bhaskara Rao, Digumarti, Editor (2000). *Education for All: Achieving the Goal*, 3 Volumes, New Delhi: APH Publishing Corporation. ISBN 81-7648-152-1.

Vol. I *The Global Consensus*. ISBN 81-7648-155-6.

Vol. II *Mid-Decade Review Reports of Regional Seminars*. ISBN 81-7648-154-8.

Vol. III *Issues and Trends*. ISBN 81-7648-155-6.

Bhaskara Rao, Digumarti, Editor (2000), *International Encyclopaedia of AIDS*, 11 Volumes in 13 Parts. New Delhi: Discovery Publishing House. ISBN 81-7141-6 (Set).

Vol. 1 *Introduction to HIV/AIDS*. ISBN 81-7141-523-7.

Vol. 2 *HIV/AIDS—Issues and Challenges*, 2 Parts. ISBN 81-7141-524-5.

Vol. 3 *HIV/AIDS—Socio Economic Realities*. ISBN 81-7141-524-3.

Vol. 4 *HIV/AIDS—Law Ethics and Human Rights*, 2 Parts. ISBN 81-7141-526-1.

Vol. 5 *AIDS and NGOs*. ISBN 81-7141-527-X.

Vol. 6 *AIDS and Home Care*. ISBN 81-7141-528-8.

Vol. 7 *STD Case Management*. ISBN 81-7141-529-6.

Vol. 8 *HIV/AIDS Prevention and Care—Teaching Modules for Nurses and Midwives*. ISBN 81-7141-530-X.

Vol. 9 *HIV Prevention Education for Education for Educational Institutions*. ISBN 81-7141-531-8.

Vol. 10 *Instructional Modules for AIDS Education*. ISBN 81-7141-532-6.

Vol. 11 *School Health Education to Prevent AIDS and STD—A Package for Curriculum Planners*. ISBN 81-7141-5338-4.

Bhaskara Rao, Digumarti, Editor (2000). *International Encyclopaedia of Science and Technology Education*, 11 Volumes. New Delhi: Discovery Publishing House. ISBN 81-7141-548-2 (Set).

Vol. 1 *Science and Technology Education.* ISBN 81-7141-568-7.

Vol. 2 *Science Education in Developing Countries.* ISBN 81-7141-570-9.

Vol. 3 *Organisational Structure of Science.* ISBN 81-7141-570-9.

Vol. 4 *Science Education in Asia and the Pacific.* ISBN 81-7141-571-7.

Vol. 5 *Science and Technology Education for All* ISBN 81-7141-572-5.

Vol. 6 *Values, Ethics, Talent and Girls in Science and Technology Education.* ISBN 81-7141-573-3.

Vol. 7 *Popularization of Science and Technology Education.* ISBN 81-7141-574-1.

Vol. 8 *Science, Power and Society.* ISBN 81-7141-575-X.

Vol. 9 *Information Technology.* ISBN 81-7141-576-8.

Vol. 10 *Teacher Training in Science and Technology Education.* ISBN 81-7141-577-6.

Vol. 11 *Teacher Training in Science and Technology: A Curriculum Framework.* ISBN 81-7141-578-4.

Bhaskara Rao, Digumarti, Editor (2001). *Distance Education in Different Countries.* New Delhi: APH Publishing Corporation. ISBN 81-7648-229-3.

Bhaskara Rao, Digumarti, Editor (2001). *Decentralised Management of Education (Management of Education in Panchayati Raj and Municipal Bodies).* New Delhi: Discovery Publishing House. ISBN 81-7141-617-9.

Bhaskara Rao, Digumarti, Editor (2001). *Electrochemistry for Environmental Protection.* New Delhi: Discovery Publishing House. ISBN 81-7141-619-5.

Bhaskara Rao, Digumarti, Editor (2001). *Global Educational Studies.* New Delhi: Discovery Publishing House. ISBN 81-7141-616-0.

Bhaskara Rao, Digumarti, Editor (2001). *Global Synthesis of Educational Assessment.* New Delhi: Discovery Publishing House. ISBN 81-7141-613-6.

Bhaskara Rao, Digumarti, Editor (2000). *International Encyclopaedia of Human Rights*. 7 Volumes in 13 Parts. New Delhi: Discovery Publishing House. (Royal Size). ISBN 81-7141-567-9 (Set).

Vol. 1 *International Instruments of Human Rights*, 2 Parts. ISBN 81-7141-595-4.

Vol. 2 *Regional Instruments of Human Rights*. ISBN 81-7141-604-7.

Vol. 3 *Human Rights and the United Nations*, 2 Parts. ISBN 81-7141-605-5.

Vol. 4 *Fact Files of Human Rights*, 3 Parts. ISBN 81-7141-606-3.

Vol. 5 *Study Stories of Human Rights*, 3 Parts. ISBN 81-7141-607-3.

Vol. 6 *International Meetings on Human Rights*, 2 Parts. ISBN 81-7141-608-X.

Vol. 7 *Professional Training in Human Rights*. ISBN 81-7141-609-8.

Bhaskara Rao, Digumarti, Editor (2001). *Jomtein Decade of Education*. New Delhi: Discovery Publishing House. ISBN 81-7141-618-7.

Bhaskara Rao, Digumarti, Editor (2001). *Nuclear Materials: Issues and Concerns*, 2 Volumes. New Delhi: Discovery Publishing House. ISBN 81-7141-611-X.

Bhaskara Rao, Digumarti, Editor (2001). *World Conference on Education for All*. New Delhi: APH Publishing Corporation. ISBN 81-7141-274-9.

Bhaskara Rao, Digumarti, Editor (2001). *World Conference on Higher Education*, New Delhi: Discovery Publishing House. ISBN 81-7141-610-1.

Bhaskara Rao, Digumarti, Editor (2001). *World Conference on Science*. New Delhi: Discovery Publishing House. ISBN 81-7141-612-8.

Bhaskara Rao, Digumarti, Editor (2003). *Inspiring Experience in Teacher Education*. New Delhi: Discovery Publishing House. ISBN 81-7141-656-X.

Bhaskara Rao, Digumarti, Editor (2003). *International Studies in Education*, 3 Volumes, New Delhi: Discovery Publishing House. ISBN 81-7141-647-0.

Bhaskara Rao, Digumarti, Editor (2003). *Military Conversion: Impact on Science and Technology*, New Delhi: Discovery Publishing House. ISBN 81-7141-578-4.

Bhaskara Rao, Digumarti, Editor (2003). *United Nations Millennium Summit*. New Delhi: Discovery Publishing House. ISBN 81-7141-632-2.

Bhaskara Rao, Digumarti, Editor (2003). *World Assembly on Aging*. New Delhi: Discovery Publishing House. ISBN 81-7141-637-3.

Bhaskara Rao, Digumarti, Editor (2004). *World Conference on Human Rights*. New Delhi: Discovery Publishing House. ISBN 81-7141-661-6.

Bhaskara Rao, Digumarti, Editor (2003). *World Education Forum*. New Delhi: Discovery Publishing House. ISBN 81-7141-639-X.

Bhaskara Rao, Digumarti, Editor (2004). *Education Employment and Human Resource Development*. New Delhi: Discovery Publishing House. ISBN 81-7141-681-0.

Bhaskara Rao, Digumarti, Editor (2004). *Successfully Schooling*. New Delhi: Discovery Publishing House. ISBN 81-7141-677-2.

Bhaskara Rao, Digumarti, Editor (2004). *European Education and Teachers*. New Delhi: Discovery Publishing House. ISBN 81-7141-702-7.

Bhaskara Rao, Digumarti, Editor (2004). *Teachers in a Changing World*. New Delhi: Discovery Publishing House. ISBN 81-7141-694-2.

Bhaskara Rao, Digumarti, Editor (2004). *Learning to Live Together*, 4 Volumes. New Delhi: Discovery Publishing House.

Vol. 1 *International Conference on Learning to Live Together.*

Vol. 2 *Globalisation and Living Together.*

Vol. 3 *Curriculum for Learning to Live Together.*

Vol. 4 *Science Education for the Contemporary Society.*

Bhaskara Rao, Digumarti (2004). *International Guidelines on Open and Distance Education*, New Delhi: Discovery Publishing House.

Bhaskara Rao, Digumarti, Editor (2004). *Adult Learning in the 21st Century*. New Delhi: Discovery Publishing House.

Bhaskara Rao, Digumarti, Editor (2004). *Educational Practices: Research and Recommendations*. New Delhi: Discovery Publishing House.

Bhaskara Rao, Digumarti, Editor (2004). *Chernobyl: Never Again*. New Delhi: APH Publishing Corporation.

Bhaskara Rao, Digumarti, Editor (2004). *Virology and Immunology*. New Delhi: APH Publishing Corporation.

Bhaskara Rao, Digumarti, C.A.P. Swami and B.S.V. Dutt (1997). *Self-Evaluation in Student Teaching*. New Delhi: Discovery Publishing House. ISBN 81-7141-374-9.

Bhaskara Rao, Digumarti and B.S.V. Dutt, Editors (2003). *Education: Programmes and Policies*. New Delhi: APH Publishing Corporation. ISBN 81-7648-470-9.

Bhaskara Rao, Digumarti and D. Naresh Kumar (2004). *School Teacher Effectiveness*. New Delhi: Discovery Publishing House.

Bhaskara Rao, Digumarti and D. Sridhar (2002). *Job Satisfaction of School Teachers*. New Delhi: Discovery Publishing House. ISBN 81-7141-652-7.

Bhaskara Rao, Digumarti and Digumarti Pushpa Latha (1994). *Achievement in Biology*. New Delhi: Discovery Publishing House. ISBN 81-7141-264-5.

Bhaskara Rao, Digumarti, C. Sridevi and K. Vijaya (1995). *Achievement in Social Studies*. New Delhi: Discovery Publishing House. ISBN 81-7141-281-5.

Bhaskara Rao, Digumarti and Digumarti Pushpa Latha (1995). *Achievement in English*. New Delhi: Discovery Publishing House. ISBN 81-7141-283-1.

Bhaskara Rao, Digumarti and Digumarti Pushpa Latha (1994). *Achievement in Science*. New Delhi: Discovery Publishing House. ISBN 81-7141-280-70.

Bhaskara Rao, Digumarti and Digumarti Pushpa Latha (1995). *Achievement in Mathematics*. New Delhi: Discovery Publishing House. ISBN 81-7141-278-5.

Bhaskara Rao, Digumarti and Digumarti Pushpa Latha, Editors (1998). *International Encyclopaedia of Women*. 5 Volumes. New Delhi: Discovery Publishing House. ISBN 81-7141-410-9.

Vol. 1 *Status of World's Women*. ISBN 81-7141-494-X.

Vol. 2 *Women, Education and Empowerment*. ISBN 81-7141-498-1.

Vol. 3 *Women Challenges and Advancement*. ISBN 81-7141-497-4.

Vol. 4 *Women and Family Health*. ISBN 81-7141-497-4.

Vol. 5 *Women and International Action*. ISBN 81-7141-498-2.

Bhaskara Rao, Digumarti, Digumarti Pushpa Latha and Digumarti Harshitha, Editors (2001). *Biological Warfare*. New Delhi: Discovery Publishing House. ISBN 81-7141-597-0.

Bhaskara Rao, Digumarti, Digumarti Pushpa Latha and Digumarti Harshitha, Editors (2001). *Women as Educators*. New Delhi: Discovery Publishing House. ISBN 81-7141-602-0.

Bhaskara Rao, Digumarti and Digumarti Harshitha, Editors (2001). *Education in India*. New Delhi: APH Publishing Corporation. ISBN 81-7141-207-2.

Bhaskara Rao, Digumarti, Digumarti Pushpa Latha and Digumarti Harshitha, Editors (2001). *Assessing Learning Achievement*. New Delhi: Discovery Publishing House. ISBN 81-7141-601-2.

Bhaskara Rao, Digumarti, Digumarti Pushpa Latha and Digumarti Harshitha, Editors (2001). *Energy Security*. New Delhi: Discovery Publishing House. ISBN 81-7141-598-9.

Bhaskara Rao, Digumarti. Digumarti Harshitha and K.R.S.S. Rao, Editors (1999). *Advanced Biotechnology*. New Delhi: Discovery Publishing House. ISBN 81-7141-516-4.

Bhaskara Rao, Digumarti and K.R.S. Sambhasiva Rao, Editors (1996). *Current Trends in Indian Education*. New Delhi: Discovery Publishing House. ISBN 81-7141-311-0.

Bhaskara Rao, Digumarti and K. Vijaya (1995). *A Text Book of Evaluation*. Ambala Cantt. The Associated Publishers.

Bhaskara Rao, Digumarti and N.V.M. Mohana Rao (2002). *Problems of Mentally Handicapped Children*. New Delhi: Discovery Publishing House. ISBN 81-7141-645-4.

Bhaskara Rao, Digumarti and S. Chandra Mohan (2002). *Sports Management*. New Delhi: APH Publishing Corporation. ISBN 81-7648-467-9.

Bhaskara Rao, Digumarti and Sk. Johni Basha (2004). *Teachers' Population Education Awareness*. New Delhi: APH Publishing Corporation.

Bhaskara Rao, Digumarti, V.V. Rao, V.V. Lakshmi and V.V. Krishna, Editors (1999). *Status and Advancement of Women*. New Delhi: APH Publishing Corporation. ISBN 81-7648-169-6.

Babu, P.C., Author and Digumarti Bhaskara Rao, Editor (2004). *Flowers of Wisdom*. New Delhi: Discovery Publishing House. ISBN 81-7141-695-0.

Bhagya Lakshmi, Lingineni, Author and Digumarti Bhaskara Rao, Editor (2000). *Reading and Comprehension*. New Delhi: Discovery Publishing House. ISBN 81-7141-543-1.

Bhuvaneswara Lakshmi, Gadde, Author and Digumarti Bhaskara Rao, Editor (2000). *Attitude Towards Science*. New Delhi: Discovery Publishing House. ISBN 81-7141-541-6.

Devraj, T.A.S., Author and Digumarti Bhaskara Rao, Editor (1997). *Trace Analysis of Uranium and Thorium*. New Delhi: Discovery Publishing House. ISBN 81-7141-375-7.

Durga Rani, K., Author and Digumarti Bhaskara Rao, Editor (2000). *Educational Aspirations and Scientific Attitudes*. New Delhi: Discovery Publishing House. ISBN 81-7141-555-55.

Dutt, B.S.V. and Digumarti Bhaskara Rao (2001). *Empowering Primary Teachers*. New Delhi: Discovery Publishing House. ISBN 81-7141-615.2.

Ediger, Marlow and Digumarti Bhaskara Rao (1996). *Science Curriculum*. New Delhi: Discovery Publishing House. ISBN 81-7141-321-8.

Ediger, Marlow and Digumarti Bhaskara Rao (2000). *Teaching Mathematics Successfully*. New Delhi: Discovery Publishing House. ISBN 81-7141-552-0.

Ediger, Marlow and Digumarti Bhaskara Rao (2001). *Teaching Science Successfully*. New Delhi: Discovery Publishing House ISBN 81-7141-600-4.

Ediger, Marlow and Digumarti Bhaskara Rao (2001). *Teaching Social Studies Successfully*. New Delhi: Discovery Publishing House ISBN 81-7141-596-2.

Ediger, Marlow and Digumarti Bhaskara Rao (2002). *Philosophy and Curriculum*. New Delhi: Discovery Publishing House ISBN 81-7141-631-4.

Ediger, Marlow and Digumarti Bhaskara Rao (2002). *Improving School Administration*. New Delhi: Discovery Publishing House. ISBN 81-7141-633-0.

Ediger, Marlow and Digumarti Bhaskara Rao (2002). *Elementary Curriculum*. New Delhi: Discovery Publishing House. ISBN 81-7141-658-6.

Ediger, Marlow and Digumarti Bhaskara Rao (2003). *Language Arts Curriculum*. New Delhi: Discovery Publishing House. ISBN 81-7141-657-8.

Ediger, Marlow and Digumarti Bhaskara Rao (2004). *Teaching Language Arts Successfully*. New Delhi: Discovery Publishing House. ISBN 81-7141-678-0.

Ediger, Marlow and Digumarti Bhaskara Rao (2004). *Teaching Mathematics in Elementary Schcols*. New Delhi: Discovery Publishing House. ISBN 81-7141-687-X.

Ediger, Marlow and Digumarti Bhaskara Rao (2004). *Teaching Science in Elementary Schools*. New Delhi: Discovery Publishing House. ISBN 81-7141-709-4.

Ediger, Marlow and Digumarti Bhaskara Rao (2004). *School Curriculum and Administration*. New Delhi: Discovery Publishing House. ISBN 81-7141-709-4.

Ediger, Marlow and Digumarti Bhaskara Rao (2004). *Modern Elementary School*. New Delhi: Discovery Publishing House.

Ediger, Marlow and Digumarti Bhaskara Rao (2004): *Relevancy in Elementary Curriculum*. New Delhi: Discovery Publishing House. ISBN 81-7141-751-5.

Ediger, Marlow and Digumarti Bhaskara Rao, (2004). *Teaching Social Studies in Elementary Schools*. New Delhi: Discovery Publishing House.

Ediger Marlow, B.S.V. Dutt and Digumarti Bhaskara Rao (2004). *Teaching English Successfully*. New Delhi: Discovery Publishing House. ISBN 81-7141-707-8.

Harshitha, Digumarti and Digumarti Bhaskara Rao, Editors (2004). *Educational Innovations*. New Delhi: Discovery Publishing House.

Indira Devi, Author and J. Prasanth Kumar and Digumarti Bhaskara Rao, Editors (2004). *Values in Language Text Books*. New Delhi: Discovery Publishing House.

Jayasree, Kandi, Author and Digumarti Bhaskara Rao, Editor (1999). *Correlates of Socialisation*. New Delhi: Discovery Publishing House. ISBN 81-7141-517-2.

John Babu, Chikati, Author and T.J.R. Prasad, G.M. Madhukar and Digumarti Bhaskara Rao, Editors (1996). *Problem Solving in Mathematics*. New Delhi: APH Publishing Corporation. ISBN 81-7648-273-0.

Lalitha, T., Author and K.S. Prabhakaram, D.S.N. Sastry and Digumarti Bhaskara Rao, Editors (2004). *Educational Philosophic Beliefs*. New Delhi: Discovery Publishing House. ISBN 81-7141-765-5.

Madhu Bala, Jampala, Author and Digumarti Bhaskara Rao, Editor (2004). *Adjustment Problems of Hearing Impaired*. New Delhi: Discovery Publishing House.

Marja, Talvi and Digumarti Bhaskara Rao, Editors (1996). *Educational Leadership and Social Changes*. New Delhi: Discovery Publishing House. ISBN 81-7141-320-X.

Nirmala Jyothi, M., Author and Digumarti Bhaskara Rao, Editor (2003). *Non-detention Systems in School Education*. New Delhi: Discovery Publishing House. ISBN 81-7141-654-3.

Prabhakaram, K.S., Author and Digumarti Bhaskara Rao, Editor (1998). *Concept Attainment Model in Mathematics Teaching*. New Delhi: Discovery Publishing House. ISBN 81-7141-424-9.

Prasanth Kumar, J., Author and Digumarti Bhaskara Rao, Editor (1998). *Effectiveness of Distance Education System*. New Delhi: Discovery Publishing House. ISBN 81-7141-437-0.

Prasanth Kumar, J., Author and G. Sundara Rao and Digumarti Bhaskara Rao, Editors (2000). *Open University Student Support Services*. New Delhi: Discovery Publishing House. ISBN 81-7141-550-4.

Ramatulasamma, K., Author and Digumarti Bhaskara Rao, Editor (2002). *Job Satisfaction of Teacher Educators*, New Delhi: Discovery Publishing House. ISBN 81-7141-655-1.

Rama Krishnaiah, D., Author and Digumarti Bhaskara Rao, Editor (1998). *Job Satisfaction of College Teachers*, New Delhi: Discovery Publishing House. ISBN 81-7141-438-9.

Rama Kumar Ratnam, M., Author and Digumarti Bhaskara Rao, Editor (1998). *Dukka: Suffering in Early Buddhism*. New Delhi: Discovery Publishing House. ISBN 81-7141-653-5.

Rathaiah, Lavu and Digumarti Bhaskara Rao, Editors (1996). *International Innovations in Education*. New Delhi: Discovery Publishing House. ISBN 81-7141-359-5.

Ramesh, Ganta and Digumarti Bhaskara Rao, Editors (1998). *Environmental Education: Problems and Prospects*. New Delhi: Discovery Publishing House. ISBN 81-7141-423-0.

Rathaiah, Lavu and Digumarti Bhaskara Rao (1997). *Achievement Correlates*. New Delhi: Discovery Publishing House. ISBN 81-7141-385-4.

Reddy, Sudhakar Y., Author, and Digumarti Bhaskara Rao, Editor (2003). *Creativity in Adolescents*. New Delhi: Discovery Publishing House. ISBN 81-7141-659-4.

Reddy, M.S., Author and Digumarti Bhaskara Rao, Editor (2004). *Creativity in College Students*. New Delhi: Discovery Publishing House. ISBN 81-7141-697-7.

Radramamba, B., Author and Digumarti Bhaskara Rao, Editor (2003). *Problems of Teaching*. New Delhi: APH Publishing Corporation. ISBN 81-7648-462-8.

Sanjeeva Rao, P.C., Author and Digumarti Bhaskara Rao, Editor (1996). *A Text Book of Geology*. New Delhi: Discovery Publishing House. ISBN 81-7141-313-7.

Satya Narayana V., Author and Digumarti Bhaskara Rao, Editor (2001). *Physical Education, Social Attitudes and Leadership Qualities*. New Delhi: Discovery Publishing House. ISBN 81-7141-593-8.

Srinivasulu Reddy, M., and K.R.S. Sambasiva Rao, Authors and Digumarti Bhaskara Rao, Editor (1999). *A Text Book of Aquaculture*. New Delhi: Discovery Publishing House. ISBN 81-7141-482-6.

Srinivasa Rao, Mandalapu, Author and Digumarti Bhaskara Rao, Editor (2004). *Achievement Motivation and Achievement in Mathematics*. New Delhi: Discovery Publishing House. ISBN 81-7141-674-8.

Vanaja, M. Author and Digumarti Bhaskara Rao, Editor (1999). *Inquiry Training Model*. New Delhi: Discovery Publishing House. ISBN 81-7141-515-6.

Vanaja. M. and N. Sneha Latha, Authors and Digumarti Bhaskara Rao, Editor (2004). *Student Shyness*. New Delhi: APH Publishing Corporation.

Valeri V. Koustiouk, Author and Digumarti Bhaskara Rao, Editor (2002). *A Text Book of Cryogenics*. New Delhi: Discovery Publishing House. ISBN 81-7141-642-X.

Valeri V. Koustiouk, Author and Digumarti Bhaskara Rao, Editor (2004). *Refrigeration and Environment*. New Delhi: APH Publishing Corporation.

Veena Kumari, Balusu and Digumarti Bhaskara Rao (1996). *Operation Black Board*. New Delhi: Ashish Publishing Corporation. ISBN 81-7024-711-X.

Veena Kumari, Balusu, Author and Digumarti Bhaskara Rao, Editor (2000). *Psycho-Social Correlates of Achievement*, New Delhi: Discovery Publishing House. ISBN 81-7141-547-4.

Vanaja, M., Author and Digumarti Bhaskara Rao, Editor (1999). *Inquiry Training Model*. New Delhi: Discovery Publishing House. ISBN 81-7141-515-6.

Venkata Rao, P. and Digumarti Bhaskara Rao (1989). *A Text Book of Zoology—Junior Intermediate*. Guntur: Vignan Publishers.

Venkata Rao, P. and Digumarti Bhaskara Rao (1989). *A Text Book of Zoology—Senior Intermediate*. Guntur: Vignan Publishers.

Venugopala Rao, K., Author and Digumarti Bhaskara Rao, Editor (2000). *Teacher Morale in Secondary Schools*. New Delhi: Discovery Publishing House. ISBN 81-7141-551-2.

Vidya, C., Author and Digumarti Bhaskara Rao. Editor (1996). *A Text Book of Nutrition*. New Delhi: Discovery Publishing House. ISBN 81-7141-309-9.

Vidya Bharathi, D., Author and Digumarti Bhaskara Rao, Editor (2000). *Educational Philosophies of Swami Vivekananda and John Dewey*. New Delhi: APH Publishing Corporation. ISBN 81-7648-309-9.

Books in Telugu Language

Bhaskara Rao, Digumarti (1986). *Dhrushya Sravana Bodhanapukaranalu* (Audio Visual Teaching Aids). Guntur: Nagarjuna Publishers.

Bhaskara Rao, Digumarti (1993). *Jeevasashtra Bodhana* (Teaching of Biology). Guntur: Nagarjuna Publishers.

Bhaskara Rao, Digumarti (1995). *Vignanasasthra Bodhana* (Teaching of Science) Guntur: Nagarjuna Publishers.

Bhaskara Rao, Digumarti (1997). *Vidya Manovignana Seshtram* (Educational Psychology). Guntur: Creative Press.

Bhaskara Rao, Digumarti (1998). *DSC Study Material*. Guntur: Nagarjuna Publishers.

Bhaskara Rao, Digumarti (1998). *Upadhyayudu Vidya*. (Teacher and Education). Guntur: Nagarjuna Publishers.

Bhaskara Rao, Digumarti (1998). *Vidya Drukpadalu* (Prespectives of Education). Guntur: Nagarjuna Publishers.

Bhaskara Rao, Digumarti (1999). *EdCET Teaching Aptitude*. Guntur: Nagarjuna Publishers.

Bhaskara Rao, Digumarti (2001). *Bharata Samajamulo Upadyayudu Vidya* (Teacher and Education in Emerging Indian Society). Guntur: Nagarjuna Publishers.

Bhaskara Rao, Digumarti (2001). *Bhoutika Sastra Bodhana Paddathulu* (Methods of Teaching Physical Science). Guntur: Nagarjuna Publishers.

Bhaskara Rao, Digumarti (2001). *Jeeva Sastra Bodhana Padhathulu* (Methods of Teaching Biology). Guntur: Nagarjuna Publishers.

Bhaskara Rao, Digumarti (2001). *Vidya Manovignana Sastram* (Educational Psychology). Guntur: Nagarjuna Publishers.

Bhaskara Rao, Digumarti (2003). *Patsala Yajamanyam/Paripalana* (School Management and Administration). Guntur: Nagarjuna Publishers.

Bhaskara Rao, Digumarti (2004). *Vidya Sanketika Sastram mariyu Computer Vidya* (Educational Technology and Computer Education). Guntur: Nagarjuna Publishers.